CW01281971

airbus.com

AIRBUS

**It took us 125 years to use
the first trillion barrels of oil.**

We'll use the next trillion in 30.

So why should you care?

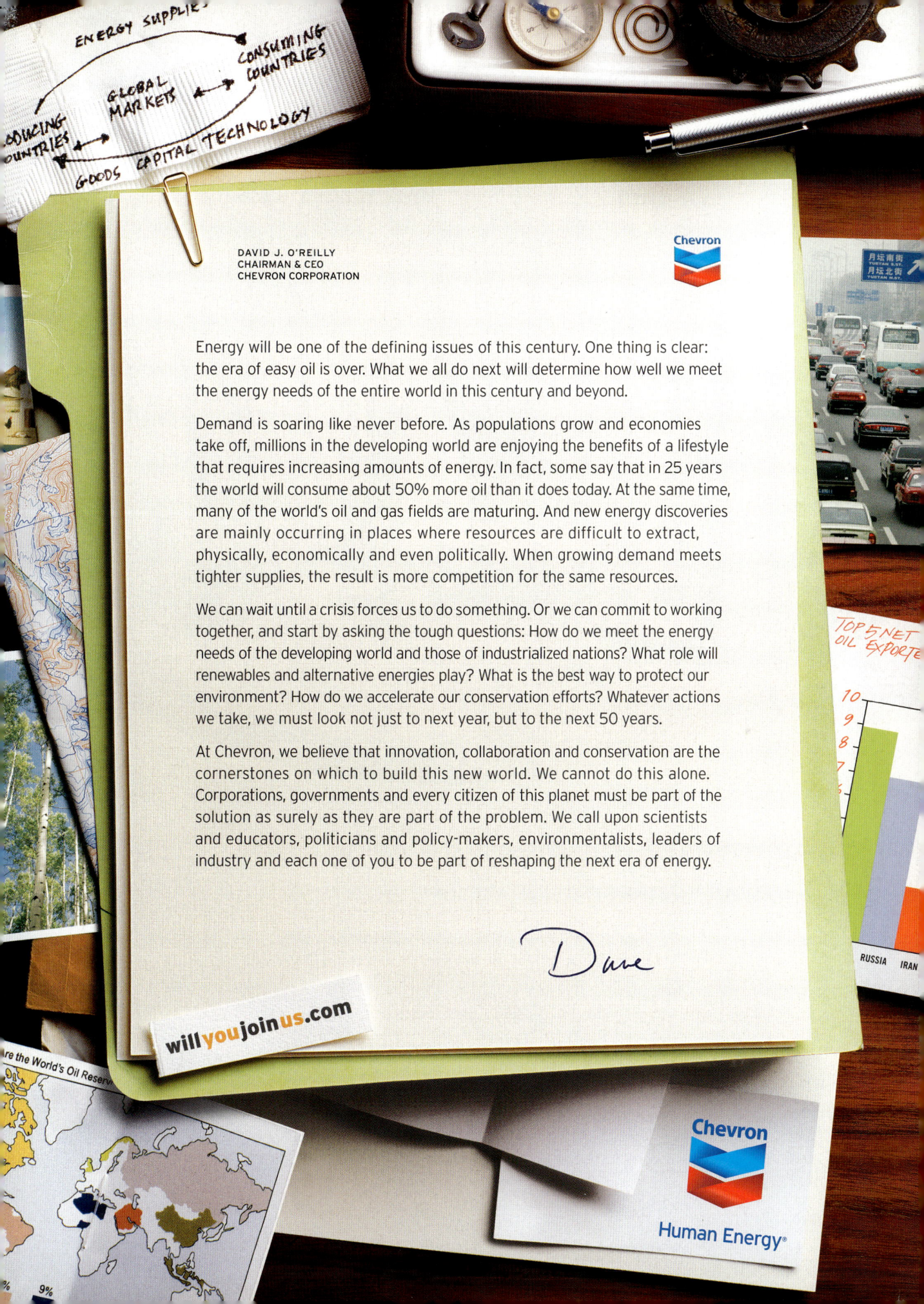

DAVID J. O'REILLY
CHAIRMAN & CEO
CHEVRON CORPORATION

Energy will be one of the defining issues of this century. One thing is clear: the era of easy oil is over. What we all do next will determine how well we meet the energy needs of the entire world in this century and beyond.

Demand is soaring like never before. As populations grow and economies take off, millions in the developing world are enjoying the benefits of a lifestyle that requires increasing amounts of energy. In fact, some say that in 25 years the world will consume about 50% more oil than it does today. At the same time, many of the world's oil and gas fields are maturing. And new energy discoveries are mainly occurring in places where resources are difficult to extract, physically, economically and even politically. When growing demand meets tighter supplies, the result is more competition for the same resources.

We can wait until a crisis forces us to do something. Or we can commit to working together, and start by asking the tough questions: How do we meet the energy needs of the developing world and those of industrialized nations? What role will renewables and alternative energies play? What is the best way to protect our environment? How do we accelerate our conservation efforts? Whatever actions we take, we must look not just to next year, but to the next 50 years.

At Chevron, we believe that innovation, collaboration and conservation are the cornerstones on which to build this new world. We cannot do this alone. Corporations, governments and every citizen of this planet must be part of the solution as surely as they are part of the problem. We call upon scientists and educators, politicians and policy-makers, environmentalists, leaders of industry and each one of you to be part of reshaping the next era of energy.

Dave

willyoujoinus.com

Chevron
Human Energy®

Mohammed Al Khwarizmi
Arab Mathematician and Inventor of Algebra

Mohammed Al Khwarizmi was an Arab mathematician whose revolutionary new ideas transformed the field of mathematics. His book, *hisab al-jabr*, gave birth to a whole new field in mathematics: algebra. In fact, the very word algebra comes from the Arabic word *al-jabr* from the name of his book.

Our investment ideas are new.
Our investment principles are not.

At Istithmar World, we're inspired by Khwarizmi's pursuit of ideas. Which is why we not only seek out the best investment ideas, we even create our own with the help of our industry-focused professionals. Then we identify industry trends, new strategies and top managers to ensure the success of our ideas. Because we strongly believe that only a great idea can result in a great investment.

Our "I" Investment Philosophy™ is based around three principles: Ideas, Inquiry and Integrity.

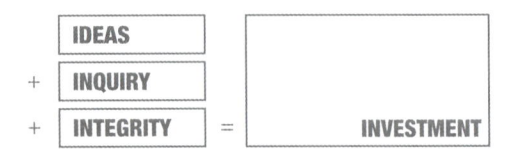

```
  | IDEAS     |
+ | INQUIRY   |
+ | INTEGRITY | = | INVESTMENT |
```

Istithmar World

a **Dubai World** company

www.istithmarworld.com

BANKER MIDDLE EAST BEST PRIVATE EQUITY HOUSE 2007 • BANKER MIDDLE EAST BEST PRIVATE EQUITY HOUSE 2008

Contents

The World in 2009

EDITOR:
Daniel Franklin
MANAGING EDITOR:
Harriet Ziegler
DEPUTY EDITORS:
John Andrews,
Leo Abruzzese
EDITORIAL ASSISTANT:
Nicola Bartlett
COUNTRIES EDITOR:
Alasdair Ross
INDUSTRIES EDITOR:
Carla Rapoport
DESIGN AND ART DIRECTION:
Mike Kenny, Bailey and Kenny
ART DIRECTOR:
Anita Wright
CHARTS:
Phil Kenny, Michael Robinson,
Peter Winfield
ILLUSTRATIONS:
Steve Carroll, Derek Cousins,
Kevin Kallaugher, James Sillavan
PICTURE EDITOR:
Juliet Brightmore
RESEARCH:
Carol Howard, Jane Shaw
EDITORIAL ASSISTANCE:
Ingrid Esling, Camilla Longin
ADVERTISING DIRECTOR:
David Weeks
ADVERTISING MANAGERS:
Harry Whitbread (UK),
Sarah Jane Lindsay (Europe),
Nick Mesquita (MEA),
Suzanne Hopkins (North America),
Terrie Lam (Asia)
CIRCULATION & MARKETING DIRECTORS:
Lisa Jamal (UK),
Anna Rawling (Europe),
Michael Brunt (Asia)
PRODUCTION:
Sharon Simpson, Michael Mann,
Andrew Rollings, Amy Brown,
Katy Wilson, Robert Banbury
SYNDICATION & LICENSING DIRECTOR:
Rebecca Cogswell
Agent: Hutton-Williams Agency
PUBLISHER:
Des McSweeney

The Economist

25 St James's Street
London SW1A 1HG
Telephone:
020 7576 8133
E-mail: worldineditor
@economist.com

11 **From the editor**

Leaders
13 **America's new hope**
Barack Obama must learn to say no, at home and abroad
14 **Buckle up**
Tougher times for the global economy
18 **The year of unsustainability**
Corporate survival responsibility
21 **Come to order**
More regulation for finance
22 **Banning the bomb**
All just talk, of course, but talk has its uses
26 **Shocking science**
A year of celebrations and screams
28 **The perils of sharing**
The surprising threat to your privacy
30 **English marks a million**
Or does it?

33 **Calendar for 2009**

Britain
35 **Maybe, prime minister**
Gordon Brown's chances of survival
36 **Straining at the leash**
The debate over Scotland 
38 **Made in Britain**
A call for a manufacturing renaissance
40 **Binary blues**
The economy: recession or slump?
41 **Spent, spent, spent**
The red hole in Britain's public finances
42 **No such thing as a free crunch**
Boris Johnson on London

Europe
45 **Nice project, shame about the voters**
Elections disturb the European agenda
46 **Ever greater union**
Travel in Europe
49 **Take your partners**
Germany's election dance
52 **A French semi-revolution**
The recession will not deter the president
54 **After the fiesta**
The party's over in Spain
56 **North stars**
New Nordic defence
56 **Same old Silvio?**
Italy's leader will show if he is a reformer
58 **Message from Madrid**
José Luis Rodríguez Zapatero on Europe
60 **Swaggering on**
But Russia will find the going harder
62 **An answer to the Russian question**
Yulia Tymoshenko on Europe and Russia
64 **Twenty years of capitalism**
Was it worth it?
65 **Frozen conflicts**
Europe's unfinished business

United States
67 **The audacity of change**
Mr Obama goes to Washington
68 **Goodbye Guantánamo**
But it won't be the end of the mess
69 **Pick your scenario**
How bad will America's economy get?
70 **The bucks stop here**
What happens when Americans save
71 **At 100, the NAACP still has a mission**
The struggle for civil rights
72 **Crime, interrupted**
Treating violent crime as a disease
74 **An end of hubris**
Henry Kissinger on a new world order

The Americas
75 **Latin drift**
Sorting pragmatists from populists
76 **Old order, new oil**
Cuba's future becomes a little clearer
77 **Canada's clashes**
New strains replace the old ones
78 **Building on the B in BRIC**
Lula da Silva on the rising powers

Asia
79 **Riders on the storm**
Solid growth and lower inflation for most
80 **A rocky and a hard place**
Afghan woes are NATO's too
81 **A subcontinent votes**
India enters an uncertain election season
82 **After the Olympics**
The next agenda for China
83 **Twitching China**
Bird-watchers are a new species
83 **Shock and aftershock**
An upheaval in Japanese politics
84 **Hurry, Murray-Darling**
Australia is running out of surface water
85 **Indonesia sets an example**
The largest Muslim country votes
86 **Large issues and medium powers**
Kevin Rudd on tackling global issues

Middle East and Africa
87 **Iraq wants its sovereignty back**
Arguments over the pace of America's withdrawal will persist
88 **Going nuclear in Iran**
Ever closer to getting the bomb
89 **Full of angst**
A disillusioned Israel on the political slide
90 **Buying the world**
The Gulf's spending plans

All change
So, Mr President, what exactly are you going to do, *page 13*? Mr Obama goes to Washington, *page 67*. End of an aura, *page 162*. Leaving Iraq, slowly, *page 87*. And Guantánamo, *page 68*. **Henry Kissinger**'s briefing on the world that awaits the new president, *page 74*.

New world order
A bad year for global diplomacy, *page 95*. **Lula da Silva** sees a bigger role for Brazil and other emerging powers, *page 78*. **Lakshmi Mittal** takes an optimistic view of the emerging new economic order, *page 134*. **Kevin Rudd** outlines the role of Australia and other medium-sized powers in global issues, *page 86*. **Yulia Tymoshenko** urges bold thinking in relations with Russia, *page 62*. Putting Africa on the map, *page 92*.

The World in 2009 online
Browse **readers' comments** on the articles in *The World in 2009*, compare this year's predictions with those from **previous editions**, play with an **interactive version** of the Countries and Industries pages and read our **predictions blog** at our website: **www.economist.com/theworldin**

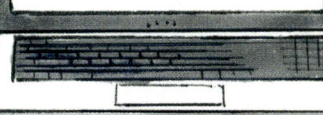

Some think breakfast.

We think research.

Since 1856, we have focused on bringing new perspectives to our clients. Understanding the past, but shaped by the future. Always looking at opportunities and challenges from a different point of view. Providing you with the information you need to give you a competitive edge. After all, our future is based on making the most of yours.
www.credit-suisse.com

Thinking New Perspectives.

CREDIT SUISSE

THE WORLD IN 2009

Contents

91 **Everything to play for**
Sub-Saharan Africa needs better policies

92 **Putting Africa on the map**
An information revolution in the making

93 **Closing the knowledge gap**
Queen Rania of Jordan on education

International

95 **A bad year for diplomats**
Multilateralists of the world, despair!

96 **About 2008: sorry**
Telling it how it wasn't

97 **Long shots for 2009**
The unlikely, but possible, turn of events

98 **The great wheel of China**
My Ferris is bigger than yours

99 **Scramble for the seabed**
Claims to underwater riches

100 **The museum-building binge**
Starchitecture and civic pride

101 **Farewell to youth**
The rich world reaches middle age

102 **Isaiah, chapter 100**
The role of public intellectuals

Environment special section

105 **Wonderful, wonderful Copenhagen?**
Don't count on a climate-change deal

106 **Actually, there is an alternative**
Real shifts in the way energy is produced

107 **Building ecotopia**
The world's first carbon-neutral city

108 **Fighting for the planet**
So much to argue about in green politics

109 **More silicon, less carbon**
How computers can cut emissions

110 **More help now, please**
How to tackle tomorrow's disasters

111 **Want to drive green?**
Your choice will widen

111 **Green games**
Sports compete to save the planet

112 **A water warning**
Peter Brabeck-Letmathe on the shortage

The world in figures

113 **Forecasts for 80 countries**
123 **Forecasts for 15 industries**

Business

129 **No more business as usual**
Now for the corporate crunch

130 **To have and to hold**
India's middle-class anxieties

132 **Flight to value**
No-nonsense brands will prosper in 2009

134 **A new economic order**
Lakshmi Mittal on emerging markets

135 **Led by the nose**
Retailers sniff out business

135 **Happy birthday, Barbie**
A superdoll at 50

136 **The Chinese are coming**
Prepare for an influx of tourists

137 **The upside of a downturn**
Fired with enthusiasm

138 **Intensive scare**
Innovations shake up health care

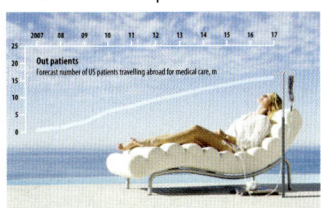

140 **The year of the CFO**
Corporate life won't be funny

142 **Old Macdonald gets some cash**
Farming after a food crisis

144 **Time to re-embrace globalisation**
Jeff Immelt on competition

Finance

147 **Whatever next**
The balance between governments and markets will shift

148 **Small is beautiful**
Microcredit's moment

150 **Dirty words**
Derivatives, defaults, disaster…

152 **No end of trouble**
More trauma for banks

153 **The return of the gentleman banker**
Introducing the winners of 2009

154 **Who's a bull?**
Some markets start to look up

155 **Currency comeback**
A lift for the dollar

156 **Lessons from a crisis**
Josef Ackermann on reshaping the system

Science

157 **A year of astronomy**
The search for life beyond Earth

158 **Life on Man**
Be happy to be a human hybrid

159 **Cancer killers**
Gene therapy gets to work

160 **Dark secrets**
The physics discovery of 2009

160 **A fin-tuned design**
The latest in biomimetics

161 **Piece of mind**
Paul Allen on the brain

Obituary

162 **End of an aura**
The Bush administration bows out

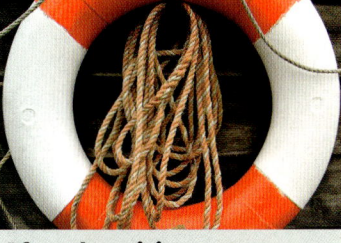

PHOTOGRAPHIC SOURCES
Alamy Images: Ace Stock, Jon Arnold Images, Big Cheese Photo LLC, Oote Boe, Patrick Byrd, Deco Images, Terry Harris, Jupiter Images, Look Die Bildagentur der Fotografen, Iain Masterton, Steven May, Frances Roberts, Ian Shaw, Robin Steward, Ken Tam. ArcelorMittal. Associated Press/AP Images: Rodrigo Abd, Franka Bruns, Ron Edmonds, Jae C. Hong, Pavel Rahman, Rajesh Kumar Singh. Corbis: Bettmann, Elio Ciol, Nigel Farrow, Brooks Kraft, Lawrence Manning, Finbarr O'Reilly, ©Andy Warhol Foundation. Getty Images: Steve Coleman, Emmanuel Dunand/AFP, Dominique Faget/AFP, Munawar Hosain, Jeff Hunter, Koichi Kamoshida, Atta Kenare/AFP, Barry King/WireImage, Jon Kopaloff/FilmMagic, Gemma Levine, Philippe Marchand, David McNew, NATO, George Pimentel/WireImage, Riccardo Savi, Keren Su, Topical Press Agency, White Packert . Mattel, Inc. Newspix/Brenton Edwards. PA Photos: Andrew Parsons, Chris Radburn. Michael Pilkington. *Punch* May 25th 1861. Reuters: Denis Balibouse, Mike Blake, China Daily, Grigory Dukor, Johannes Eisele, Gary Hershorn, Ciro De Luca/AGN, Mahmoud Raouf Mahmoud, Andreas Manolis, Brendan McDermid, Ho New, Enny Nuraheni, Enrique de la Osa, Punit Paranjpe, Alessia Pierdomenico, Suzanne Plunkett, Marcelo Del Pozo, Baz Ratner, Jason Reed, Jayanta Shaw, Jorge Silva, Bob Strong, Goran Tomasevic, Ajay Verma, Darren Whiteside, Philippe Wojazer, Shamil Zhumatov. Michael Rufo/Boston Engineering Corporation. Still Pictures/Biosphoto/Ruoso Cyril. Ricardo Stuckert. Vulcan, Inc. Vernon T. Williams.

Printed by St Ives PLC, Plymouth, England

Printed on UPM-Kymmene Star 80gsm

© 2008 The Economist Newspaper Limited. All rights reserved. Neither this publication nor any part of it may be reproduced, stored in a retrieval system, or transmitted in any form or by any means, electronic, mechanical, photocopying, recording or otherwise, without the prior permission of The Economist Newspaper Limited. Published by The Economist Newspaper Limited.

ISBN 978-0-86218-210-6

Where opinion is expressed it is that of the authors and does not necessarily coincide with the editorial views of the publisher or The Economist.

All information in this magazine is verified to the best of the authors' and the publisher's ability. However, The Economist Newspaper Limited does not accept responsibility for any loss arising from reliance on it.

♺ recycle

After the crisis

Buckle up for the recession, *page 14*. Deutsche Bank's **Josef Ackermann** outlines how to fix the financial system, *page 156*. Bring on the regulators—or can finance heal itself, *pages 21* and *147*? Spot the bulls, *page 154*. Now for the corporate crunch, *page 129*. Welcome to the year of the CFO, says **Lucy Kellaway**, *page 140*. Don't give up on globalisation, argues GE's **Jeff Immelt**, *page 144*.

Warming up

A stern test for "sustainability", *page 18*. The climate changes: arguing all the way to Copenhagen, *pages 105* and *108*. Chicago v Tokyo for the greenest of Olympics, *page 111*. The world's first carbon-neutral city, *page 107*. Australia's drought, *page 84*. Nestlé's **Peter Brabeck-Letmathe** gives a water warning, *page 112*.

Happy birthday to you

Celebrating 20 years of capitalism in eastern Europe, *page 64*. The rich world turns 40, *page 101*. Barbie at 50, *page 135*. Isaiah Berlin at 100, *page 102*. One hundred years of America's struggle for civil rights, *page 71*. Two hundred years for Darwin and 400 for Galileo's telescope: shocking science, *page 26*. **Paul Allen** expects the birth of a new era in brain research, *page 161*.

"TELL ME ABOUT THE RELATIONSHIP WITH YOUR LAWYER"

It turns out, there was no relationship. Most lawyers only do what is necessary, probably perfectly well. But we know that our clients' service needs are broader, so we use our knowledge of the law to be a business partner. Perhaps that's why our 3,700 lawyers are now in the world's leading and emerging markets—25 countries and counting. It's all part of our commitment to our clients. Because if it matters to our clients, it matters to us.

www.dlapiper.com

EVERYTHING MATTERS

DLA PIPER

Nigel Knowles, Chief Executive Officer
DLA Piper is a global legal services organisation, the members of which are separate and distinct legal entities

From the editor

Anyone hoping for a period of calm after the turbulence of the past year will be disappointed. For the economy and for business, as well as for politics, 2009 promises to be a year of bracing adjustment to a changed world.

In politics the most obvious change will be in the White House: in January Barack Obama will become America's first black president. This is a remarkable achievement—and a remarkable opportunity. Abroad, President Obama can restore America's standing after the damage of the Bush years. At home, together with a Democratic Congress, he has a chance to bring about bold reform, notably in America's health-care system. Indeed, such are the expectations of Mr Obama that one of his biggest challenges will be to manage them so that he does not disappoint too much.

Beyond America, too, it will be a busy year for politics, with a large chunk of humanity involved in elections. India, the world's biggest democracy, holds a general election. So does Germany, Europe's largest economy, and in June the whole 27-country European Union votes in elections for the European Parliament. There will be presidential polls in Indonesia, the world's most populous Muslim country, and in pivotal places such as South Africa, Iran and Afghanistan. Voters everywhere will focus mainly on local issues, as they always do, but in the background will lurk broader arguments over the changing attitudes to markets and the role of the state.

That is because the aftershocks of the financial crisis of 2008 will be rumbling on. After an extraordinary boom, in which the world's GDP rose year after year by between 4% and 5%, global growth will slide below 3%. The rich economies face recession, with all that comes with it: bankruptcies, belt-tightening and rising unemployment. Within companies, cherished perks will disappear and power will ebb from visionary bosses to the chief financial officer. Those with cash and cunning will find opportunities to buy competitors on the cheap.

In the emerging world, meanwhile, growth will be less spectacular than before, but in many countries it will—with luck—remain relatively robust. So the shift in global power to places such as Brazil, Russia, India and China will, if anything, quicken. These countries will expect a bigger say in how the world is run.

One aspect of running the world will draw increasing attention as the year progresses: how to tackle global warming. At the end of 2009 a gathering in Copenhagen will attempt to reach a post-Kyoto agreement to cut greenhouse emissions. It may well fail to do so, but climate change and related issues (such as carbon trading, water shortages and alternative energy) will loom large in 2009, which is why we publish a special section on the environment.

If all this sounds a bit earnest, don't worry: there will be plenty of fun in 2009 as well. Dubai will open the world's tallest building, China the world's biggest Ferris wheel. Barbie and Astérix will celebrate their 50th birthdays. Africans will enjoy a new fascination with maps, thanks to the internet, while soaring numbers of twitchers in China will indulge in a new fascination with birds. Scientists will map the brain as well as search for Earth-like planets—in what will be the International Year of Astronomy, 400 years after Galileo first peered through a telescope

As always this volume is full of predictions, a few of which may actually prove right. This time we've even included several things we think probably won't happen, though they just might: forecasts whose chance of coming true falls roughly between 5% and 20%. Might 2009 see a peace deal between Israel and Syria, a cure for cancer or the abdication of Queen Elizabeth II? Probably not. But you read it here first.

Daniel Franklin
editor, *The World in 2009*

> The shift in power to places such as Brazil, Russia, India and China will quicken. These countries will expect a bigger say in how the world is run

No. 1 in Modern Energy

Believe in the Wind

Wind is an important source of homegrown energy for most countries in the world. And with soaring prices and global climate change, this clean natural resource holds more promise today than ever before.

How far can we go with wind? A lot further than you might think. We know, because Vestas is a global leader in technologies that use wind to generate electricity. And wind is the sole focus of our business.

The world has an abundance of wind resources, and Vestas is here to help harness them. Believe in the wind.

vestas.com

Vestas.

America's new hope

But in 2009 Barack Obama will have to learn how to say no both at home and abroad, argues **John Micklethwait**

So, Mr President, what exactly are you going to do? As Barack Obama stares down at the cheering crowds at his inauguration on January 20th 2009, America's first black president may well remember the great buzzword of his campaign—and smile ruefully. His mantra of "Change" propelled him all the way to the White House in some style. Mr Obama did not just win the electoral college handsomely; he has the full backing of a Democratic Congress and the overwhelming support, if national polls are to be believed, of most of the rest of the world. George Bush never had such a broad political mandate.

Yet change will constrain what President Obama can actually do in 2009. Most obviously there is the cathartic change over the past year in the economy: whereas Mr Bush inherited a healthy budget surplus in 2001, in 2009 America's budget deficit is projected to be as high as $1 trillion. But there is also foreign affairs. Back in 2000 the United States, the undisputed hegemon, was mainly at peace with the world. In 2009 Mr Obama will have troops under fire in Iraq and Afghanistan, and power is shifting away from America towards the faster-growing economies of the emerging world.

How Mr Obama deals with these very different changes will determine the success of his presidency. A man who has often been accused of being all things to all people will have to start making choices. Many of these choices may disappoint his own party as well as some of his most fervent supporters around the globe.

The immediate focus in 2009 will understandably be on the economy. Mr Obama promised a lot of things to a lot of people. Even if there were more money available, he would have had to concentrate on just a few core things, such as his middle-class tax cut and his health-care plan; with fewer funds, that will be essential. He may even be able to turn the need to economise to his advantage. On health care, some of the mooted reforms in Congress look more efficient than his own one (and still deliver the universal coverage America ought to have). Meanwhile, the empty government coffers provide a perfect excuse to escape from his more pork-laden commitments.

Nevertheless, frustrations will mount, especially in his own party. With an economy in recession there will be protectionist growling from Congress which needs to be firmly resisted. There will also be reams of regulation. Many of the main Democratic constituencies have waited a long time to get their man in the White House: the unions will demand new labour rules; lawyers will want liability laws; greens will wage new environmental campaigns. All of these could slow down any economic recovery.

> Around the world the young new president has become a symbol of what people think America should be

Young ambitious presidencies can get derailed by small causes early on: think of what the "gays in the military" fuss did to Bill Clinton in 1993. A particular worry about Mr Obama is that in his brief political career he has never obviously crossed his party on any significant issue. He will need to start saying no to Democrats soon in 2009 if he is not to betray the many independent voters who believed his campaign talk about rep- ▶

John Micklethwait: editor-in-chief, *The Economist*

resenting the whole country.

If expectations are too high for Mr Obama in domestic policy, they are off the scale when it comes to the world abroad. Once again, the Democratic base will be a problem: it expects him to extract America from Iraq rapidly and smoothly. That was what Mr Obama once promised; but he now seems to realise that a rapid retreat from Iraq would be disastrous both for that country and for America's reputation in the region. Meanwhile, he will also need to re-sell the Afghanistan campaign to a weary electorate: the West's chances of prevailing depend on having more troops there, not fewer.

That brings in the issue of America's allies. Around the world the young new president has become a symbol of what people think America should be. Merely because he is not the loathed Mr Bush, he may be able to deliver some things. The rapid closure of Guantánamo Bay would be a good start. But other things the world hopes for, such as a global-warming pact, will take a long time. Peace in the Middle East will not break out just because the new president's middle name is Hussein: hard compromises need to be made. Mr Obama needs to spell out what he will do; and he also needs to demand more from America's allies. That so few of them help in Afghanistan, for instance, is a disgrace, and he should say it loudly.

Just as much as at home, the new president will be tested by events abroad. There are plenty of troublemakers like Iran who will want to test the new president's mettle. Yet, as he scrambles to deal with these immediate challenges, Mr Obama should also look to the long term—and to one thing in particular.

Salesman to the world

When historians look back on his presidency, they may well judge him most on whether he managed to bring the emerging powers into the world order and unite them behind Western values. By the time Mr Obama leaves office, which, assuming he serves two terms, will be 2017, powers like China, India and Brazil will surely have taken larger roles in the world economy. At the moment, none of them is in the G8 club, and only China has a spot on the UN Security Council. If America cannot find a way to bring China and India into the existing global power structure, they will start drifting away to form their own clubs.

It is not just institutional. China especially is nervous about Western values. The financial crisis coupled with the shredding of America's reputation over the past eight years has given weight to those people in the regime who argue that Western capitalism and democracy are flawed, old models. The new president will have to re-sell what America stands for. That will be a long process; but, even allowing for all his other priorities, President Obama needs to start work on it in 2009. ■

Buckle up

Robin Bew expects even tougher times ahead for the global economy

Yes, it has been a traumatic year. The financial crisis swept away venerable banks, American house prices fell more steeply than at any time since the Great Depression, there were food riots in developing countries and scary gyrations in the price of oil. Yet the news was not all bad. Beyond banking and housing, other bits of the American and European economies managed for much of the year to struggle on. Emerging economies generally delivered robust economic growth. All in all, despite the turmoil in finance and a sharp turn for the worse towards the end of the year, with GDP growth of around 3.8% the global economy wasn't nearly as bad in 2008 as many feared. Can it repeat the trick in 2009?

Sadly, no. For some professions, things will get better—since they could hardly get worse. Investment banking as an independent activity virtually ceased to exist in 2008, as famous names collapsed, merged or converted into deposit-taking institutions. Investment bankers spent the year fearing for their jobs (or tending their gardens). But for many investment banks, the rapid downsizing seen in 2008 means that by mid-2009 most of the firings will be over. Indeed, the more adventurous will be looking for opportunity in adversity, and hunting for new business by late 2009.

> The go-go years of 2003-07 are over, replaced by the go-slow years of 2009 and beyond

Similarly for the housing industry. Builders have been through a bruising 2008, as housing activity practically ground to a halt. But with prices in America likely to bottom out in the spring (and Europe perhaps six months behind), the industry should at least stabilise—although a recovery in housebuilding seems unlikely before 2011.

However, other sectors will find 2009 much tougher than 2008. The choking of bank credit, combined with general gloom about the economic outlook, is leading non-financial businesses to retrench. Having dithered for much of the past year, companies are getting serious about cost-control. So layoffs and cuts are moving from banking and construction to the wider economy. This by itself will reduce growth; and the resulting rise in unemployment will further sap consumer de-

Robin Bew: editorial director and chief economist, Economist Intelligence Unit.

THE FUTURE JUST LOST ITS LEAD.

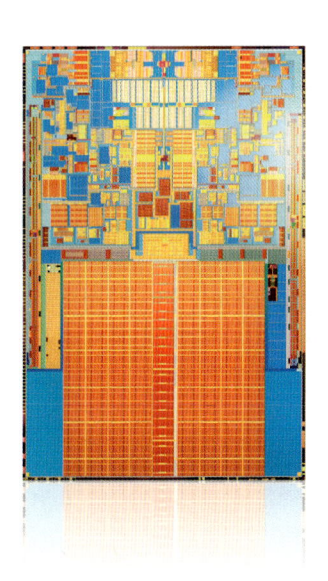

INNOVATION IS ALWAYS IN AT INTEL.

We're relentless about invention. Our latest technology includes hafnium-based circuitry, mobile technology for a new generation of MIDs, and our forthcoming 32 nanometer processing. See our newest advancements at intel.com/inside

GREAT COMPUTING STARTS WITH INTEL INSIDE.

To see how FedEx will work behind the scenes to help your business succeed, go to **experience.fedex.com**. FedEx, behind a great experience.

FedEx Express

© 2008 FedEx.

mand for everything from PCs to restaurant meals.

Weakness in the broader economy will also make it harder for consumers and businesses to service their debts. In 2008 default rates remained relatively low (although you might not have thought so from the newspaper headlines). The picture will be much worse in 2009, as currently good credit risks start to shirk their debts. As a result, banks will experience a second wave of financial difficulties, as their commercial and retail arms go through similar pain to their investment-banking divisions. This will lead to yet more swingeing write-downs and desperate capital-raising—and more household names will go under.

This pressure on commercial and retail banking will mean that the credit crunch continues for much of 2009. Indeed, for most people the situation will feel worse than in 2008: it's one thing to read in the newspapers about investment-banking blow-ups, quite another to see your own home-town bank going to the wall. The trickle of retail-bank failures we saw in 2008 will become a flood.

Down but not out

Does all this mean that the developed world is heading for a depression, of the sort seen in the 1930s? Almost certainly not. Times will be tough and many of the world's largest economies will shrink in 2009. But policymakers demonstrated during 2008 that they were prepared to step in to prevent individual banking failures from turning into a broader economic crisis and they will do so again during 2009. Lower inflation will allow interest-rate cuts too, supporting the economy more broadly. Yet while depression will be avoided, recession will not and recovery will be more gradual than many commentators hope. The go-go years of 2003-07 are over, replaced by the go-slow years of 2009 and beyond.

Those wanting a more optimistic outlook may be tempted to turn to the emerging world. For much of 2008 these markets seemed only marginally affected by the slowdown in the developed West. They were sustained by burgeoning domestic demand and strong revenues from the sale of high-priced commodities. But rapid growth fuelled inflation. And, after a lot of soul-searching, the result was a tightening of policy everywhere from eastern Europe to Asia, which in turn caused local financial markets to crash.

That leaves many emerging markets facing a double whammy in 2009. Exports to America, Europe and Japan will weaken further, as imports in those big markets start to shrink. Much more significantly, domestic spending in the emerging world will come under pressure. Food is still expensive, leaving less cash for shopping sprees. Foreign cash, which flooded into emerging bond and equity markets during the good times, will be harder to come by (although inflows of longer-term foreign direct investment should hold up). And, as softer economic growth weakens demand for commodities, exporters of raw materials will start to feel the pinch. None of this need be crisis-inducing. But it will lop up to a third off economic growth rates in the developing world in 2009 compared with the boom year of 2007.

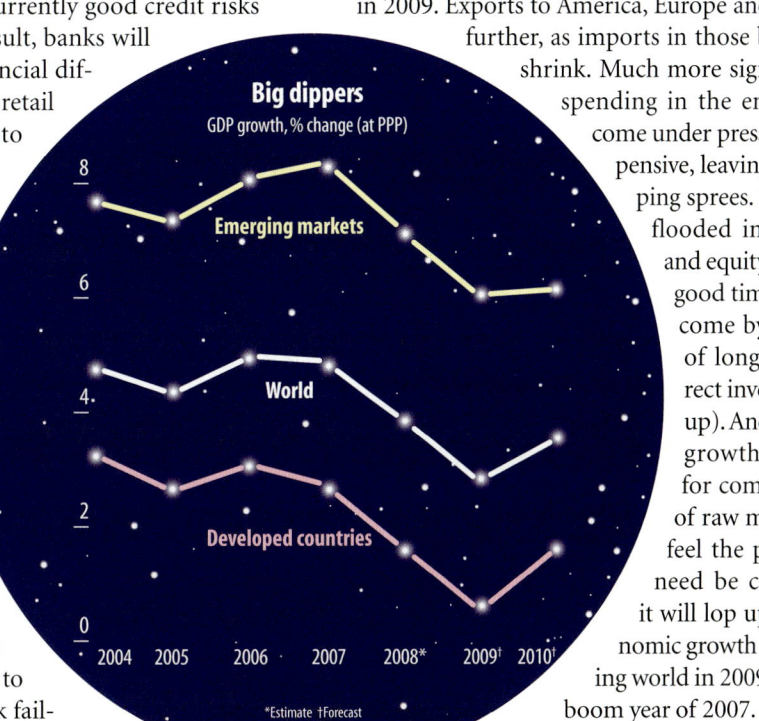

Big dippers
GDP growth, % change (at PPP)

Emerging markets
World
Developed countries

2004 2005 2006 2007 2008* 2009† 2010†

*Estimate †Forecast
Source: Economist Intelligence Unit

Put the developed and the emerging world together and 2009 looks set to be the weakest year for the global economy since the aftermath of the tech wreck in 2002. For the developed world alone, it could be the worst year since the early 1980s recession. That sounds a grim prognosis. But it is important to remember that it could be worse: given the scale of the financial and housing crisis, not to mention the commodity-price shock, we could have been staring at a rerun of the 1930s. That we aren't says much for the handiwork of policymakers during 2008. They will need to remain as active during 2009.

And in one respect, at least, they ought to be bolder still. In 2008, governments let slip the chance to reach agreement in the Doha round of global trade liberalisation. The talks fell apart. The last thing a fragile world economy needs is an outbreak of protectionism—yet that could be all too tempting a response to the tougher times ahead. A far better response would be to give investors and businesses confidence that markets will remain open and trade will flow freely. And nothing would do the job like a Doha deal. ■

The year of unsustainability

We will see whether business and governments are serious about sustainability, says **Daniel Franklin**

For business, the buzzword of 2008 was "sustainability". Never properly defined, it meant different things to different people, which of course added to its charm. In part it was a new way of packaging the clumsy old "corporate social responsibility" (CSR). And it added a virtuous green dimension: sustainable business would help to save the planet. So companies appointed chief sustainability officers and printed (or, to avoid felling more rainforest, electronically distributed) sustainability reports full of photographs of green fields and blossom.

But that was then. In 2009 sustainability will take on a new meaning in boardrooms: staying in business. As recession bites and growth slows, bankruptcies will soar. To sustain profits, companies will slash costs and cut jobs, while consumers will be even less prepared to pay extra for organic food or air-travel offsets.

In these harsher circumstances many companies will tone down their loud green initiatives and instead quietly emphasise value for money. The budgets for worthy projects in the developing world, let alone for supporting opera houses, will be trimmed or cut altogether as their champions find the spending impossible to defend amid the lay-offs. Even the easy wins in the sustainability business—saving both money and the planet by cutting energy usage—will be less rewarding with lower oil prices.

The good, the bad and the ugly

Some of this will be salutary. In the face of the fashion for CSR, companies have tended to make two mistakes. First, they have been too defensive about the benefits they bring to society by the simple fact of being in business. They provide employment, as well as the goods and services that their customers want—and the threat of job losses and even bankruptcies will serve as a powerful reminder of this basic reality.

Second, many companies pretend that their sustainability strategy runs deeper than it really does. It has become almost obligatory for executives to claim that CSR is "connected to the core" of corporate strategy, or that it has become "part of the DNA". In truth, even ardent advocates of sustainability struggle to identify more than a handful of examples. More often the activities that go under the sustainability banner are a hotch-potch of pet projects at best tenuously related to the core business. The coming shake-out will help to remove some of this froth.

Yet it would be wrong for companies to conclude that they can forget about trying to be good. The forces that have pushed companies to fret about sustainability—the scrutiny from the internet, multiplying lobby groups, popular concern about global warming, the threat of lawsuits for misbehaviour on human rights—are not about to disappear. Nor will the desire of potential recruits to work for companies with "values" suddenly vanish. In the competition for the best business-school graduates and other high-flyers, especially once the economy starts to recover, companies that show that they were not mere fairweather friends of sustainability will be at an advantage.

And if companies are not seen to take their social responsibility seriously, governments will intervene to change the rules by which they operate. Some will force companies to sell greener products (for example, by banning the sale of incandescent light bulbs). Others will legislate on executive pay, or oblige banks to lend money in ways the state deems desirable. After rescuing the financial system, many Western governments will imagine that they are the best judges of how to run businesses responsibly.

Yet in 2009 governments face their own test on "sustainability". A summit in Copenhagen at the end of the year is supposed to hammer out a post-Kyoto agreement to cut greenhouse gases. Already pressure is growing to avoid the growth-inhibiting restrictions needed to meet ambitious carbon-cutting targets. Failure to reach a deal will mean, in effect, that the world gives up seriously seeking to stop global warming (see our special section on the environment). Instead, attention would turn to ways the world might adapt to climate change rather than prevent it.

Governments and businesses alike have talked up their commitments to sustainability in recent years. In 2009 both will have to show whether they really meant it. ■

> It would be wrong for companies to conclude that they can forget about trying to be good

Daniel Franklin: editor, *The World in 2009*

Direct Relief INTERNATIONAL
healthy people. better world. since 1948.

Since 1948, Direct Relief International has assisted people in need – both in poor regions of the world and wherever disaster has struck – by providing essential resources to locally-run health programs.

In 2007, Direct Relief provided $136 million in direct aid through medical material assistance and targeted cash grants, providing 34.8 million courses of treatment in 59 countries worldwide. To learn more, visit www.directrelief.org.

Partners in disaster relief

BD Helping all people live healthy lives

Natural and man-made disasters take an alarming toll on their victims. Those who survive often are left tragically devastated. Helping them requires compassion and teamwork to ensure that the necessary medical and humanitarian supplies are distributed quickly to all those who desperately need them.

With the aid of BD and other donors, Direct Relief International has delivered emergency medical supplies and health services to millions, from refugees displaced by war to victims of hurricanes and earthquakes.

These efforts provide the poor, sick and needy with the care they require and the hope they need. BD donates syringes, surgical instruments, blood collection devices and other medical supplies in support of these efforts.

Named one of *America's Most Admired Companies*[1] as well as one of the *World's Most Ethical Companies*,[2] BD provides advanced medical technology to serve the global community's greatest needs.

BD – *Helping all people live healthy lives.*

[1] *FORTUNE*, March 2008
[2] *Ethisphere® Magazine*, June 2008

Please visit www.bd.com
BD and BD Logo are trademarks of Becton, Dickinson and Company. © 2008 BD

Photo ©STR/Reuters

THE ENGINE

ONE OF MANKIND'S BIGGEST CHALLENGES IS TO MAKE OUR WORLD WORK IN A WAY THAT SUSTAINS EVERYTHING THAT IS WONDERFUL ABOUT THIS PLANET. TO DO SO WILL TAKE A SPECIAL KIND OF SKILL. SOME CALL IT ENGINEERING. WE CALL IT CREATIVE PROBLEM-SOLVING. REAL ENERGY SOLUTIONS FOR THE REAL WORLD. WWW.SHELL.COM/REALENERGY

Come to order

There will be a struggle over how to regulate finance and it will not be pretty, says Edward Carr

The coming year will be the one in which financial services fight back. Not in the sense that all those bombed-out banks will suddenly start to make a lot of money. After the wild-eyed panic of 2008, that moment is still some years off. Instead, the fight will be over regulation, and it will be messy.

In 2008 the authorities turned the rules of everyday finance upside down. Their struggle to save the system saw them cut interest rates and widen the collateral they would accept; they poured the state's money into the banks; they guaranteed deposits and creditors; they stood behind the money markets; and they lent directly to companies. But the guarantor-state does not only give: it also takes away. Having saved finance, people want to put those bankers in their place and society needs to redraw the line between government and market.

When their survival was in doubt, financiers had no choice but to accept what the politicians demanded. When the danger passes and markets lie stunned, they will still have to accept some change. The fight will be over how much. Forget any brotherhood or gratitude forged in the greatest financial salvage operation since the 1930s. The rescuers will demand broad regulation, and the rescued will do their best to keep it at bay. Their conflict almost guarantees a bad outcome.

That is a pity because change is essential. The system needs transparency and timely information. The machinery of derivatives was supposed to spread risk from those who wanted to shed it. In theory those who bought risk could rely on the opinions of the rating agencies and buy protection against default. In fact, the rating agencies failed; the insurers went bust; and the shadow banking network of off-balance-sheet vehicles and lightly regulated financial firms hid vast, opaque liabilities. When that became apparent, nobody trusted the firms they did business with.

In addition, the system needs to act against behaviour that fuels the boom and exacerbates the bust. For instance, highly leveraged investment banks lend more when credit is easy and pull back faster in the crash. In future, banks will have to lay more capital aside in the good times—even though that will lower their profits. And America and Europe need to sort out their fragmented regulation. Centuries of manias and panics teach that financiers always have a better hand than their regulators, but the outdated and chaotic structure of regulation only add to their advantages.

Beware bad regulation

And there is almost unlimited scope for bad regulation. Banning short selling did not stop shares from falling, but it did make the market more volatile. Suspending accounting rules that peg assets at their market value has its attractions, because firesale prices are probably too low. But the alternative—book prices that reflect managers' judgments—commands no authority at all: instead it adds to the doubt out there. In general, using regulation to create a pared-down financial industry will be costly. And even then it does not guarantee stability.

After intervening on such a grand scale, the state must use 2009 to prepare for the day when it can credibly say that it no longer guarantees everything. And that, in turn, will call for a restoration of the balance in which investors are confident enough to lend their money, but fearful enough to ensure they lend it wisely. Just now, many people will criticise regulation for being too lax. But remember that regulation can also be costly and distorting. And who will suffer if finance works badly? One thing that became agonisingly clear in 2008 is that we all will. ■

Edward Carr: editor, business affairs, *The Economist*

Banning the bomb

It will just be talk, of course—but, as **Peter David** points out, talk has its uses

One prediction about 2009 can be made with absolute confidence: nuclear weapons will not be abolished. However wonderful it may be in theory to remove the threat of nuclear annihilation once and for all, the idea of simply banning the bomb has long seemed like so much pie in the sky. But here's a paradox. Talk about abolition is going to grow louder. And the talkers will not be only the usual dreamers. Some hard-headed practitioners of realpolitik will be joining the fray.

Oddly enough, what will drive the growing talk about outright abolition is the world's failure to achieve the much more modest objective of preventing new countries from joining the nuclear club. George Bush made stopping "evil" regimes such as North Korea and Iran from getting the bomb a big part of his presidency. In neither case did he succeed. North Korea let off some kind of bomb in 2006, and nobody is certain that it will honour a later promise to disarm. Iran has meanwhile ignored United Nations resolutions (and sanctions) calling on it to stop enriching uranium, which many governments think, despite Iran's denials, it intends to use for a nuclear weapon.

If dangerous-looking countries such as Iran and North Korea build nuclear weapons, why should the official nuclear-armed powers (America, Russia, Britain, France and China), let alone the "unofficial" ones (India, Pakistan and Israel), give up theirs? They won't. But their recent failure to halt actual proliferation in North Korea and potential proliferation in Iran has taught the nuclear powers a lesson. The haves have learnt that unless they start at least to talk about their own eventual disarmament they will find it hard to get many of the have-nots on their side when it comes to preventing further proliferation.

This is because the have-nots have a grievance. The Nuclear Non-Proliferation Treaty (NPT) does not just require the non-nuclear powers to give up the idea of acquiring nukes. It also obliges the official five to work towards the abolition of their existing arsenals. If the haves show no sign of living up to this side of the bargain, the have-nots' resentment will grow and they will become less and less willing to agree to the sharper inspections that will be needed as nuclear know-how and materials spread more widely round the world.

> Talk itself will have real-world consequences

This is one reason why a number of arch-"realists" in America, including former secretaries of state Henry Kissinger and George Shultz, have been calling for more serious thinking about a nuclear-free world, starting off with big new cuts in the arsenals of Russia and America. How realistic, though, is total abolition?

Not very. "Make me perfect," said Saint Augustine, "but not yet." That is the attitude of many nuclear powers. They hint that they would give up their nukes when it is safe, but do not really expect ever to feel safe enough. Israel, for example, says it favours a Middle East free of weapons of mass destruction, but not until all the local powers, including Iran, make peace and agree to verification. And not all nuclear states favour abolition even in principle. France, for one, holds that its nukes are a useful deterrent against all sorts of threats, not just the threat from other nuclear powers.

Let's pretend

Even in the unlikely event of all the nuclear powers deciding to abolish their weapons, the practical difficulties of doing so would be immense. Who would go first? How could each be sure that one of the others had not kept a few nukes—or the ability quickly to rebuild them—in reserve? No nuclear state is likely to move towards disarmament unless there are simultaneous moves to strengthen the safeguards against proliferation. But serious dialogue on this between the haves and have-nots has all but stopped during the bad-tempered wrangles over Iran.

If abolition is just a pipe dream, why put it in a list of predictions about 2009? Because the talk is going to grow, and talk itself will have real-world consequences. In 2010 the haves and have-nots will hold their next five-yearly review of the NPT. It will be far easier to prevent the non-proliferation rules from collapsing if the nuclear powers sound as if they are at least a little serious about their obligation to work towards disarmament. Some will call this hypocrisy: the haves will pretend to believe in abolition and the have-nots may pretend to believe them. But productive diplomacy often requires a measure of mutual pretence. ■

Peter David: foreign editor, *The Economist*

Cities that consume 30% less energy?

As a leading producer of energy-efficient solutions, ABB helps deliver major power savings, without compromising performance. Our lighting control systems can deliver power savings of up to 50 percent, and our building automation up to 60 percent. While everyone else is talking about energy prices, power shortages and climate change, ABB is doing something about it, right here, right now. www.abb.com/energyefficiency

Certainly.

Power and productivity
for a better world™

ABB

Thank you

You allow a moment in which our engines don't need to run – s
now available across the BMW range. Revolutionary cars wit

BMW EfficientDynamics

www.bmw.co.uk
Tel. 0800 325 600

BMW
The Ultimate Driving Machine

stop sign.

ney don't. Auto Start-Stop is just one technology in our EfficientDynamics initiative, a programme
MW EfficientDynamics.

BMW EfficientDynamics
Less emissions. More driving pleasure.

Shocking science

Geoffrey Carr expects scientists to provide a year of celebrations and screams

"Starry Messenger" does not sound a particularly controversial sort of title. "On the Origin of Species" doesn't sound controversial, either. But, between them, these two books poked their fingers in the eyes of the religious establishment so sharply that they provoked screams which are still heard today, making 2009 a good year for anniversaries of scientific controversies. Though Galileo Galilei's book was not published until 1610, he first picked up the telescope that provided the material for it in 1609. Charles Darwin, born in 1809, published his masterwork in 1859. Four centuries, two centuries, and one-and-a-half centuries: 2009 offers a fine excuse to celebrate two of the great iconoclasts of history.

The echoing screams from these books are, oddly, loudest in America. It is a paradox that the world's greatest scientific power is also the one that protests most audibly against the acceptance of scientific truths when they conflict with revealed ones. The coming year is likely to hear more screaming as science pushes further into areas that some people would prefer it kept its inquisitive nose out of.

One likely announcement, which may happen any day of the year, is of the world's first artificial living creature. The announcer will almost certainly be Craig Venter, an American biologist who has been working on making such a creature for over a decade. It will not be quite as billed. *Mycoplasma laboratorium*, as the bacterium is expected to be dubbed, will need the shell of a natural bacterium to get going. But the genes themselves will have been made and stitched together, as the name suggests, in a laboratory—and it is the genes, not the shell, that define the organism. Someone once accused Dr Venter of playing God. His reply was, "We're not playing." And though a completely artificial life form is the ultimate in synthetic biology, 2009 will also see the widespread deployment of natural bugs that have been highly tinkered with in the creation of advanced biofuels, as well as the planting of yet more genetically modified crops. Scream on.

The heat may, however, go out of another controversial field. Embryonic-stem-cell research should become more acceptable in 2009. One reason will be the exit of George Bush from the White House. And the science itself is moving on. Several groups of researchers think they can now make pretty good simulacra of such cells without killing anything that remotely resembles a potential human being.

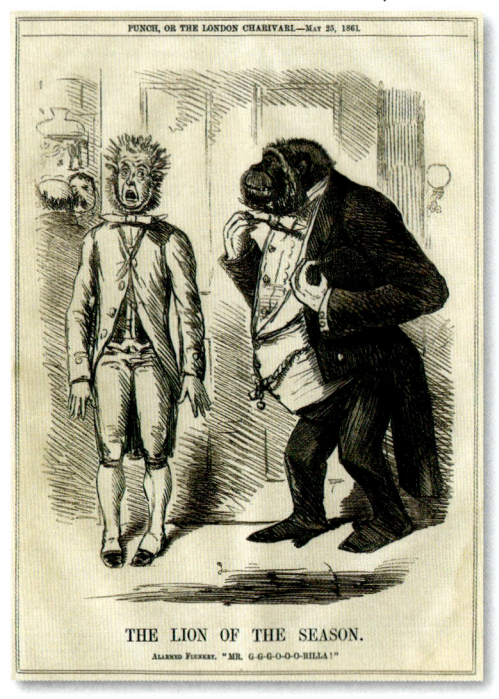

No end of controversy

Science will also be arguing with itself, as it always does. Expect ructions in the field of climate change as people seek to reconcile the smooth curves of computer models with the messy reality of the atmosphere, and thus explain why things have not been heating up recently in the way the models suggest they should have. More esoterically, the first results from the world's largest particle accelerator, the Large Hadron Collider near Geneva, should be coming in. Here, too, theory could clash with reality as the models of the sub-atomic world built up by physicists are tested.

Perhaps the most controversial field of all is one after Darwin's own heart: the evolution of religion itself. Some academics suggest that science and religion are different ways of looking at the same questions. Peaceful co-existence is the way forward. But that is not good enough for the evolutionists.

They see a propensity to religion as a natural human characteristic, like a propensity to language. Examining the biological and evolutionary causes of language is a respectable endeavour, so why not apply the same approach to religion? This sort of science seeks not to transcend religion, but to absorb it and reduce it to just another natural phenomenon that can be prodded, measured and explained. Such research is now going on apace—and set to provoke screams that will echo well beyond 2009. ■

> Perhaps the most controversial field of all is one after Darwin's own heart: the evolution of religion itself

Geoffrey Carr: science editor, *The Economist*

HEAVEN

EARTH

Where will you find your Shangri-La?

SHANGRI-LA
HOTELS and RESORTS

www.shangri-la.com

The perils of sharing

The surprising threat to your privacy is closer than you think, cautions **Andreas Kluth**

Something new has recently occurred in the timeless human activity of socialising, and it will begin to cause a lot of grief in 2009. The fashionable term for it is "sharing". In its new context, this refers to volunteering personal information that used to be considered off-limits to all but the most intimate friends and relatives—but that is now taking on a life of its own.

It may consist of daily photos to chronicle a pregnancy, uploaded to websites such as Flickr or Facebook and adorned by comments from "friends", real and imagined. Or video clips of bacchanalia by the hockey team. Or geo-tagged and time-dated clips of the girls' softball team's weekly practice, with each girl's name tagged and pointing to a MySpace page.

But things can go wrong in pregnancies, and prying eyes that are not those of friends suddenly witness tragedies or a cruel hiatus in updates. College-admissions deans and potential employers browse bacchanalian footage. Perverts can plot detailed schedules of a particular girl's movements on a given practice day.

People have always tried to manage their reputation, and today's new media give them powerful tools to do just that. So most people participate, and share, enthusiastically. This is rational, says Edward Felten, a privacy expert at Princeton University, because they get benefits: inclusion into a community and more control in crafting and presenting their own image.

The problem is that they quickly lose that control. This has to do with what Steven Rambam, a professional investigator, modestly calls "Rambam's Law": whatever purpose a piece of information may have been created and shared for, it will eventually be used for something else. There was a time when the likes of Mr Rambam got paid big bucks to snoop out somebody's picture, sexual history, mother's maiden name (still a popular password) and list of friends. Today, this is a matter of minutes spent stitching together data from a few web sites. An identity thief, a political rival, a bitter ex-spouse, a litigant—anybody who is savvy and wants information—can get it.

Most of the paranoia about privacy in the internet era has focused on the power of companies, primarily Google, to collect information about all our doings online. Google installs cookies in web browsers that record the search history of users; it analyses the text in e-mails to insert relevant advertisements; it takes photos of private homes—occasionally with the residents visible—and adds them to its online maps.

This makes it necessary for the public to scrutinise Google and similar companies, and to hold them accountable for any breaches of privacy. But Sergey Brin, one of Google's two founders, is also right to point to the risk of an asymmetrical hysteria. The public may have overreacted to the perceived threat of Google. Google ensures that computers, rather than humans, "read" user data. And Google has a powerful incentive to protect its users' information, rather as the self-interest of banks includes proper custody of depositors' data.

The enemy within

Meanwhile, the public has mostly ignored the bigger danger: ourselves. Anybody with a mobile phone that is also a camera is today a potential producer of an autobiographical documentary. She may upload this for fame, friendship and fun, but it may come back to hurt her.

Does that mean that it is prudent to opt out of Facebook, Flickr, Twitter, MySpace, YouTube and their ilk? Probably not. Participation has become automatic. Even as the camera phone makes each individual an autobiographer, it also makes all the people around her into freelance paparazzi, with their own tabloid-style press (the web). Those paparazzi capture, tag and gossip about her in their own photos, clips and "twitters".

So there we are, a Google search away, for all to see in places and company we should not have been in, the unwitting backdrop of other people's documentaries.

The only remaining choice is whether or not to inject our own perspective, with our own media, into this never-ending stream of narratives, to preserve whatever control remains in presenting our own image. The wise will still share things about themselves in 2009. But they will become hyper-sensitive about sharing collateral information about others, in the hope that reciprocity and a new etiquette will eventually limit everybody's vulnerability, including their own. ∎

> Anybody who is savvy and wants information can get it

Andreas Kluth: San Francisco correspondent, *The Economist*

www.barcap.com

LOOK INTO THE CENTRE OF BARCLAYS CAPITAL AND YOU'LL FIND OUR CLIENTS.

Whatever changes the world is facing in 2009, one thing will stay exactly the same.
We will continue to put our clients at the centre of everything we do, every day.

Earn Success Every Day

BARCLAYS CAPITAL

ed by Barclays Bank PLC, authorised and regulated by the Financial Services Authority and a member of the London Stock Exchange, Barclays Capital is the investment banking division of Barclays Bank
which undertakes US securities business in the name of its wholly-owned subsidiary Barclays Capital Inc., an SIPC and FINRA member. © 2008 Barclays Bank PLC. All rights reserved. Barclays and Barclays
al are trademarks of Barclays Bank PLC and its affiliates.

English marks a million

Or does it? **John Grimond** has some infrequently offered answers

Some events in 2009 may be more momentous, but surely not many: on April 29th the number of words in the English language will pass 1m. This astonishing fact prompts a host of frequently asked questions or, as wordsmiths call them, FAQS.

First, who says—or, in tabloid (this meaning coined in 1902) journalese (1882), who sez? The answer is the Global Language Monitor, a company based in Austin, Texas. It keeps an eye on the use of language, especially English, and tracks changes.

And by what authority does the Global Language Monitor say a new coinage is a genuine new word? None. Some countries, such as France and Spain, have academies that claim the right to regulate their national languages, and to repel invasive terms, usually from English. Neither England nor the United States attempts such an exercise in futility. English is a mongrel language that keeps its vitality by absorbing new words, uses and expressions. It promiscuously plunders other languages and delights in neologisms. It is the language of free traders and inventive entrepreneurs such as the staff of the Global Language Monitor.

Stick to the FAQs

So is it really a fact that English will have 1m words on the predicted date in April? Of course not. For a start, the global monitors explain that the actual date could be five days either side of April 29th. Then they say that English already has well over 1m words, if you accept the statement in the introduction to the Merriam-Webster dictionary that the language contains "many times" the 450,000 words it lists. Yet the Oxford dictionary lists only half as many.

Who's right? How many words are there? That depends on what counts as a word. Should "write", "writes", "wrote", "written" count as four words or one? If one, what about "be", "am", "are", "is", "was", "were"? What about the numberless words with different meanings? Should "set" and "stock", for instance, each count as one, though their meanings are manifold? And what of winespeak, computer drivel and other jargon?

Och aye, and whit aboot Scots? Yes, English gathers variants as it travels and, my, how it has travelled. Is the Scots "thrapple" just the same as the English "thropple" (throat)? Is the Australian "donkasaurus" (car engine) English or Australian or Greek?

Come to that, what about all the words that English picks up abroad? "Hobson-Jobson", written in 1886, lists over 2,000 Anglo-Indian expressions. "Shampoo" and "bungalow" have certainly earned their place in the English dictionary, but what of the Hindi "dam", the Indian coin once used in English phrases like "I don't give a dam" but now consigned to history or misspelt, and so misunderstood, as "damn"? Or what of "roué", a "French" word common enough in English but now almost unknown in French? List them all, you may say, along with jihad, tsunami, schadenfreude and béarnaise sauce. But the line must be drawn somewhere, so where?

The global monitors would have the world believe that their lines are drawn scientifically: take the bulk of the best-known dictionaries, chuck in all the words in Shakespeare, Chaucer and the Bible, and then apply their proprietary algorithm, which trawls through the press, the internet and every other medium for new words. After that, apparently, the words must meet criteria about frequency of use in print and speech and their ability to stand the test of time. Words drop out of use as well as into it—Oxford lists 47,156 it considers obsolete—and most neologisms die almost as soon as they leave the lips of the rapper, valley girl or blogobore who utters them.

So, last question, is the 1m-word claim meaningless? Yes, largely. But English does indeed have lots of words, almost certainly more than any other tongue. That is the consequence of its evolution. Basically Germanic, it was expanded by the conquering Normans, who introduced French, and the medieval scholars and clergy, who used Latin. As the global language of the modern world, it now has lots of local variants—some recompense perhaps for the words it helps to obliterate as more and more languages become extinct. ■

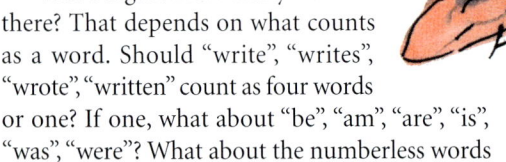

> English does indeed have lots of words, almost certainly more than any other tongue

John Grimond: writer at large, *The Economist*

MALAYSIA
Your Profit Centre in ASIA

WHY MALAYSIA:

Political and economic stability ■ Strong economic fundamentals ■ Pro-business government
Liberal investment policies ■ Transparent policies ■ Policy of welcome
Well developed infrastructure ■ Harmonious industrial relations
Trainable and educated workforce ■ English language widely spoken ■ Quality of life
The Nation's track record

MIDA is the first point of contact for investors who intend to set up projects in the manufacturing and services sectors in Malaysia. With its headquarters in Malaysia's capital city of Kuala Lumpur, MIDA has established a global network of 19 overseas offices to assist investors interested in locating their operations in Malaysia.

MIDA provides:
- Investment Information and Assistance
- Business Matching
- Other Advisory Services

Malaysian Industrial Development Authority
Block 4, Plaza Sentral, Jalan Stesen Sentral 5, Kuala Lumpur Sentral, 50470 Kuala Lumpur, Malaysia
Tel: (603) 2267 3633   Fax: (603) 2274 7970   Website: www.mida.gov.my   E-mail: promotion@mida.gov.my

MIDA

Everyday, we make the world a little smaller.

Welcome to our expanding global network.

It's a world where cities are coming closer together. One where gaps no longer separate the continents. It's an extensive network that touches every corner of the globe. So fly with us on your next journey. After all, we cover the world with over 80 destinations.

World's 5-star airline.
qatarairways.com

Europe	Middle East	Africa	South Asia	Northeast Asia
Athens	Abu Dhabi	Alexandria	Ahmedabad	Beijing
Berlin	Amman	Algiers	Chennai	Guangzhou
Frankfurt	Bahrain	Cairo	Colombo	Hong Kong
Geneva	Beirut	Cape Town	Delhi	Osaka
Istanbul	Damascus	Casablanca	Dhaka	Seoul
London	Dammam	Dar es Salaam	Hyderabad	Shanghai
Madrid	Doha	Johannesburg	Islamabad	**Southeast Asia**
Manchester	Dubai	Khartoum	Karachi	Bali
Milan	Jeddah	Lagos	Kathmandu	Bangkok
Moscow	Kuwait	Luxor	Kochi	Cebu
Munich	Mashad	Nairobi	Kozhikode	Ho Chi Minh City
Paris	Muscat	Seychelles	Lahore	Jakarta
Rome	Riyadh	Tripoli	Maldives	Kuala Lumpur
Stockholm	Sanaa	Tunis	Mumbai	Manila
Vienna	Tehran		Nagpur	Singapore
Zurich			Peshawar	**USA**
			Trivandrum	Houston (30th March 2009)
				New York
				Washington, DC

QATAR AIRWAYS القطرية

Calendar for 2009

Our selection of events around the world

JANUARY

The Czech Republic assumes the presidency of the European Union, and Linz in Austria and Vilnius in Lithuania become European "Capitals of Culture".

America welcomes its 44th president to the White House.

The Swiss resort of Davos hosts the great and good from politics, business and the media to the annual meeting of the World Economic Forum.

Star-gazers welcome the International Year of Astronomy, celebrating the 400th anniversary of the first use of an astronomical telescope by Galileo Galilei.

Chinese around the world begin the Year of the Ox, supposedly enduring hardship without complaint and achieving prosperity through patience and hard work.

FEBRUARY

Praying for good snow, the world's best skiers compete at the Alpine World Ski Championships at Val d'Isère in France.

Iran celebrates the Ten-Day Dawn, marking the 30th anniversary of the Islamic revolution.

Lovers around the world celebrate St Valentine's day, a week before the lovers of Rio de Janeiro revel in its annual carnival.

Hollywood hands out its annual Oscars, for the 81st time, to the film world's best—a day after the award of Golden Raspberries, or Razzies, to the film world's worst.

MARCH

Fashionistas gather for the Paris Fashion Week, ogling the ready-to-wear designs women will want for the coming autumn and winter.

Barbie, the world's most popular doll, turns 50, but looks as young as ever.

Battling against the Anglophone tide, the world's 200m French-speakers celebrate the international day of la francophonie.

China's National People's Congress holds its annual plenary session. Voters in Congo-Brazzaville elect a president.

Masochistic runners attempt Morocco's Marathon des Sables, a race which covers 151 miles (243km) of the Sahara desert and takes six days.

APRIL

Tricksters across the world delight in April Fool's Day.

Beirut becomes the ninth World Book Capital, chosen by UNESCO for "its focus on cultural diversity, dialogue and tolerance".

South Africa holds both parliamentary and presidential elections around now.

Peace-seeking scientists, scholars and public figures gather in The Hague for the annual Pugwash Conference on Science and World Affairs, aimed at reducing the risk of armed conflict.

MAY

Russia hosts the Eurovision Song Contest, normally marked by camp performances and politically biased voting.

Deadline for India, the world's most populous democracy, to hold a general election to the People's Assembly.

Star Trek XI is released, delighting the film saga's fans as it delves into the early days of the Star Trek crew.

Rome hosts the final of the UEFA Champions League, pitting Europe's best football teams against one another.

JUNE

Voters in the 27-nation European Union elect a new European Parliament to a five-year term. Few citizens will afterwards know the name of their MEP.

Those who prefer life without clothes are invited to celebrate World Naturist Day.

The art world gathers in Italy for the Venice Biennale, held every two years to exhibit contemporary art.

Roger Federer tries, again, and despite Rafael Nadal, to win the French Open, the only tennis grand-slam title to have escaped him.

The deadline passes for all EU states to include biometric data in their passports.

JULY

Sweden takes its turn as president of the European Union.

Horse-riders race around the main square of Siena, Italy; bulls run through the streets of Pamplona, Spain; and cyclists gather in Monaco for the Tour de France.

Indonesia begins its presidential election.

Finland hosts the Wife-Carrying World Championships. The winner gets his wife's weight in beer.

Arts performers of all kinds gather in France for the annual Avignon Festival and in Lebanon for the Baalbeck International Festival.

AUGUST

Montreal hosts the World Science Fiction Convention, where an author's fantasy can lead to a Hugo Award.

Forbes magazine releases its list of the world's most powerful women (the 2008 list was headed by Germany's chancellor, Angela Merkel; America's Condoleezza Rice was seventh).

In contrast to America, much of Europe takes a month-long holiday.

SEPTEMBER

NASA launches the Mars Science Laboratory rover, a robot vehicle with an estimated arrival date on Mars of July-September 2010. Meanwhile, NASA's Messenger spacecraft flies by Mercury.

The UN General Assembly meets in New York.

The bling-bearing pop-music world gathers in Los Angeles for the annual MTV Video Music Awards.

OCTOBER

The IMF and World Bank meet in Istanbul, to discuss the economic woes of the world.

The International Olympic Committee announces the host city for the 2016 Summer Olympics, choosing from Chicago, Madrid, Rio de Janeiro and Tokyo.

Tunisia holds a presidential election as Zine El Abidine Ben Ali, head of state since 1987, ends his latest five-year term. Uruguay holds presidential and legislative elections.

Astérix, the heroic Gaul of the French comic-book genre, turns 50, having been translated into more than 100 different languages and dialects.

The Royal Swedish Academy of Sciences chooses a galaxy of Nobel laureates, from economics to literature, and the Norwegian Nobel Committee awards the peace prize.

NOVEMBER

Singapore hosts the Asia-Pacific Economic Co-operation forum, a gathering of 21 Pacific-rim nations, from America to Brunei.

The Pew Research Centre releases its poll on America's place in the world. In the previous poll, in 2005, some 42% of Americans thought the country should "mind its own business internationally".

Britain's Queen Elizabeth will open the two-yearly summit, this time in Trinidad and Tobago, of some 53 Commonwealth heads of state and government. They may discuss a bid for membership by Rwanda, formerly a Belgian colony.

Word-lovers compete in the World Scrabble Championships, held every two years.

The UN Climate Change Conference opens in Copenhagen, with delegates striving to reach a new agreement on cutting greenhouse gases beyond the expiry in 2012 of the Kyoto protocol.

DECEMBER

Chile holds presidential and parliamentary elections, as does Mozambique, and Iraq elects a new Council of Representatives.

The Finnish-made Oasis of the Seas, the largest cruise ship ever built, at a cost of $1.2 billion, and with some 5,400 passengers, undertakes its maiden voyage.

At the end of the month, the third deadline set to accommodate protests from America and other exponents of non-metric measures, the European Union bans all imports that are not labelled with metric measurements.

With the help of contributions from
foresightnews
www.foresightnews.co.uk

TALKING
USES ENERGY.
DOING
CREATES IT.

IBM is working with companies to develop intelligent utility networks – automated, responsive power delivery systems that can help provide greater service reliability, reduce outages and promote energy efficiency. Start rethinking the way you do business at **ibm.com/doing/uk**

STOP TALKING **START DOING**

IBM, the IBM logo and ibm.com are registered trademarks or trademarks of International Business Machines Corporation in the United States and/or other countries. Other company, product and service names may be trademarks or service marks of others. ©2008 IBM Corporation. All rights reserved.

Britain

Also in this section:
The debate over Scotland 36
The case for manufacturing 38
Recession or slump? 40
Going deep into the red 41
Boris Johnson: London after the credit crunch 42

Maybe, prime minister

Andrew Miller

Gordon Brown's chances of surviving the year in office

It will be more of the same at Westminster in 2009—or it will be a year of dramatic change. Gordon Brown will continue unhappily as prime minister, boosted only temporarily by his handling of the financial crisis and trailing David Cameron and the Conservative Party in the polls. Or Mr Brown will be deposed in a Labour coup, and a new prime minister installed—who in turn may feel obliged to call an early general election.

Dissatisfaction with Mr Brown's leadership among Labour MPs erupted in the autumn of 2008, when around a dozen called for a leadership contest. Some senior ministers share the rebels' concerns, and in 2009 may say so publicly—especially if Mr Brown attempts a more thorough cabinet reshuffle than October's, in which he surprisingly brought Peter Mandelson, a talented but controversial politician, back into government. Actually ousting Mr Brown, however, would require a concerted strike by a gang of high-ranking figures: by threatening to resign, they could try to force Mr Brown out instead. The members of this putative cabal have been pre-emptively dubbed "the men in grey suits" (some Labourites joked in 2008 that they had been avoiding grey attire, lest they be mistaken for assassins).

If Mr Brown goes, who might take over? David Miliband, the young and clever foreign secretary, seemed the likeliest successor until Labour's annual conference in September, when his palpable eagerness for the top job, plus a couple of silly-looking photographs (including one of him wielding a banana) damaged his prospects. Other contenders include Jack Straw, the justice secretary, one of the wiliest Labour survivors; and Harriet Harman, who in 2007 won the race to become Labour's deputy leader. For some in the party, the idea that the erratic Ms Harman might inherit Mr Brown's crown is reason enough to make sure he keeps it.

So much for the "how" and the "who". If there is to be a putsch, the final question is, when? The day of greatest peril for Mr Brown is likely to be June 5th—the day after elections to the European Parliament. If Labour does as badly as it did in assorted votes in 2008, more Labour MPs will see that under him they are doomed to defeat,

> The day of greatest peril for Mr Brown is likely to be June 5th

It's getting late

perhaps a catastrophic one, in a general election too.

Even some of those who argued against deposing Mr Brown in 2008 think the summer of 2009 will be more propitious. A new prime minister would be Labour's third in a single parliamentary term; Mr Cameron, and much of the media, would howl at him or her to go to the country quickly. But a summer leadership contest, yielding a new prime minister in the early autumn, might let a new leader avoid calling an election until the following year.

Yet the factors that have preserved Mr Brown in ▸

Andrew Miller: political editor, *The Economist*

Britain

2009 IN BRIEF

International **Twenty20 cricket**, a bastardised but popular quick-play offspring of test cricket, comes to the home of cricket with the Twenty20 World Cup at Lord's, in London.

Number 10 until the start of 2009 may keep him there until the end of it. One is disagreement among his critics about who should replace him. More important, however, is the economic downturn, whose gravity deterred his rivals from moving against him. The crisis enabled him to argue that, having served ten years as chancellor of the exchequer, he was uniquely qualified to govern now. "This", he quipped, "is no time for a novice."

His bold and (relatively) timely intervention in the banking sector seemed to corroborate this view. The argument may prove mistaken in 2009. If Mr Cameron manages to persuade the public that Mr Brown is the cause of the problem rather than its solution, the prime minister's economic record will damage him. Meanwhile, as the mayhem in the financial sector bequeaths rising unemployment and falling tax receipts, Mr Brown will have to decide how far to back up his pledge to protect voters with tangible policies—and find a way to pay for them. For his part, Mr Cameron will have to exchange his sunny, optimistic version of Conservatism for a more astringent kind. The debate between the two leaders will be rancorous: they dislike each other intensely. It may also become refreshingly ideological.

As for the rest of the political cabaret: Nick Clegg, the affable leader of the Liberal Democrats, will rely on his excellent shadow chancellor, Vince Cable, to maintain his party's visibility. Alex Salmond—leader of the Scottish National Party (SNP), and first minister of the devolved Scottish government—will continue to pick fights with Westminster. But his personal popularity will not (yet) translate into greater support for the SNP's ultimate goal of Scottish independence (see box). Northern Irish politics will remain deadlocked. Boris Johnson, the eccentric mayor of London, will amuse Londoners and occasionally embarrass himself.

At the start of 2009, Mr Johnson wields more executive power than any other Tory. Will that be true at the end of the year—or will Mr Brown be out, Mr Miliband or Mr Straw in, perhaps quickly followed by Mr Cameron? The best bet is on Mr Brown struggling through 2009, lame but unmovable, before facing the country, and Mr Cameron, in a general election in 2010. ■

Straining at the leash

Merril Stevenson

The debate over just how free Scotland should be will change in 2009

Among Gordon Brown's woes in 2009 the ongoing row with his native land will not be the least. Displaced in Scotland's local elections in 2007, his Labour Party went on to lose one Westminster by-election there in July 2008 and fought in November to retain another seat. Alex Salmond, head of the Scottish National Party (SNP) and first minister of devolved Scotland, has lost no chance to tear critical strips off Mr Brown. He also wants a referendum in 2010, with a view to taking Scotland out of the union.

For all Mr Salmond's growing popularity, most Scots are still keener on more devolution than on independence, and most English are only irritated by the fact that Scots seem to get a better deal on central-government spending. But the debate will be different in 2009, for two reasons.

First, the Tories' lead in England, though whittled in 2008, has proved enduring. Polls suggest that the likelier a Tory victory is at Westminster, the more Scots will favour independence.

Unless, that is, the economy takes even more of a turn for the worse—the second reason why the terms of the debate will change. Scotland suffered less than England during the downturn of the early 1990s; its citizens are less in hock on their homes and more of them work for the state, which will be loth to lay them off. But this time the financial system is compromised: one Scottish bank is already down; Edinburgh fund managers will suffer; and Scottish firms too need bank loans. Frightened by signs of collapse, the Scots may well cling to nanny instead.

There will be two telling moments in 2009. The first is the European elections in June, in which the SNP is likely to advance. The second is the report of the Calman commission on Scottish devolution, which is expected to recommend giving Scotland more power over taxes. If adopted (and it could prove popular in both England and Scotland), this might reduce demands for separation.

The debate on independence is mostly couched in terms of what Scotland would lose or gain (cue heavy breathing over North Sea oil revenues and fiscal flows). A second argument is over whether the United Kingdom as a whole, and its weight in the world, would be diminished.

But more specific consequences are worth pondering. If Labour loses its hinterland, what remains of the union might lurch to the right under an entrenched Tory majority. It would lose many nuclear-power and renewable-energy sites, a disproportionate chunk of its best soldiers and its only world-class tennis player. Most tellingly, it might have to wrap up its nuclear-submarine base on the Clyde. Food for thought for all parties, which have 2009—but not much longer—to make up their minds just where they stand on devolution. ■

Merril Stevenson: Britain editor, *The Economist*

a) 🛢 oil

b) 🔥 natural gas

c) 🌬 wind

d) ☀ solar

e) 🌱 biofuels

✓ f) all of the above

The answer to the big question of how to secure future energy supplies isn't one of the above. It's all of the above. That's why, as the largest single producer of oil and gas in the UK North Sea, BP is using the latest technology to find new reserves and to increase recovery from existing fields. We are also investing in a major biofuels facility in Hull and expanding our global wind power generation and production of solar panels. It all adds up to a more dependable energy future. Learn more at bp.com

london official partner

bp

beyond petroleum

Made in Britain

John Rose

A leading industrialist puts the argument that the time is ripe for a manufacturing renaissance

Paradoxically, today's challenging economic conditions provide a unique opportunity for Britain. A fundamental examination of how this nation earns its living is long overdue. The credit crunch could provide the impetus we need to answer a question that has defeated policymakers for more than 50 years: how can manufacturing be encouraged to create wealth as part of a competitive, high-value British economy?

Manufacturing's problems began with the misguided notion that Britain should become a "post-industrial" economy: that we would focus on services and the creation of ideas, with other nations taking on the less attractive task of making the finished product. The results speak for themselves. Manufacturing now generates just 13% of GDP, compared with 32% in 1970.

The credit crisis has exposed the risks of an unbalanced economy. At a recent conference a senior British industrialist, about to address German government and industry representatives on our industrial policy, was introduced as follows: "Our speaker is now going to explain how you run an economy based on real estate."

These imbalances have also prompted our politicians and commentators to consider seriously, some for the first time, the importance of high-value-added manufacturing in a developed economy. The government has published a new manufacturing strategy; the Conservatives are reviewing their policy towards industry. Our objective as a country must be to build on this work and define the policy and financial mechanisms required to encourage an expansion of manufacturing as part of a more balanced economy. We have to be ruthlessly honest about both the scale of the competition we face and the focused action which other countries are already taking to promote manufacturing.

The first priority should be to stop treating manufacturing as a relic of the industrial revolution. High-value-added manufacturing brings huge benefits. It penetrates the economy of the entire country, not just London and the south-east. It pays well but avoids bewildering distortions of income. It drives and enables a broad range of skills and stimulates the growth of services. In short, it creates wealth.

The benefits are seen clearly in Derby, where around 11,000 people are employed by Rolls-Royce and a further 15,000 in its supply chain. Nearly 12% of the city's workforce is involved in high technology, the highest figure in the country, and the number of skilled employees is 2.4 times the national average. Derby's contribution to the British economy, measured by gross value added, is growing faster than that of any other city.

Manufacturing generates over three-quarters of R&D investment made by British businesses. This creates a strong technology base which opens new options for all businesses.

That is why Britain's decision to proceed with new nuclear is so important: it has the potential to catalyse a manufacturing renaissance. If we can become a nuclear "first mover" we will develop our nuclear capability and supply chain, enabling us to benefit from a growing global market. This industry also demands a very broad range of skills, from project management to materials science, most of which are transferable to other sectors.

What is true of civil nuclear is true of high-value-added manufacturing more generally. I am struck by the fact that almost all developed and emerging economies have well articulated plans to capture and promote this sort of manufacturing. Britain risks being the only country out of step. We need an economic route map for attracting and retaining high-value-added investment, identifying Britain's competitive advantages with ruthless honesty and prioritising both public and private investment accordingly.

This is not about protectionism or "picking winners". It is simply an acknowledgment that most nations with these goals have a clear strategy for achieving them, with that clarity being part of their competitiveness. Britain's success in the 2008 Olympics was based on precisely the sort of competitive assessment and focused investment that we must bring to our economic decisions. It has sent a strong signal to aspiring young sportsmen and women. The same will, I submit, be true of the signals sent to young people in education if we bring a similar clarity to addressing our economic competitiveness.

So how do I see British manufacturing faring in 2009? We still retain a strong industrial capability and science base. By setting the right priorities we can develop within a generation a more broadly based economy, with greater resilience and stronger exports. We will see a high-value-added manufacturing sector with deep product knowledge enabling growing services, and renewed demand for science-based subjects in schools and universities. It is entirely feasible that this new direction can be set in 2009 and that today's economic difficulties will create the right conditions to inform this fundamental shift in attitude and policy. ■

> **Stop treating manufacturing as a relic of the industrial revolution**

Sir John Rose: chief executive, Rolls-Royce

Back to the heyday?

2009 IN BRIEF
Cambridge University becomes 800 years old.

FOR DECISIONS THAT MATTER, INFORMATION THAT MATTERS.

Information. The world runs on it. Industries are built on it. But for the people who matter, who make the decisions that matter, information alone is not enough. They require insight. They demand relevance. They need intelligent information.

Ordinary information is passive. Intelligent information is anything but. It thinks for itself. It takes the nebulous and focuses it. It provides a competitive advantage, in forms that can be acted upon instantly. Cross-platform. Cross-industry.

Intelligent information begins with data. And Thomson Reuters has an unmatched ability to gather it and verify it. To separate the meaningless from the meaningful and set that information to work. In databases that share ideas. With algorithms that reinforce and multiply each other's capabilities. Filtering data until actionable knowledge emerges.

Then, before information is delivered to decision makers in law, science, finance, healthcare, tax or media, it is filtered again. By experts who know what you do, because they do what you do. Knowledge that arrives when needed. Knowledge that finds you. In real time.

It is knowledge that is trusted by the Fortune 500. Knowledge relied on when decisions matter. And it makes us the leading source of intelligent information for businesses and professionals around the world. It is knowledge of consequence, for people of consequence. It is knowledge to act.
thomsonreuters.com

FINANCIAL — Applications used by over half a million professionals globally.

LEGAL — Westlaw relied upon by 98% of the world's major law firms.

TAX & ACCOUNTING — Checkpoint used by 99 of the top 100 U.S. accounting firms.

SCIENTIFIC — Used by more than 20 million researchers worldwide.

HEALTHCARE — Informs healthcare decisions affecting over 150 million lives.

MEDIA — Reuters News reaches over one billion people daily.

THOMSON REUTERS
KNOWLEDGE TO ACT

©2008 Thomson Reuters. Thomson Reuters and the Kinesis logo are the trademarks of Thomson Reuters.

Binary blues

Anatole Kaletsky

Will the economy experience a common-or-garden recession, or a severe slump?

The tradition of *The World in* is to make clear predictions, avoiding conditionals or qualifications. Any rational assessment of the British economy in 2009, however, requires a modification of this approach. The problem is not that the outlook is cloudy; uncertainty is a permanent feature of economics. What makes 2009 unusual is actually the clarity of the outlook: this will be a binary year. Two very different economic scenarios are not just possible, but almost certain, depending on what has happened to the British financial system by the start of 2009. But before considering these distinct scenarios in greater detail, let us begin with the elements they both have in common—the "known knowns" of 2009.

One thing we know for sure is that the British economy will suffer its first recession for 18 years in 2009. To be more precise, the recession will be officially confirmed in early February with the release of GDP figures for the fourth quarter of 2008. These figures will show a second consecutive quarter of GDP decline, satisfying a common definition of a recession. For observers more concerned about the state of business than semantic arguments among economists, these figures will also confirm that the recession deepened dramatically towards the year-end and that the first half of 2009 will see the economy suffering its deepest slump since the 3.4% annualised rate of decline in the second half of 1991.

As a result of this recession, unemployment will rise sharply in the first few months of the year—to around 2.5m or 8% of the workforce, compared with only 1.7m or 5.6% before the autumn banking meltdown. And the housing market will continue its collapse, with prices falling by some 15% in the 12 months to mid-2009, a fall which will imply a decline of at least 25% from the house-price peak in August 2007.

With tax revenues shrinking and unemployment spending rising, the government deficit will soar in 2009 (see "Spent, spent, spent" on next page)—attracting stern admonishments from the European Commission for breaching the 3% of GDP Maastricht limit. But Alistair Darling, the chancellor of the exchequer, will allow the deficit to expand unchecked. Indeed, he intends to bring forward planned public investments to cushion the economy in 2009. In a recession, measures to increase taxes or reduce public spending would be politically impossible and economically foolish.

With the "fiscal rules" invented by Gordon Brown at the dawn of New Labour reduced to rubble, Mr Darling will doubtless introduce a new "fiscal framework" designed to bring borrowing under control in the medium term and restore credibility to the government's economic management. However, nobody will take this seriously—not with pressures for public spending intensifying as unemployment rises and as a general election draws near.

The "known" good news about 2009, which seems even more certain than the catalogue of woes above, is that interest rates and inflation will be much lower by the spring of 2009 than anyone would have expected six months earlier. The Bank of England's base rate will at least match the 50-year low of 3.5% established in 2003 and may well dive further. In fact, for the first time since 1952, British interest rates may well boast a "two" in front of the decimal point. A weak pound, especially against the dollar, is another near-certain consequence of the British economy's recessionary troubles. Although the pound may hold its own or even rise a bit against the euro, it is bound to fall much further against the dollar, with the 2003 level of $1.60 merely one milestone and $1.40 quite possible before the end of the year.

Fears that the weakness of the pound, combined with ultra-low interest rates, will stoke inflation will prove unfounded. The Bank of England will have no problem reconciling an ultra-easy monetary policy with its 2% inflation target and will actually welcome the decline of the pound, because inflation will have vanished from the list of economic worries by the spring. With house prices collapsing, the labour market in the doldrums and oil and commodity prices roughly half their year-earlier levels, the inflationary worries of early 2008 will seem like distant dreams.

On the other hand

Now for the bad news—and for the binary, even bipolar, nature of the 2009 outlook. If something like normal functioning of the banking system has been restored by the beginning of 2009, then the first half of the year will see nothing worse than a common-or-garden recession, as described above, followed by a decent recovery in the second half of the year, driven by ultra-low interest rates and a competitive exchange rate. Unemployment may continue to rise until the year-end, but other economic indicators—including business confidence, stockmarket

> The British economy will suffer its first recession for 18 years

2009 IN BRIEF
Britain acquires a **Supreme Court** in October, taking over some functions from the House of Lords and so further separating the judiciary from the legislature.

Doleful prospect
Unemployment rate, average %
Source: Economist Intelligence Unit
*Forecast

Anatole Kaletsky: partner, GaveKal Research; editor at large, the *Times*

Spent, spent, spent

Paul Wallace

The red hole in Britain's public finances

Britain has been spared a big budgetary drama for many years. The closest shaves the Labour government has experienced in over a decade in office have been about specific taxes, such as the protests against high fuel duty in 2000. More recently Gordon Brown's reputation took a battering when it emerged that his last budget as chancellor would leave 5m poor families worse off, forcing a humiliating U-turn to try to make amends.

But the real crises occur when governments lose control over the public finances. That is what threatens in 2009 as a weakening economy pushes the exchequer into the biggest deficit since the mid-1990s. That earlier loss of fiscal control wrecked the Conservatives' low-tax reputation as they had to push up taxes in order to plug the hole. The budgetary crisis of 2009 will prove just as damaging to Labour's credibility as a governing party able both to deliver high public spending and to keep the nation's finances in good shape.

Britain's fiscal difficulties have surprisingly little to do with the big banking rescues the government has mounted. As financial transactions, these are not counted in the usual measure of the budget deficit, although they have raised national debt since the Treasury has borrowed to finance its capital injections and banking liabilities have been placed on the public books to reflect state control. Taxpayers are at risk from loan losses, but the bail-out's impact on the deficit will be small.

Rather, the budgetary crisis of 2009 has its roots in Mr Brown's increasingly unsound management of the public finances. Emboldened by an early big surplus, he let spending rip. When the budget moved back into deficit, he failed to push up taxes enough to plug the gap. Mr Brown's imprudence sapped the nation's finances. Whereas other European economies, such as Germany's, restored fiscal order, Britain stayed in the red even when the economy was booming. By 2007 the deficit as a share of GDP was the second highest among the 15 old members of the European Union.

This has left the exchequer vulnerable to the downturn. Britain's public finances are in any case especially sensitive to the business cycle because so much revenue comes from finance and property. As a result, they will be hit particularly hard by a recession concentrated in those two sectors. The deficit in the fiscal year from April 2009 to March 2010 could easily reach 6% of GDP, the highest for 15 years.

The mood swings

The budgetary crisis of 2009 will hand the Conservatives the first opportunity for more than a decade to regain the initiative on tax and spend. Labour kept them on the back foot in the past two elections by successfully exploiting fears that Tory pledges to cut taxes would come at the expense of public services. That led to a new policy under David Cameron: the Tories would "share the proceeds of growth" between higher spending and lower taxes. But that formula, too, no longer looks appropriate now that there will be no economic growth to share.

What might appear a setback may instead be an opportunity for the Conservatives. As the deficit widens, Labour's plans for spending and taxation will increasingly lack credibility. Mr Cameron can seek a freer hand, presenting the Tories as the party of fiscal responsibility that will do what it takes to clear up Labour's mess.

The Conservatives will benefit from a sea-change in the public mood. By 1997, when Labour won power, the electorate had become more worried about decrepit public services than high taxes. In 2000 an international poll for The Economist found that Britain was alone among 17 countries in having a majority of people prepared to pay more taxes to finance more spending on public services. By 2008 that generosity had vanished, as a rising tax burden had squeezed incomes and as it became clear that public services had failed to improve that much despite the spending spree. A YouGov poll in March 2008 found two-thirds of people agreeing that the government "should tax less and spend less".

The economic downturn of 2008 shattered Mr Brown's claim to have done away with boom and bust. The budgetary crisis of 2009 will undermine Labour's credibility on tax and spend, and open the way to an overdue period of retrenchment. ■

Paul Wallace: Britain economics editor, *The Economist*

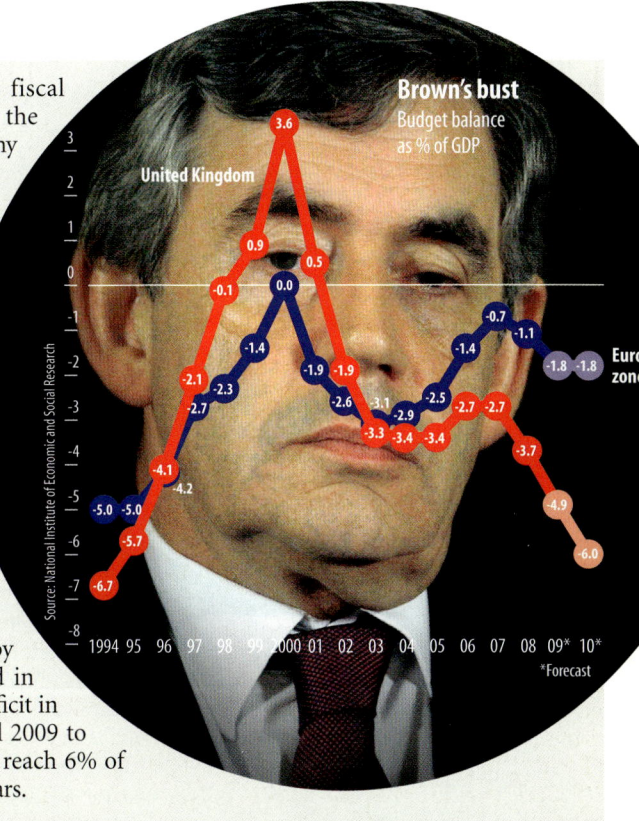

---

prices and even housing—should show clear signs of improvement by the third quarter. In short, the downturn will be painful, but nowhere near as traumatic as the inflationary recessions of the early 1980s and 1990s. In these circumstances, Britain by the end of 2009 will again be seen as a fundamentally strong economy.

Suppose, on the other hand, that the global financial implosion continues into 2009 and bank nationalisations around the world turn the allocation of capital into a governmental responsibility, in a bizarre resurrection of Soviet-style central planning. In that case, the outlook for capitalist economies everywhere will drastically deteriorate through 2009, instead of improving. And Britain, as the world's most financially oriented economy, will suffer more than any other country.

Britain, with its clear comparative advantage not only in finance but in all business services associated with free capital movements, has most to lose if global capitalism is permanently hobbled. But it has most to gain from a long-term revival in global finance. ■

2009 IN BRIEF

First **English translations** of the Bible from Latin celebrate their 600th birthday.

No such thing as a free crunch

London will rebound from the financial crisis, but it has work to do to stay competitive, argues the city's mayor, Boris Johnson

Two decades ago Londoners used to fret about whether their city was faring better or worse than Paris. A decade ago, around the time of the launch of the euro, Londoners worried that Frankfurt would gain the upper hand. But in 2008 London can claim to be the financial centre of not just Europe but the world, on a par with (or by some accounts surpassing) New York. The twin cities of NY-Lon, the diamonds on the opposite coasts of the Atlantic, are now the only two truly world cities, global magnets for talent and business.

But there is no perch more perilous than the top one, especially when a hurricane hits. London has traditionally been super-cyclical, experiencing the ups and downs of the British economy in magnified form. With financial services playing such a large part of its economy, it is particularly vulnerable. The collapse of American banks such as Lehman hits London as hard as British ones such as HBOS.

London has also been at the forefront of Britain's debt-fuelled house-price boom, and is at the forefront of the collapse. By October 2008, house prices had fallen by around 10% from their peak, and only Pollyannas can persuade themselves that the widespread predictions of further falls are wrong.

History is little help in forecasting how this financial and housing turmoil will affect the wider economy, but there is cause for sensible optimism. Comparisons with the 1930s are wildly overblown—then around a quarter of adults were unemployed, whereas now the figure is only around 5%. The fall in the stockmarket and the rise in inflation are a fraction of what they were then. Indeed, by some measures stocks already appear underpriced.

The diverse and dynamic London economy may take a hit, but it is fundamentally very sound. Londoners are highly productive, and in many industries besides finance, such as creative ones, they are world-class. My economists predict that the London economy will grow—albeit marginally—in 2009, before rebounding in 2010.

NY-Lon, maybe, but not TefLon

But the financial crisis is bringing to the fore many of the longer-term challenges that London faces. The most immediate danger is that we over-regulate and over-tax ourselves into a second-class city. The British government must not respond to the crisis by imposing so many new rules on bankers that we drive them elsewhere, as the American government did with the Sarbanes-Oxley act after the Enron scandal. You can't regulate your way out of a recession, but you can regulate your way into one. It is essential at this time to defend financial services from its many detractors. The masters of the universe may not be popular here, but there are many other parts of the universe that would welcome them with open arms.

Rising taxes are also making us uncompetitive. The British government has steadily increased the tax burden on multinational corporations, making London increasingly unattractive as a base for global headquarters. Some companies have already left, and at the end of 2008 around 40 of the FTSE 100 companies are considering relocating. It is a cause of intense anxiety to the industry leaders of my International Business Advisory Council, who have warned me that high taxes—particularly on foreign earnings—are making London an unattractive base. Our once predictable tax regime has become unpredictable, with Treasury U-turns and threats of windfall taxes on energy companies.

Personal taxation, too, has become less favourable with the botched introduction of the levy on non-doms and the increase in capital-gains tax. It is not in my powers to change such taxes, and unless the national government adopts a strategy of global tax competitiveness, the exodus of HQs from London will accelerate.

A review of London's financial services has shown that, although London has many strengths, its competitiveness in many areas is decreasing. Global wealth is moving east, a trend that the financial crisis can only deepen. Asian and Middle Eastern financial centres pose a growing challenge to our financial dominance. There are concerns that London's IT infrastructure is not up to future demands. The transport network is overstretched, and even airlines admit that Heathrow is a disgrace—not just a hassle for travellers, but giving a poor welcome to visitors, with long immigration queues. There are continuing concerns about London being one of the world's most expensive cities. Although, like most Londoners, I believe London is the greatest city on earth, it performs poorly in many rankings of quality of life.

As mayor, I must make sure that everything is done to retain our global pre-eminence. London has an extraordinary resilience, based on the diversity and drive of those who reside in it. This resilience ensured it surmounted the challenges it faced in the past, and will ensure we surmount those in the years ahead. ∎

It is essential at this time to defend financial services from its many detractors

DISCOVER WHAT YOUR SIGNATURE CAN DO FOR THE CLIMATE.

If we all help out to change the system, global warming can be resolved. Discover how your signature can support politicians and decision makers to take the necessary actions to combat climate change: visit www.vattenfall.com/climatesignature

VATTENFALL
ENERGY FOR THE EMPOWERED

Where a compact city allows business visitors to make the most of their time.

SINGAPORE
WHERE GREAT THINGS HAPPEN

Singapore's integrated environment and seamless infrastructure ensure every spot in the city is just a short ride away. This allows visitors to make the most of the great networking and business prospects from a wide base of industries. In addition to the benefits of interaction with top global talent the city draws to itself, Singapore's compactness also allows for a little extra time to enjoy its vibrant cityscape and unique culture. Choose Singapore for your corporate meetings, conferences, exhibitions and incentive travel. visitsingapore.com/businessevents

UNIQUELY
Singapore
visitsingapore.com

THE WORLD IN 2009

Europe

Also in this section:
Travel in Europe 46
Germany's coming election 49
France's semi-revolution 52
The party's over in Spain 54

Nordic defence 56
Can Silvio Berlusconi reform Italy? 56
José Luis Rodríguez Zapatero: Message from Madrid 58

Russia swaggers on 60
Yulia Tymoshenko: On Russia 62
Capitalism, 20 years on 64
Europe's frozen conflicts 65

Nice project, shame about the voters

David Rennie BRUSSELS

One vote after another disturbs the European agenda

The European Union is rarely mistaken for a vibrant democracy. The club deserves its reputation for deals forged in backrooms, under the sway of unelected bureaucrats. Yet in 2009 the EU will, for once, have to devote much of its energy to elections, and the aftermath of national votes.

In common with the rest of the world, the EU will start the year pondering a new American president. European public opinion may imagine that the departure of George Bush will transform relations overnight. EU officials and diplomats know better.

It will be a bumpy year for transatlantic ties, especially over trade. There will be heavy EU pressure on the new American administration to return to the Doha talks on trade liberalisation that foundered in 2008. The World Trade Organisation will hand down rulings on a pair of tit-for-tat complaints—the first an American complaint about public subsidies for Airbus, the European maker of civilian airliners; the second a retaliatory European complaint about taxpayers' money shovelled to Boeing, America's aerospace giant.

Adding to the toxic atmosphere, the new president will inherit an unresolved row over the purchase of 179 new aerial-refuelling tankers by the American air force. In February 2008 there was rejoicing (and some disbelief) in Europe when the $35 billion contract was awarded to a joint American-European bid involving modified Airbus freighters. Months later, the deal was halted and handed to the next president to oversee, following complaints from Boeing. If the win for the Airbus tankers is reversed, the political fallout will be serious: even friendly EU politicians will accuse America of protectionism beneath a cloak of national security.

From the spring, legislative business in the EU will slow to a near-halt, as the European Parliament prepares for elections across 27 countries in June. Federal elections in Germany, due in September 2009, will leave the EU's largest member distracted for months.

One big consequence is that March is the absolute deadline for EU leaders to agree on a European proposal to take to the climate-change talks that will be held in Copenhagen in November-December.

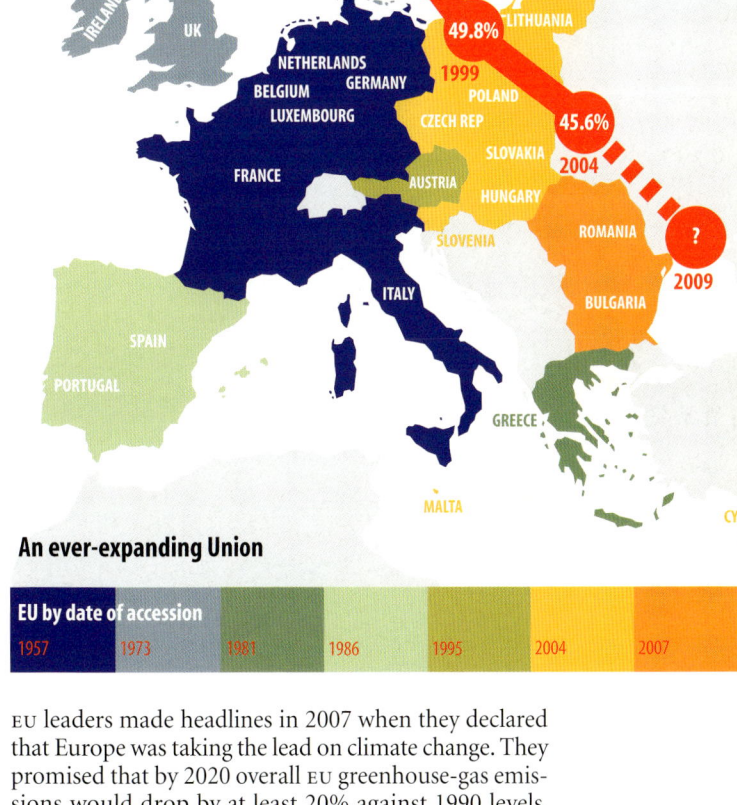

Turnout at European elections
63.0% 1979
61.0% 1984
58.5% 1989
56.8% 1994
49.8% 1999
45.6% 2004
? 2009

An ever-expanding Union
EU by date of accession: 1957 | 1973 | 1981 | 1986 | 1995 | 2004 | 2007

EU leaders made headlines in 2007 when they declared that Europe was taking the lead on climate change. They promised that by 2020 overall EU greenhouse-gas emissions would drop by at least 20% against 1990 levels, and that by the same date 20% of overall EU energy needs would be met by renewable sources such as wind, water and solar power. Yet soon afterwards those pledges were cast into doubt by intense national lobbying, ranging from French and German calls to protect jobs in energy-hungry industries to Polish pleas for gentler treatment of a power sector dependent on coal. Wrangling over a final EU proposal may go right up to the March 2009 deadline (though original plans said a deal should be finished in December 2008).

Members of the European Parliament boast they are the directly

> The Lisbon treaty is dead, at least in its current form, and in 2009 devoted fans will at last come to terms with that fact

2009 IN BRIEF
Slovakia becomes the 16th country to adopt the euro.

David Rennie: European Union correspondent, *The Economist*

elected representatives of half a billion EU citizens. They have gained hefty power over the years. Yet since direct elections started in 1979, at five-yearly intervals, turnout has fallen each time, to 46% in 2004 (an average that hides lower turnout in countries like Britain, and truly appalling turnout statistics in some new member states which joined in 2004). Voter indifference is explained by the lack of partisan passion in debates: the place acts like a giant coalition government, in which all deals have to be compromises.

Death of a treaty

The 2009 Euro-election will be haunted by another vote: the Irish rejection by referendum in June 2008 of the Lisbon treaty, which was supposed to usher in institutional reforms to make an enlarged EU work better. As an international treaty, it cannot come into force until it is ratified by all EU member states. That was painful for the European Parliament, which under Lisbon would gain the same rights as national governments to oversee new laws in a wide range of policy areas.

After the Irish voted to reject the treaty, there was intense pressure from some EU leaders for Ireland to hold a second vote quickly (and get the answer right). Eurodevotees express fears that uncertainty over Lisbon will affect the European Parliament elections, turning the June poll into a debate about the treaty. They should be so lucky. Voters care little about the Lisbon treaty. Instead, a real danger is that economic misery will fuel protest votes for extremists from left and right.

The Lisbon treaty is dead, at least in its current form, and in 2009 its fans will at last come to terms with that fact. Expect some desperate attempts to get it ratified: there will be more pressure on Ireland to hold a second referendum on Lisbon in 2009, and a deep recession might just scare the Irish to fall into line. More likely, when it becomes clear that a fresh vote would lead to another rejection, several countries will demand that the Irish government find some legal wheeze for ratifying the treaty through parliament, removing the need for another referendum. But for the Irish government, bypassing voters like that would be legally risky. It would also be political suicide.

A nasty row will break out among the 27 EU leaders, and it can only be hoped that pragmatists gain the upper hand quickly. They will have to persuade others that the loss of the treaty is not the end of the world, and that Lisbon's biggest innovations, such as changes in voting rules and the creation of a full-time "president of the European Council" to speak for national governments, can be tucked into the next day-to-day EU treaty that comes along (in this case meaning the treaty admitting Croatia). With Europe's economy set to be in a grim state in 2009, pragmatists should be in a stronger position than usual. Europe cannot afford more institutional navel-gazing: voters will not stand for it. ■

> **2009 IN BRIEF**
> EU **travellers to America** under the visa-waiver programme must first have an electronic travel authorisation before boarding a US-bound airliner or ship.

Ever greater union
John Andrews

Travel brings everyone closer

Forget the boasts of European Union officialdom and all the Eurospeak of directives and regulations. The real force behind European integration is easy travel, especially when it's cheap. Companies like Ryanair and easyJet will do more in 2009 for "the European project" than any politician struggling to revive the Lisbon treaty. And there will be more than 40 other budget airlines competing to transfer northern Europeans south to the sun, be it to "second homes" in Tuscany or beach resorts in Spain. Transavia will fly Dutch families from Amsterdam to Montpellier; Meridiana will fly Polish workers from Cracow to Turin.

Or so cheap-ticket fans will assume. But recession could lead to more route cuts and bankruptcies in 2009. This is rapidly overtaking earlier concerns about the price of oil, which had started to strain the ability to keep aloft without raising ticket prices. And failure, for whatever reason, is common: a score of budget airlines have either collapsed or lost their independence in the past five years.

Yet the underlying reality is that cheap and convenient European travel is here to stay. One reason is that the airlines face increasing competition from the railways. The Eurostar service between London and Brussels had a 40% share of the market in 2003 and 70% in 2008, and the TGV service between Paris and Marseille has had a similar impact on air services between the two cities.

So if you can't beat them, join them: Air France-KLM will spend much of 2009 perfecting plans to start a high-speed rail service of its own, designed to compete with Eurostar and to link Paris with London and Amsterdam in time for the 2010 liberalisation of the EU's international rail services. Meanwhile, the Railteam collaboration of Europe's leading high-speed operators will be modernising and extending high-speed track. It will also be refining its one-ticket approach to travel with different companies across frontiers.

Add to all that the preparations by several companies for competitive cross-frontier services. Virgin's Sir Richard Branson, for example, is said to be mulling the idea of a European high-speed rail service, and Deutsche Bahn would like its trains to link London to Cologne. With or without the Lisbon treaty, good Europeans can rejoice: the "ever greater union" of the EU's founders is indeed taking place. ■

John Andrews: deputy editor, *The World in 2009*

Common interests
Imagine if confronting climate change and solving energy needs were inseparable

For Total, satisfying energy needs sustainably and controlling the environmental impact of our activities are our top priorities. In our search for new sources of fossil and renewable energy (such as solar and biomass), the Group is working hard to achieve greater energy efficiency and optimise processes to cut greenhouse gas emissions. With a pilot project to capture and store CO_2 in France's Lacq basin, Total is developing innovative technology to confront global warming. *www.total.com*

Our energy is your energy

TOTAL

AKBANK

The most valuable financial brand of Turkey.*

* "World's Most Valuable 500 Financial Brands" 2007 survey conducted by Brand Finance and The Banker.

The innovative power of Turkey

AKBANK

www.akbank.com

Take your partners

Brooke Unger BERLIN

Germany's election dance

Two oddities will shape 2009's main German event, the parliamentary elections to be held on September 27th. The first is that the current chancellor, Angela Merkel, will run against her foreign minister (and vice-chancellor) Frank-Walter Steinmeier. The second is that much of the attention will focus on the party least likely to gain a share of power: the Left Party.

Ms Merkel's Christian Democratic Union (CDU) and Mr Steinmeier's Social Democratic Party (SPD) are normally rivals. The "grand coalition" government they formed in 2005 was awkward from the start. Its final months will be spent coping with the consequences of the financial crisis. Each partner yearns to form a government with a more congenial smaller party: the CDU with the liberal Free Democrats (FDP) and the SPD with the Greens. The obstacle is the Left Party. The brash newcomer has pulled German politics leftwards and turned a cosy four-party system into a chaotic five-way mêlée, in which no traditional two-party coalition can form a majority. Its strong showing in the 2005 elections brought about the grand coalition; since then it has gained more ground.

Today's Left Party is the result of a 2007 merger between ex-communists from the old East Germany, still its stronghold, and disgruntled western Germans, many of them trade unionists. Exploiting popular anger over economic reforms and stagnant living standards, it has grown in western Germany mainly at the expense of the SPD. In recent elections it has entered the legislatures of four of western Germany's ten *Länder* (states). In an August 2009 election in Saarland, home of its populist leader, Oskar Lafontaine, it may finish ahead of the SPD for the first time in a western state. In Thuringia in eastern Germany it could lead its first state government.

The Left Party is accumulating power without respectability. It is a foe of NATO and the independence of the European Central Bank. Mr Lafontaine, a former finance minister and chairman of the SPD, accused George Bush and Tony Blair of terrorism in Iraq. The SPD dallies with the Left Party in the *Länder*, hoping that it will mature through proximity to power. But, so far, the SPD has ruled out co-operation at national level.

Colourful coalitions

Once again, therefore, the Left Party may be the spoiler in the Bundestag, the lower house of parliament. That would leave open the possibility of an unwieldy three-party government: either a "traffic light" coalition consisting of the "red" Social Democrats, the (yellow) FDP and the Greens; or a "Jamaica" coalition (after the colours of Jamaica's flag) combining the two smaller parties with the (black) CDU. There is hope for a CDU-FDP tandem, good for economic reform. As likely is another grand coalition, which neither of its parts wants.

Whether Ms Merkel or Mr Steinmeier prevails may depend on which of them Germans find more reassuring during an anxious year. Germany's export-driven economy may not grow at all in 2009. A VAT hike in 2007 and surging oil prices in 2008 thwarted the spending spree consumers normally enjoy in an upswing. Unemployment will rise. Now the slowdown endangers one of the coalition's central goals, balancing the federal budget by 2011. Hardship will shape the messages of both parties. The CDU will stress its economic competence, the SPD its tradition of defending a robust role for the state.

The candidates bring into battle similar temperaments: both sparkle less in the limelight than behind the scenes. They will offer voters different flavours of moderation. Mr Steinmeier wants to pull his divided SPD toward the political middle but must watch his left flank. Ms Merkel, who nearly lost in 2005 running as a reformer, will try to look more compassionate than conservative.

Herr Steinmeier, I want a majority this big

> Germany's export-driven economy may not grow at all in 2009

She is instinctively pro-American and sterner than her foreign minister with Russian and Chinese autocrats; Mr Steinmeier sneers at her "display-window policies". With approval ratings approaching 70%, Ms Merkel is likely to deliver a "chancellor bonus" to the CDU. Mr Steinmeier is popular but has never run for anything. The parties' first trial of strength will be in May, when the Bundestag, and delegates chosen by state legislatures, are likely to re-elect Horst Köhler as Germany's president, a largely ceremonial job. He is backed by the CDU. The first popularity contests will be local and European elections on June 7th.

Germany will also look back in 2009. May 23rd is the 60th birthday of the Federal Republic; November 9th marks 20 years since the fall of the Berlin Wall. What happens in Afghanistan, with up to 4,500 German troops, and in the European Union will pose questions about Germany's place in the world. These anniversaries will ensure that the answers are informed by a sense of its past. ■

2009 IN BRIEF
The European Union's single market gets a boost with new rules cutting the cost of **mobile-phone calls** when roaming from one EU country to another.

Brooke Unger: Germany correspondent, *The Economist*

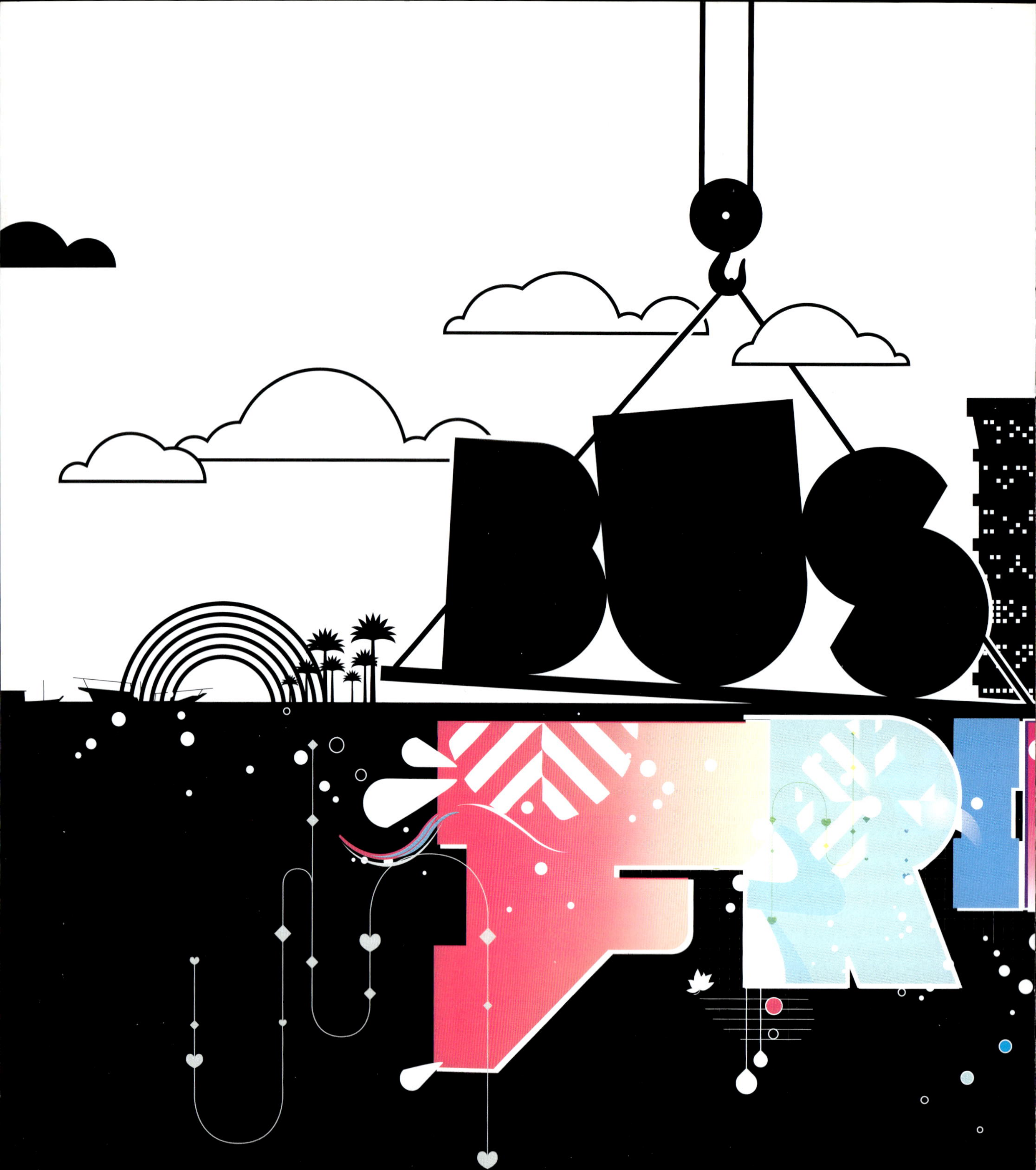
BUS

The Gulf's most liberal business environment.
The Gulf's best access to all the region's markets.
And the Gulf's lowest taxes and operating costs.
For more information visit www.bahrain.com

BAHRAIN

A French semi-revolution

Sophie Pedder PARIS

The recession will not deter the reformist president

2009 IN BRIEF
Ireland starts to phase out the sale of incandescent **light bulbs**.

Nothing of ease or comfort awaits President Nicolas Sarkozy in 2009. The French economy will face recession, bank losses will mount, companies will cut output and jobs, social malaise will grow. Abroad, he will surrender France's presidency of the European Union, and thus the mandate he has relished as globe-trotting European diplomat-in-chief. And yet 2009 could be the year that Mr Sarkozy begins to get it right.

Mr Sarkozy is impatient to prove he can achieve what eluded his predecessors: change in France. Harsh economic times will delay results, and squeeze options. He has no room to cut taxes. The budget deficit is likely to breach the euro zone's limit. Yet, although Mr Sarkozy will urge more state intervention in financial markets, he will not use the downturn as an excuse to ease off on broadly liberalising reforms. He will try to coax the French into adapting to get the economy into better shape. This will include trimming the civil service, tightening welfare rules, cutting red tape for entrepreneurs and ensuring that schools stay open during strikes.

The nature of public discontent will change. Sporadic factory strikes, in protest at job cuts, will break out. Disorganised street protests could turn nasty. But public-sector strikes will be less effective. Mr Sarkozy will undermine union leaders by appealing to the broader interests of the French, as consumers, commuters or parents. With strike days no longer paid, and minimum service guaranteed on public transport during strikes, unions' power will ebb.

Mr Sarkozy will keep the discreet François Fillon as prime minister until after elections to the European Parliament in June. Reckoning on two prime ministers during his five-year term, he will delay the selection of a new one as long as possible. Candidates include Xavier Bertrand, his labour minister, and Xavier Darcos, his education minister. Real power will stay firmly in the Elysée presidential palace.

Mr Sarkozy's sometimes capricious use of this power—over public nominations, say, or ties with the media—will grate. But he will face no mainstream opposition. The Socialist Party will have a new boss. Yet this will not resolve its internal rivalries.

A leader to watch will be Olivier Besancenot, a revolutionary postman-cum-politician. He will launch an "Anti-Capitalist Party", catching the market-hostile mood. This will further split the left—much as, in the past, the right was splintered by the far-right National Front. The National Front itself will find things tougher, after its combative leader, Jean-Marie Le Pen, hands over to his daughter, Marine.

Man of the world

Abroad, Mr Sarkozy will dream of graduating from diplomat to elder statesman. Impatient and bullying, with a tendency to settle for headline-grabbing fixes, he will infuriate as much as impress. Yet, with German and British leaders distracted by internal battles, he will have few west European rivals for the diplomatic limelight.

One of his first meetings will be with the new American president. On a trip to Washington in 2006, when interior minister, Mr Sarkozy met just two senators: remarkably, they were John McCain and Barack Obama. Underlining his Atlanticism, he will reaffirm France's place in the "Western family", rejecting the neo-Gaullist doctrine of equidistance from Russia and America. He will try to sell his plan to overhaul international financial institutions.

Seventy years after the outbreak of the second world war, Mr Sarkozy will jointly host, with Germany, NATO's 60th-anniversary summit at a symbolic cross-border event on the Rhine. If he secures support for joint European defence, he will announce France's return to NATO's integrated command. To prove his commitment, Mr Sarkozy will keep French forces in Afghanistan. Having warmed up France's formerly cool relations with Israel, he will build on this friendship to try to act as an intermediary with the Islamic world. He will draw in Syria, keep up pressure on Iran, and re-orient French diplomacy towards the Gulf and the Horn of Africa. To this end, he will close one French military base in sub-Saharan Africa, its traditional sphere of influence.

All this frenetic activity may yield only limited diplomatic success. But the French will like having their country taken seriously again. With his stylish wife, Carla Bruni, Mr Sarkozy will be a calmer figure, no longer simply the bling-bling caricature of yesterday. It may not be a year of headline-grabbing reform. But France in 2009 will be nudged by circumstance and leadership gently out of its comfort zone. And this, in a country that has long found it hard to change in evolutionary ways, will itself be semi-revolutionary. ■

> Mr Sarkozy will be a calmer figure, no longer simply the bling-bling caricature of yesterday

Sophie Pedder: Paris bureau chief, *The Economist*

Hard head versus hard hats

There's a business opportunity worth £1.2bn in the UK. Let us introduce you to it.

Not only can the Carbon Trust help UK business save money by cutting carbon, we can also help you make money from low carbon opportunities.

ACT ON CO₂

Join the low carbon world
0800 085 2005
www.carbontrust.co.uk/opportunity

CARBON TRUST

Europe

2009 IN BRIEF
Norway mandates the use of **open document formats** for government papers published on government websites.

After the fiesta

Thomas Catan MADRID

The party's over in Spain

Over the past decade Spain has reaped huge benefits from its membership of the single European currency. Easy access to cheap credit and a surge of foreign investment set off an economic boom that has raised the living standards of millions of Spaniards and drawn millions more migrants to its shores. And, as if the country wasn't already fizzy enough, the national team won the Euro 2008 football championship.

In 2009, however, Spain will experience the downside of euro membership as its economy slides into a stinging recession. Without its own currency, Spain will not be able to devalue its way out of trouble, as it did during its recession in 1993. Nor will it be able to cut interest rates to aid its debt-laden households and businesses. For the most part, all that Spaniards will be able to do is grin and bear it.

Some things could be done. High inflation, paltry productivity and rising wages have made Spain a less competitive place in an increasingly competitive world. Spain could reform its labour markets to regain much-needed flexibility.

But if the Socialist government of José Luis Rodríguez Zapatero did not undertake meaningful reform during the good times, labour unions are unlikely to agree to it when job losses loom. In any case, Spain's prime minister has already breezily promised them that he would not take any economic measures without their consent—a vow he will come to regret in 2009 as labour unrest returns to haunt Spain.

Mr Zapatero largely squandered his first term in office fighting culture wars with the country's right when he should have been fixing Spain's underlying problems. Warning signs had been flashing for years, but the prime minister cheerfully ignored them, and was rewarded with a second term in office in elections last March (though he fell short of an absolute majority in parliament).

It won't be fun

True, the economy has slumped even faster than pessimists had predicted. And Spain's home-grown problems—a high current-account deficit, over-dependence on construction and over-borrowing by consumers and businesses—have been compounded by an international financial crisis.

But Mr Zapatero has been slow to react. Rather than tackling Spain's antiquated education system, encouraging entrepreneurship or weaning young Spaniards off their predilection for government jobs, the prime minister has instead announced yet another round of hostilities with Spain's Catholic bishops. Reforms of Spain's laws on abortion and euthanasia may provide some red meat for the Socialist Party rank-and-file, but they are hardly the central concerns of most Spaniards, for whom 2009 will be a miserable year after 15 years of rapid economic growth.

The best scenario for Spaniards is two years of anaemic growth, with wages losing value in real terms until the economy regains competitiveness. A recovery could begin in 2010—but not before the unemployment rate reaches an eye-watering 15%. A worse scenario is that Spain, unable to face the needed reforms, will settle into the type of long-term economic sclerosis suffered by European laggards such as Italy or Portugal.

Spain's banks and financial regulator have been rightly praised for avoiding the sort of risky investments in exotic financial instruments that got so many other banks into trouble. But Spanish banking is still uncomfortably entangled in the property sector, which will remain moribund in 2009 as the market digests a glut of 1.5m unsold homes.

With more Spaniards defaulting on their loans and construction companies collapsing, Spanish banks are facing a dire year. Many of Spain's savings banks are heavily exposed to the construction industry and some are thought to be harbouring big losses. But most have strong connections to the country's powerful regional governments, making them politically too important to fail. The government will have to engineer a series of shotgun weddings between smaller entities to keep them afloat.

Mr Zapatero made governing Spain look easy during his first term despite lacking an overall majority in parliament. This time his government will struggle to pass a controversial slate of social reforms while keeping the lid on simmering labour discontent and placating regional governments, which will fight furiously over a shrinking share of national resources. Mr Zapatero is a shrewd politician and his opponents underestimate him at their peril. But he will need more than his famously sunny disposition to steer his country through tough times in 2009.

Grin and bear it

Thomas Catan: Spain correspondent, the *Times*

> The best scenario for Spaniards is two years of anaemic growth

BT

Bringing it all together

Do you speak global?

As a leading global networked IT services provider, we believe every business can benefit from Bigger Thinking. We understand that ideas are the most valuable business asset and that technology can play a role in freeing the imagination.
Take part in the debate on Bigger Thinking – visit www.biggerthinking.com/global

www.biggerthinking.com/global

North stars

Edward Lucas VISBY

Introducing the Nordic Atlantic Treaty Organisation

2009 IN BRIEF
The first written mention of **Lithuania** is 1,000 years old.

Designed to keep the Germans down, the Russians out and the Americans in, NATO will celebrate its 60th birthday in 2009 in a sorry state. Its campaign in Afghanistan is not going well. Its members are at odds about how to deal with Russia. But look north and the European security picture will be brightening.

Sweden and Norway, once prickly friends, are striking up a new defence relationship. This might look odd: Sweden is non-NATO and a member of the European Union; Norway is a keen member of NATO, but has stayed out of the EU. But now those differences are being set aside. Co-operation on airspace monitoring, combined military procurement, joint training and co-ordinated intelligence work will all be bearing fruit in 2009.

Panting to catch up is Finland, neutral in theory but in practice also spooked by an increasingly assertive Russia. That's clever psychology by the Norwegians and Swedes: Finland would resist if it felt pressured to join in. But it hates being left out of anything its Nordic neighbours get up to. For the core three, 2009 will bring calls for higher defence spending and new efforts to extend Nordic security co-operation to other countries.

The two pressing tasks for the new Nordic security partnership (don't call it an alliance, or you will get a very chilly Scandinavian scowl) are to work out how to help the Baltic states, and to make plans for what they call the "high north", the energy-rich area that lies between Europe and the North Pole. The Baltic states (Estonia, Latvia and Lithuania) have been full members of NATO since 2004. But the alliance has made no plans to defend them, not wanting to break the taboo on counting Russia as any kind of threat. That will change in 2009, as NATO's bureaucracy in Brussels works out the practicalities.

But no NATO efforts to defend the Baltics in a crisis make sense without help from Finland and Sweden. As EU members, they will offer political support. And Sweden's airspace would offer the best way to bring reinforcements if needed. The Baltics will be keen to join in the new Nordic nexus, starting with airspace monitoring.

America is watching the Nordic efforts with increasing interest, as is Canada, once a peace-monger but now deeply alarmed by Russian adventurism in the Arctic. Add Britain for good measure, beef it up a bit, and this could turn into a handy new outfit to deal with the hottest spots of what some people are calling the new cold war. All it needs is a snappy name. What about the Nordic Atlantic Treaty Organisation? ■

Edward Lucas: central and eastern Europe correspondent, *The Economist*, and author of "The New Cold War" (Palgrave Macmillan and Bloomsbury)

Same old Silvio?

John Hooper ROME

Italy's leader will show if he really is a reformer

In a general election last April, Silvio Berlusconi and his right-wing alliance won healthy majorities in both houses of parliament that should allow them to see out a full term to 2013. Elsewhere, one might confidently use "will" instead of "should". But this is Italy, where the only thing that is inevitable is the unexpected.

There are other reasons for caution. One is Mr Berlusconi's age: despite appearances (that owe a little to cosmetic surgery), he is 72, has had both cancer and heart trouble. And his parliamentary majorities depend on the Northern League, led by Umberto Bossi. So far, Mr Bossi and his supporters have been kept happy by promises of greater fiscal autonomy for the richer north of Italy and a stiff law-and-order programme (implemented by one of their number, the interior minister, Roberto Maroni). But the Northern League are natural mavericks and Mr Bossi has threatened once already that, if he fails to get what he wants, he could switch his votes to the opposition. What is more, the going for the government will get tougher.

Italy's economy in 2009 will be in the doldrums. It probably entered recession in mid-2008. In a world labouring to break free from the credit crunch, Italy will not be alone in having economic difficulties. Indeed, it may be better placed than other countries—its banks were initially untouched by the subprime crisis.

Yet, to a far greater extent than in most rich countries, Italy's problems are structural rather than cyclical. It is now a well-established tradition that when the rest of the European Union expands, Italy grows by less; and when the other EU economies contract, Italy shrinks by more. The result is that a country once widely admired for its dynamism and inventiveness is gradually but relentlessly becoming poorer than its neighbours.

If they are to reverse this, Italians must begin to implement the reforms they have been putting off for a decade or more. Some of Mr Berlusconi's ministers realise the urgency. But will they be able to count on their boss's support when the flak starts? Mr Berlusconi has yet to show that he knows how to impose economic reform. His role in the Alitalia fiasco in 2008, pulling together a consortium to defend the failing airline's "Italian-ness", showed that, at heart, he is a nationalist, a populist and an interventionist. There is not much chance that that will change in 2009. ■

Italy unravelling
GDP per head (at PPP)
EU average = 100
1990–2009†
*Estimate †Forecast

John Hooper: Italy correspondent, *The Economist*

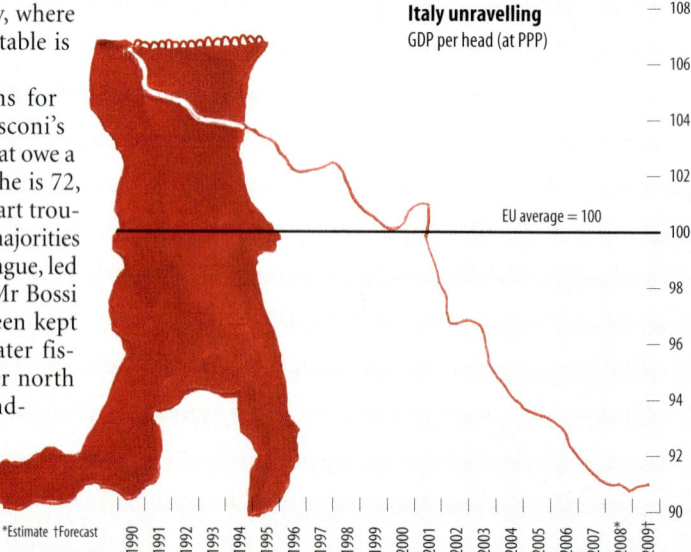

FOR THE LAST 60 YEARS OUR VEHICLES HAVE WORKED ON FARMS. NOW ONE OF THE ENGINE PLANTS IS POWERED BY ONE.

For years we've helped farmers and now we're helping them in a different way, by using a wind farm to cut our emissions. The two turbines in the wind farm generate renewable energy, which powers the Dagenham plant where all our TDV6 and TDV8 engines are produced. And in the last 10 years we've also reduced the emissions from our Solihull plant by 30%. We're very aware of our responsibility towards our planet and there are many more examples of our involvement on our website.
To find out more about our progress visit landrover.co.uk/ourplanet

🌐 landrover.co.uk/ourplanet

LAND ROVER
GO BEYOND

RANGE OF FUEL ECONOMY FIGURES FOR THE LAND ROVER RANGE (L/100KM): URBAN 30.6 (9.2) – 12.6 (22.4), EXTRA URBAN 45.5 (6.2) – 23.2 (12.2), COMBINED 37.7 (7.5) – 17.7 (16.0), CO_2 EMISSIONS 194 – 376G/KM. DRIVE RESPONSIBLY ON AND OFF-ROAD.

Message from Madrid

José Luis Rodríguez Zapatero, prime minister of Spain, sets out priorities for Europe

In their struggle for freedom, Spanish democrats have always seen the hope of progress and democracy in Europe and, having joined the European Union, Spanish society has developed a deeply pro-European feeling which my government fully supports. I believe that a stronger, more integrated Europe is fundamental to the development of our nations and for world stability and I am convinced that, despite the difficulties in ratifying its new treaty, Europe will be strengthened, with the means to face new challenges.

In these times, facing despondency, we should be aware of the enormous potential of our values: passion for freedom, a constitutional state, respect for human rights, tolerance, equality between men and women, recognition of diversity, the deepening of solidarity both inside and outside our borders. Europe is not just a beautiful idea but is also an efficient organisation that demonstrates its usefulness every day. It is therefore essential to decide on priority actions.

First, Europe must continue to develop the value of solidarity and adapt it to new realities. The policy of cohesion between member states is central, but this should be modernised and widened to include new areas such as access to R&D networks. The shared Europe we are aiming for should also take on leadership of the war against hunger and poverty, and provide the means to protect the most disadvantaged, victims of marginalisation and victims of all kinds of violence.

Europe's support of the United Nations and the peace process in the Middle East should be more visible. It should develop its co-operation with Russia and the great Asian countries, and promote its relationship with Latin America, concluding negotiations with regional groups there. Likewise, Europe should set out the necessary reforms in candidate countries, Croatia and Turkey, and offer a perspective of stability in the Balkan area.

I would like to highlight three current issues to which Europe should provide effective answers: the new economic situation; immigration; and our policy in the Mediterranean.

The situation of the world economy has created uncertainty among our people. It is important that Europe should send out a calming message and maintain a solid base in the European welfare system to alleviate the effects of the economic slowdown for the people who are most affected.

At the same time we should work on initiatives to drive forward a more productive, more energy-efficient Europe that has cleaner emissions. To do this, we must accelerate reforms in the priority areas of the Lisbon strategy for competitiveness (knowledge and innovation, business development, improvement of safety at work and flexibility of employment, and European policies on energy and global warming) with all the regulatory and budgetary instruments at our disposal.

It is clear that there have been supervisory errors and a lack of transparency in financial markets. Europe should promote the necessary reforms in the security mechanisms of these markets, both in Europe and globally.

The European Union should also promote greater transparency in the markets for oil and food, and support the proper functioning of financial derivatives for raw-materials markets, limiting excess speculative movements in primary consumer products. We are facing a humanitarian emergency that requires food aid for the countries affected and, in the medium to long term, needs improved productivity and rural output in order to achieve a sustainable food supply.

As regards immigration, it is essential to develop a common European policy. Europe should promote the appropriate integration of immigrants. This is not just about reaching an agreement on rights and duties, it is about achieving positive results in social development. Europe should also establish a bilateral, regional dialogue with the countries of origin and transit in order to provide on-the-spot alternatives, with Africa a priority area for action. And Europe should be extremely efficient in its border controls, reinforcing FRONTEX, informing potential illegal immigrants about the risks they are taking, and relentlessly fighting mafia groups.

Mediterranean mission

Finally, I would like to highlight the importance of the Mediterranean. Europe should offer its values without imposing them, and lay the foundations for shared prosperity. The great difference in per head income in southern countries and the need for dialogue and understanding require a special effort under the new initiative "Barcelona Process/Union for the Mediterranean".

For all these reasons, Spain assumes its responsibilities to drive forward this necessary new Europe alongside our colleagues, with the prospect of our presidency of the EU during the first six months of 2010. ■

The world economy has created uncertainty among our people. It is important that Europe should send out a calming message

Panasonic
ideas for life

OUR RANGE OF TVs WITH FREESAT HD BUILT-IN IS GETTING BIGGER

AND SMALLER

Panasonic's 81 series of Viera televisions has more choice than ever before, with screen sizes ranging from 32" to 50". And as they're the first televisions with Freesat HD built-in, they offer more viewing options too – enabling you to watch programmes from BBC HD – and a growing line-up from ITV – in detail like you've never seen before, without subscription.

There's even an SD card slot so you can easily view digital images in stunning HD. With so many unique features, the next generation of television is here.

The biggest and the smallest details matter,

EVERYTHING MATTERS.

32"   37"   42"   46"   50"

HOME CINEMA Choice BEST BUY 46" JUNE '08

WHAT HI·FI? SOUND AND VISION ★★★★★ 50" - SEPT '08 46" - OCT '08

To find out more about the full range visit:
panasonic.co.uk/freesat
0844 844 3852

Official Worldwide Olympic Partner — London 2012

Swaggering on

Arkady Ostrovsky MOSCOW

But Russia will find the going harder

A few minutes before midnight on December 31st 2008, President Dmitry Medvedev will stroll out of the Kremlin and stand before cameras in Red Square, steam coming from his mouth. In his first new-year address to the nation he will speak about Russia's resurgence and its demand for respect; he may talk about his difficult decision to send troops to Georgia; he is likely to mention the turbulent economic climate and Russia's ability to weather the storm. Then the clock on the Kremlin tower will strike 12 and millions of Russians will click glasses to the tune of the old Soviet anthem, restored by Vladimir Putin eight years ago.

> Russia is heading into its first truly difficult years since Mr Putin took power

What will happen next and how much Mr Medvedev's reassuring words will correspond with reality is harder to predict. But all the signs are that Russia is heading into its first truly difficult years since Mr Putin took power in 2000. Its small victorious war in Georgia was the culmination of Mr Putin's era, which was marked by high oil prices and the sense of restored pride. In practical terms, however, this escapade did not win Russia anything that it did not have already while pushing its relationship with the West to a new low. Russia's hurried recognition of South Ossetia and Abkhazia, which it controlled anyway, has created the prospect of a prolonged stand-off with the West.

When Mr Putin announced his choice of Mr Medvedev as his successor some foreign pundits, bankers and home-bred liberals rejoiced: at last, after the belligerent Mr Putin, comes a mild-speaking young lawyer with no background in the secret services and few memories of the cold war. Only unrepentant pessimists, such as Andrei Illarionov, who had worked with Mr Medvedev at one stage, gloomily predicted that Mr Medvedev would try to overcompensate for his civilian background. So far the pessimists have the upper hand: Mr Medvedev has tried to prove himself not by diverging from Mr Putin, but by imitating Mr Putin's bellicose style and sounding even tougher than his patron.

The West may not have much leverage over Russia, but the rift in the relationship is coming at a time when Russia can least afford it. One reason Mr Putin was able to ignore Western opinion on human rights or the worsening business climate was that Russia was swimming in money. The Kremlin never paid the price for destroying the Yukos oil company or revising the terms of production-sharing agreements with foreign firms. Rising oil prices and a steady flow of cheap credits from foreign banks made Mr Putin feel all but invincible and masked structural problems in the economy.

In 2009 Russia will face a much tougher economic reality. Credits from foreign banks have dried up. Oil prices have fallen sharply. Imports are rising faster than exports, so that Russia's trade surplus, which had been growing strongly, will start to shrink. To make up for this, the government will spend more money from its oil-fuelled stabilisation fund, but some of this money will go into inefficient state corporations, increasing the state's share in the economy and complicating efforts to bring down inflation, which is in double digits. Russians will see their real incomes grow more slowly.

No more mister tough guy?

In the past, the Kremlin had to worry only about a marginalised group of Russian liberals. Now it may face discontent from a wider public which cheered Mr Putin's tough stance with the West while incomes rose.

Russia's economic growth will become a lot more dependent on foreign investments. The optimistic scenario is that Russia's economic needs will tame its hostility towards the West and that the political system created by Mr Putin and inherited by Mr Medvedev will become more flexible. The war in Georgia makes this scenario less likely than it would have been a year ago. Instead, the self-sustained logic of the Putin regime suggests that Russia will continue to search for enemies both outside the country and within. This may mean more hostile rhetoric and possibly actions in the former Soviet republics which Russia considers its own sphere of influence.

But it would also make Russia's economic modernisation less likely. Several years of unchecked xenophobia have made Russians much more receptive to authoritarian and nationalistic rule than to liberal ideas. On the other hand, the more oppressive the Kremlin becomes, the more resistance it will face from its own ethnically Muslim republics, particularly in Ingushetia, where people are fed up with corrupt leadership and the constant abuse of human rights. In the short term, Russia's war in Georgia has served as a reminder to places like Ingushetia and Chechnya that Moscow is ready to steamroll any opposition. But in the longer term, having undermined Georgia's territorial integrity, Russia has inadvertently put its own at risk as well. ■

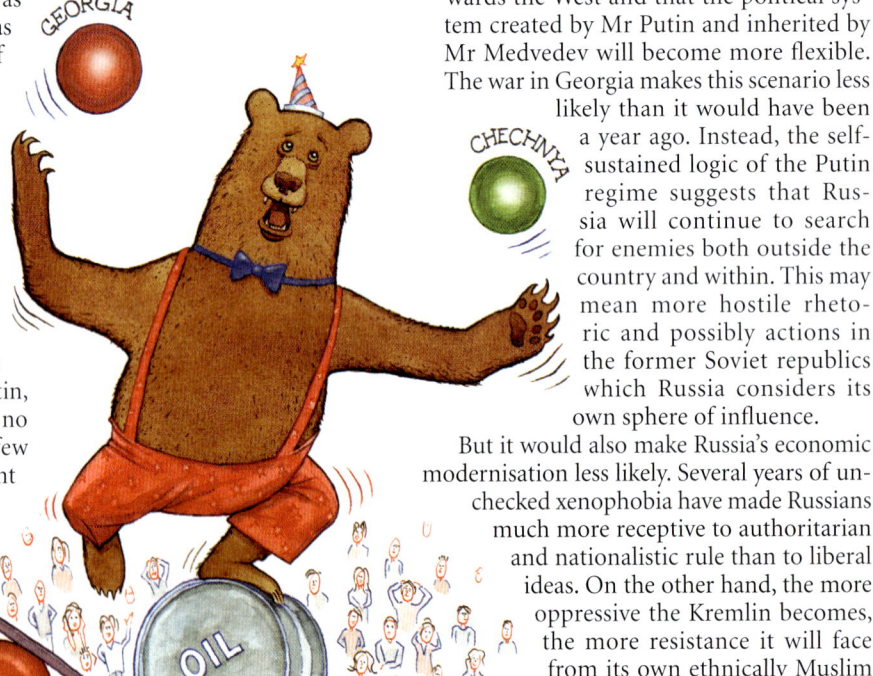

2009 IN BRIEF

The European Union signs a deal with **Ukraine** to strengthen economic and political ties.

Arkady Ostrovsky: Russia correspondent, *The Economist*

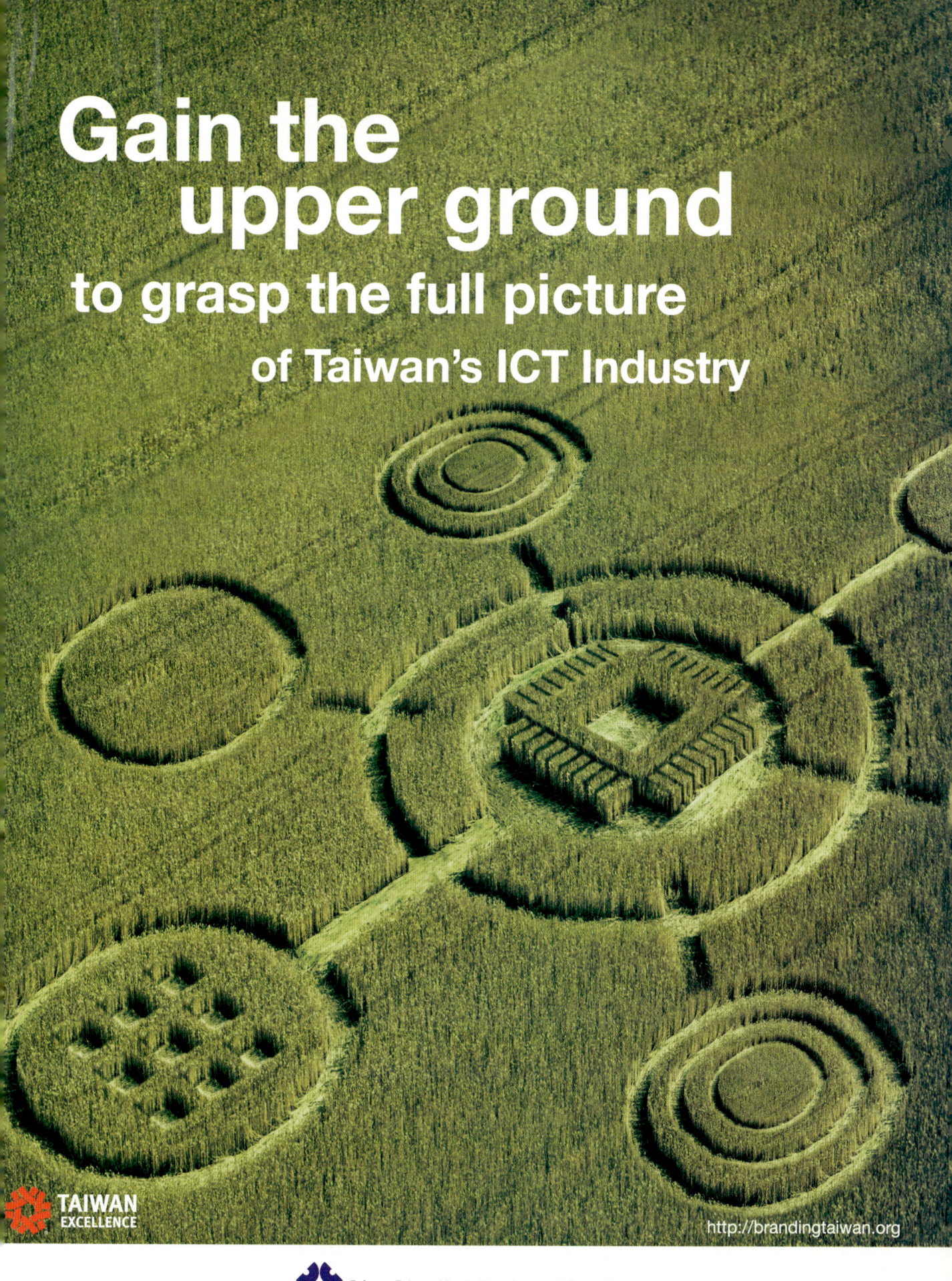

Gain the upper ground
to grasp the full picture
of Taiwan's ICT Industry

TAIWAN EXCELLENCE

http://brandingtaiwan.org

Taiwan External Trade Development Council

An answer to the Russian question

*In the post-war reconciliation between France and Germany **Yulia Tymoshenko**, prime minister of Ukraine, sees a useful precedent for relations with Russia*

The finest achievement of Europe's post-1945 leaders was their recognition that, unless Germany was integrated into the evolving Western system, insecurity would reign across the continent. In 2009 Europe will begin to recognise that only by securing the European vocations of both Russia and Ukraine can the European Union continue on its path of stability and prosperity.

But recognising a need and finding the diplomatic means to carry it out is rarely straightforward. Diplomatic relations between Russia and Ukraine are, in historical terms, very new. Ukraine's status within the Russian and Soviet empires froze history. Then, in a few dramatic months in the early 1990s, the Soviet Union folded. Suddenly, there was a need to forge diplomatic ties, and to define independent national interests, among peoples that had been living side by side for centuries. The success of Franco-German reconciliation over the past half-century represents a hopeful model.

Indeed, in 2009 Europe will begin to address a strategic task left over from the great revolutions of 1989-91: the vacuum in security that arose in the countries that lay between the EU and Russia. For to avoid confrontation in the years since 1989, a strategic and conceptual no-man's-land had taken hold. In place of the iron curtain, new and invisible borders arose in Europe between states that were protected by security guarantees and those where such guarantees were absent. This was bound to tempt countries dissatisfied with the post-cold-war settlement, and demoralise potential victims.

In 2009 the European Union must acknowledge the task of ensuring that the ongoing changes taking place in the lands between the EU and Russia proceed in an orderly, peaceful—and, most important—mutually beneficial fashion. The aim is clear: Russia and Ukraine on the road to becoming two prosperous and friendly neighbours in the manner of today's France and Germany.

To achieve this outcome, there is an urgent need to establish mechanisms that could contribute to reform and renewal in both countries without breeding tension. Such a reconciliation is particularly vital for Russia. By demonstrating that it can live amicably with its neighbours, Russia's claim to have become a reliable member of the world community would appear more convincing. It would also mollify China's leadership, which is understandably reluctant to see a reconstituted Russian power appear on its doorstep.

But Russia is not accustomed to intensively co-operative international procedures. Soviet diplomatic processes left it ill-prepared for them, and the country's yearning for great-power status has made it difficult to integrate Russia into Europe's co-operative institutions, which is why it wants only a partnership arrangement with the union. (Ukraine, on the other hand, is fixed on a course of future EU membership.) But keeping Russia outside the European framework of consultation, co-ordination and compromise only strengthened the sense of isolation that many Russians have felt since the Soviet collapse. Some, sadly, could succumb to the temptation to define their country's interests in ways irreconcilable with those of Russia's neighbours.

A European solution or a European problem

So Russia faces a strategic test in 2009: can it accept a framework that provides it with both benefits and obligations for working with the EU in fields ranging from energy security to migration and global warming? Greater confidence and stability would also come to Russian-Ukrainian relations, because they would be set within the wider European context.

The existence or absence of a framework of co-operation often determines whether diplomatic disputes mutate into a crisis. Effective international frameworks, however, usually demand a grand bargain. The settlement between France and Germany over steel in 1952 resulted in a sharing of sovereignty over a vital state function. This agreement set a precedent for the entire European project. In 2009 the challenge for the EU is to begin to shape a bargain involving Russia and Ukraine.

Another such "1952 moment" could be at hand. Energy, in particular natural gas, offers an opportunity to replicate the insights that animated the EU's founders in 1952. Finding a united voice on energy is the key to a new act of reconciliation for the EU. Ukraine will play its part and share the common burden as Europe seeks to shape such a unified policy.

In our Orange revolution, Ukraine made a choice, not between Russia and the West, but between democracy and authoritarianism. That choice was irrevocable, but is still challenged by some. This is why relations between Ukraine, Russia and the EU must not be allowed to drift. Only by creating firm institutional links will common political and economic projects come to dominate relations across the region, not fears about security. ■

The challenge for the EU is to begin to shape a bargain involving Russia and Ukraine

SEVEN ROUND THE WORLD SEATS.

VOLVO OCEAN RACE 2008-2009

The Volvo Ocean Race is no pleasure cruise. Following it, however, is much more civilised. Wherever in the globe you lose yourselves, you'll find The Volvo XC90 Ocean Race Edition the perfect travelling companion. All Wheel Drive, Roll Stability Control and its advanced chassis, make this seven seater one of the most advanced SUV's in the world. Safely on board, even the luggage travels first class.

VOLVO XC90 OCEAN RACE EDITION

IFE IS BETTER LIVED TOGETHER

lvocars.com/Rush

VOLVO

Volvo. for life

EL CONSUMPTION IN MPG (L/100KM) FOR VOLVO XC90 OCEAN RACE EDITION RANGE: URBAN 26.6 (10.6) – 14.3 (19.8), EXTRA URBAN ,5 (6.8) – 29,4 (9.6) COMBINED 34,4 (8.2) – 21,2 (13.3), WITH 217 – 317 G/KM OF CO_2 EMISSIONS.

Twenty years of capitalism: was it worth it?

Laza Kekic

Yes—but it's not so simple

In 2009 there will be cause, surely, for unqualified celebration: the 20th anniversary of the fall of the Berlin Wall. The events of 1989 did away with political tyranny, stultifying central planning, shoddy output and shortages. A generation on, the transition from communism to capitalism has been remarkable.

Yes, a few nostalgics lament the demise of the Soviet Union (Russia's Vladimir Putin has called it the greatest geopolitical catastrophe of the 20th century). But it has been a resounding success. The reforms worked and central and eastern Europe has been among the world's fastest-growing regions in recent years. Ten countries have "rejoined Europe" by becoming members of the European Union. The pain—the unemployment, inequality and crime—was either unavoidable or a price worth paying.

Or so conventional wisdom says. But is it really true?

One caveat emerges from public-opinion surveys, which reveal a deep dissatisfaction in the region (under communism there was misery but fewer pollsters). For example, the region-wide "Life in Transition" survey released by the European Bank for Reconstruction and Development in 2007 showed that only 30% of people in the region believe they live better today than in 1989. There is a strong nostalgia for the past (both in economic matters and, astonishingly, even in politics). Only 15% believe there is less corruption now than in 1989. Support for core values associated with the transition, such as markets and democracy, is underwhelming.

Surveys show that "life satisfaction" has been improving in recent years in line with economic recovery, after plunging in the 1990s. People who say they are generally satisfied with their lives now outnumber those who say they are dissatisfied—but not in all countries.

Pain and gain

Why the gloom? There is no great mystery. Behind people's assessment of satisfaction with their lives lie real experiences—of their incomes, jobs, family and social life, health, political freedom and personal security. Aside from the crucial issue of freedom, most of these have had a bumpy time.

Take the economic performance across the region. It is a tale of two halves, with a marked difference between the experience of the first and second decades of the transition.

Average output fell by more than a third to the mid-1990s, then stagnated until 1999. Since 2000 all countries have returned to growth, some at very fast rates. The region at last regained its 1989 level of output in 2006 and by 2009 it will be some 25% above that. The 1990s recession widened the income gap with the West (Poland is a notable exception). Growth since 2000 has led to a fast catch-up, although by 2009 average income per head relative to the EU15 average will be slightly below what it was in 1989—and the credit crunch has hit some countries hard.

These data are notoriously dodgy. How can you compare today's market economies with output under central planning, which was great at producing tractors that broke down, consumer goods that nobody wanted and long queues at drab shops for things people needed? Yet physical indicators (such as electricity consumption) and the results of income comparisons based on purchasing-power parity (PPP) suggest that the GDP picture may not be entirely misleading.

If so, with various assumptions—notably about hypothetical growth rates without the disruption of switching to capitalism—it is possible to estimate the opportunity cost of the transition. It is high: between $0.5 trillion and $1 trillion (in 2000 PPP dollars). Assuming, generously, future regional growth of 4-5% a year, it would take another decade for the transition to have been economically "worth it".

The regional aggregate, of course, hides big differences. The Balts and central Europeans have experienced a catch-up in living standards undreamed-of under communism.

To die for

It is often said that the transition has been among the most peaceful revolutions in history. However, civil wars have claimed tens of thousands of lives. There has also been a large unseen death toll, especially among men. In most countries, death rates in 2009 will be higher than they were in 1989. Eastern Europe is the only region in the world that has experienced a population decline over the past two decades, of some 7m.

The history and degree of demographic stress varies from country to country, and it should not be forgotten that by its latter years the Soviet Union had already become a demographic disaster area. But much of the region has experienced a calamity in this respect, with many fewer births and many more deaths than would otherwise have been the case. Such changes are clear indicators of societies in extreme

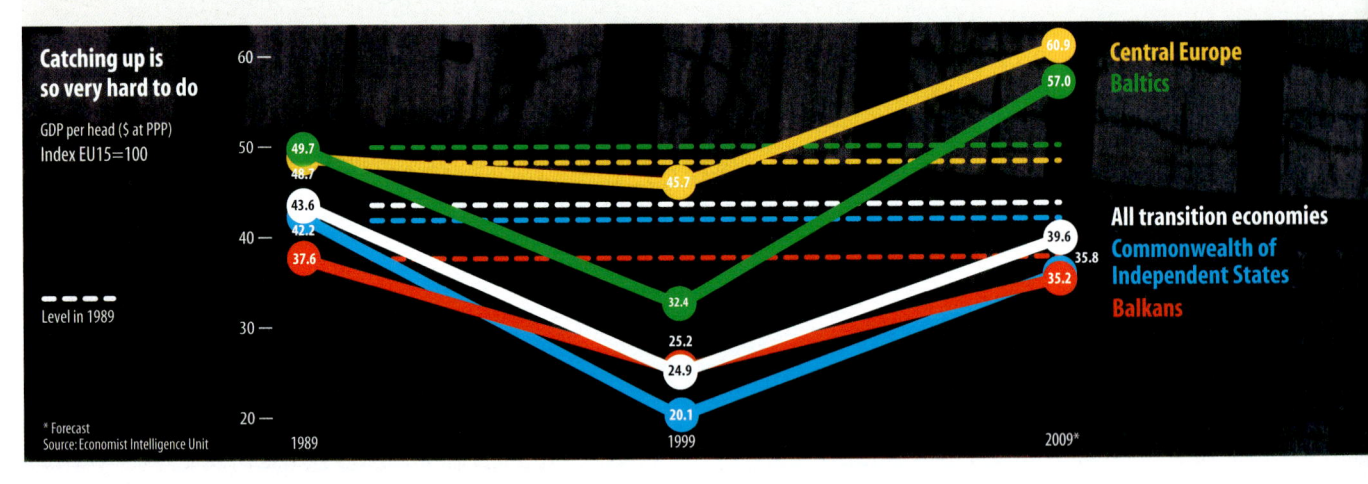

Catching up is so very hard to do

GDP per head ($ at PPP)
Index EU15=100

- - - - Level in 1989

*Forecast
Source: Economist Intelligence Unit

	1989	1999	2009*
Central Europe	49.7	45.7	60.9
Baltics	48.7	32.4	57.0
All transition economies	43.6	25.2	39.6
Commonwealth of Independent States	42.2	20.1	35.8
Balkans	37.6	24.9	35.2

stress and have previously been observed only in wartime.

On any estimate, the number of "excess deaths" since 1989 runs into the millions: that is, the number of actual deaths since 1989 is far greater than the number of deaths that would have occurred had pre-transition trends in death rates continued. The vast majority of the excess deaths occurred in Russia and Ukraine.

Rip Van Grzebski
The transition has been a giant social experiment. Some argue that freedom cannot be weighed against other things. And in central Europe at least—politically free and now richer than ever—success has become increasingly evident.

But alongside the gains, the upheaval has turned lives upside down. Human beings are adaptable but most do not react well to shocks.

In 2007 a railwayman, Jan Grzebski, woke from a 19-year coma and marvelled at what he saw in Poland. He could not understand why his countrymen were moaning and hankering after the past—but he had not experienced the transition. Mr Grzebski had, so to speak, "slept through the relentless triumph of capitalism". ∎

Laza Kekic: regional director, central and eastern Europe, Economist Intelligence Unit

Frozen conflicts
John Peet

Europe's unfinished business

The end of the cold war did not produce a thaw throughout the continent. A peculiarity of today's Europe is the variety of "frozen conflicts" it contains. From Cyprus, through the Balkans and into the former Soviet Union, a string of nasty small wars have been settled not through peace deals but simply by freezing each side's positions.

The trouble with frozen conflicts is that they have a nasty habit of turning hot. Witness the war in 2008 between Georgia and Russia over the enclaves of **South Ossetia** and **Abkhazia**, over which Georgia lost control after wars in the early 1990s. The experience of a sudden war in Georgia will draw more attention in 2009 to all of Europe's frozen conflicts—and lead to renewed efforts to resolve them.

At last, 35 years after the division of **Cyprus** into a Turkish-Cypriot north and a (legally recognised) Greek-Cypriot south, there will be a settlement, based on the notion of a bi-communal, bi-zonal federation. For years, the biggest barrier to peace was the hardline Turkish-Cypriot president, Rauf Denktash, and a hardline Greek-Cypriot president, Tassos Papadopoulos. With both men out of the way, having lost support from their voters, their successors, Mehmed Ali Talat and Demetris Christofias, will strike a deal.

Key to a settlement is the European Union, which admitted (a divided) Cyprus as a member in 2004. Indeed, the main obstacle will be Turkey, if it concludes during 2009 that its own chances of joining the EU have vanished.

The EU is also the reason why a lingering conflict between **Kosovo** and Serbia is edging towards a solution. When most Western countries recognised independent Kosovo in February, there were dire warnings of ethnic cleansing and of Serbia turning its back on Europe. But pro-European moderates in Serbia are back in the ascendant. In 2009 Serbia will accept, de facto if not de jure, the independence of its former province, in exchange for a promise of EU membership negotiations.

The problematic conflicts that are left all involve bits of the former Soviet Union, for which the lure of EU membership does not work. After their defeat of the Georgians, the Russians will throw their weight around the neighbourhood. They will try to bully Moldova into accepting a peace deal that leaves Russian troops and a breakaway regime running **Transdniestria**. There is a better prospect of a settlement in **Nagorno-Karabakh**, the enclave of Azerbaijan controlled by Armenia since a vicious war in 1994, not least because Turkey and Armenia are moving towards restoring normal relations. But here too the Russians will interfere enough to prevent a deal in 2009.

Worst of all will be the Russians' efforts to create new conflicts in 2009. They will foment trouble in all three Baltic republics, where there are large Russian-speaking minorities. And the Russians will stir things up in Ukraine, where 8m people, or almost a sixth of the population, are ethnic Russians.

The focus of this activity will be **Crimea**, a southern province of Ukraine. Crimea is majority-Russian, was transferred from Russia to Ukraine only by a stroke of Khrushchev's pen in 1954, and hosts the Russian Black Sea fleet in Sebastopol, under a lease due to expire in 2017 that the Ukrainians say they do not want to extend. In 2009 Crimea will become the hottest spot in which to assess just how tense relations between Russia and the West get. ∎

John Peet: Europe editor, *The Economist*

BOMBARDIER + eco⁴ = A new formula in energy saving

Bombardier Transportation already leads the way with close to zero-emission and almost fully recyclable trains. And now our revolutionary energy-saving *ECO4* technologies are again changing the equation – setting new standards in profitable, sustainable mobility. Built on the four cornerstones of energy, efficiency, ecology and economy, *ECO4* products are easily customized to any fleet, for optimized energy use and minimized energy waste. Which equals dramatic new benefits for operators, passengers and the whole planet

More than ever,
a new world demands a new equation.

More than ever,
The Climate is Right for Trains.

BOMBARDIER
The Global Leader in Rail Technology

www.bombardier.com

ECO4 and *The Climate is Right for Trains* are trademarks of Bombardier Inc. or its subsidiaries.

THE WORLD IN 2009

United States

Also in this section:
Goodbye Guantánamo 68
America's economy in a funk 69
What happens when Americans start to save 70
The NAACP turns 100 71
Tackling violent crime 72
Henry Kissinger: An end of hubris 74

The audacity of change

Adrian Wooldridge WASHINGTON, DC

Mr Obama goes to Washington

The United States will start its next political season with a remarkable event. On January 20th a country that, within living memory, denied some black citizens the right to vote will inaugurate its first black president. A man with a funny name and African blood will stand where 43 white men have stood before him and take the oath of office.

Barack Obama's inauguration will do much to improve two things that desperately need improving—America's reputation abroad and its mood at home. The Bush era had produced a dramatic decline in America's global image, with anti-Americanism taking root around the world, from European capitals to the Arab street. In October 2008 only about 10% of Americans thought that the country was on the right track.

In these circumstances Mr Obama is as close to a cure-all as you can get. His inauguration will mark the culmination of the civil-rights revolution. It will also help repair America's relations with the rest of the world. It will be hard for Muslims to accuse America of prejudice when its president is a man whose first name means "blessed" in Arabic and whose middle name is Hussein. And it will be hard for Europeans to accuse America of being a land of yahoos when its president is the highly educated author of two excellent books.

The balance of power in Washington will also be favourable to the new president. Democrats will be in charge of both Houses of Congress, in particular with a large majority in the Senate, the chamber that can most often frustrate presidents. Moreover, the Republicans, who have a history of tormenting ambitious Democrats, will be in no condition to torment anybody but themselves. Repudiated at the ballot box and locked out of power in the White House and Congress, they will spend the next few years squabbling among themselves.

However fortunate his position, Mr Obama will face three big problems in 2009. The first is inflated expectations. Mr Obama made numerous promises during his campaign—universal health care, investment in infrastructure and green energy, a cap-and-trade system to reduce greenhouse-gas emissions, and much else. Democrats on the Hill also

> Mr Obama will inherit one of the most difficult legacies of any president since Truman

2009 IN BRIEF
The **Clinton Global Initiative** holds its annual meeting in New York, with the former president pressing world leaders to tackle problems from poverty to climate change.

Adrian Wooldridge: Washington bureau chief, *The Economist*

2009 IN BRIEF

The **New York Yankees** open their new stadium—just across the way from the old one.

have their own shopping list.

But Mr Obama will inherit one of the most difficult legacies of any president since Truman: two wars, a dodgy economy and a fiscal black hole. The national debt is more than $10 trillion, and in 2009 the federal budget is projected to run as much as a $1 trillion deficit, having taken into account the cost of recent bail-outs.

The second problem is the status quo in Washington, DC. A candidate who ran against the old politics of tribalism and insider-ism will have to grapple with the fact that Washington's power is in the hands of his own party. Nancy Pelosi's Democrats have proved just as keen on earmarking bills, feeding lobbyists and humiliating the opposition as their Republican predecessors.

The third problem for Mr Obama will be more personal—deciding what he actually stands for. In 1992 Bill Clinton represented a coherent New Democratic creed: embrace globalisation and market economics, use the state to offer public goods like education and tinker with income distribution. Mr Obama has devoted more effort to appeasing interest groups than he has to crafting a political philosophy. He will also face a more difficult philosophical problem: the forces that seemed to be carrying all before them in 1992 are now being widely questioned, particularly on the left of his party.

Mr Obama will have to tackle profound questions about globalisation and reregulation. He will also have to deal with a confused electorate. It will become fashionable to describe Mr Obama as a liberal Reagan—a charismatic president who embodies change. But the 2008 election represented a repudiation of George Bush more than an embrace of big-government liberalism.

The biggest danger for the Obama administration is that, after an initial burst of goodwill, it will simply drift, lacking the money to deliver its promises, battered by tough economic and international circumstances, and torn between Mr Obama's desire to adopt post-partisan positions and the unforgiving logic of Washington partisanship. Still, it would be a mistake to underestimate Mr Obama. In 2008 he took on two of the most formidable politicians in Washington—Hillary Clinton on his own side and John McCain on the other—and beat them. In 2009 we will see a remarkably gifted politician confronting a remarkably difficult set of challenges. ■

Goodbye Guantánamo

Robert Guest WASHINGTON, DC

But it won't be the end of the mess

The prison at Guantánamo Bay will be closed in 2009. But anyone who thinks that this will also close an ugly chapter in American history will be disappointed. Loading the prisoners onto planes will be easy. Figuring out what to do with them next will be anything but.

The inmates of Guantánamo exist in a legal black hole. The camp is on a slice of Cuban territory, leased by the American government. George Bush put them there specifically so that they would be beyond the reach of the American legal system—although the Supreme Court ruled in 2008 that, at least as far as habeas corpus suits are concerned, they are not. Still, many have been held for years without a proper trial.

As American forces toppled the Taliban regime in Afghanistan, they rounded up suspected followers of Osama bin Laden. Many were undoubtedly jihadists. But some were innocent bystanders, often sold by local ruffians for a bounty. Hundreds were shipped to Guantánamo.

About 250 prisoners are still there (from a peak of some 700). They can be divided into three groups. First are those against whom there is enough evidence to press war-crimes charges. Between 60 and 80 of these may face military tribunals.

The next group, of about 50 inmates, consists of those who have been cleared for release but cannot be sent home. This may be for fear that they will be mistreated. More than a dozen Muslim separatists from China are to be released; they pose no threat to America but can expect rough justice if repatriated. In other cases, the Pentagon will not repatriate men to countries whose governments it does not trust to keep an eye on them, such as Yemen. Finally, there are more than 100 inmates who are considered too risky to release, but against whom there is not enough evidence to prosecute them.

In 2009 all the inmates at Guantánamo will be moved somewhere else. The knottiest problem will be what to do with those who cannot be prosecuted but cannot sensibly be freed—and are still dangerous. Mr Bush asserted a right to hold them indefinitely. Barack Obama will work with Congress to devise a fairer set of rules, but he will be reluctant to free those who openly threaten Americans.

This will be a moral minefield. Make it easy to detain suspected terrorists in the future, and you lock up innocents. Make it hard, and you create perverse incentives: soldiers will be loth to let their enemies surrender. Congress and the president have a problem. ■

Robert Guest: Washington correspondent, *The Economist*

The end is in sight

Pick your scenario

Greg Ip WASHINGTON, DC

America's economy is in a funk. How bad will it get and how long will it last?

The coming year will be the most perilous in modern history for the American economy. The forces at work are unlike any the country has seen since the Great Depression and could result in anything from anaemic growth to a severe contraction.

If only the fundamental determinants of growth were involved, America could look forward to a mild recession in the first part of 2009, giving way to sluggish recovery by year-end. But the economy is hostage not just to fundamentals but to the hurricane blowing through financial markets. That has toppled some of Wall Street's biggest firms, remade the financial landscape and produced pervasive, self-reinforcing investor mistrust that is scaring away credit. The course the economy takes depends critically on whether unprecedented fiscal and monetary counter-measures succeed in calming this storm.

America entered this recession (as it will eventually be designated) in fair shape. Seven years of restraint meant businesses did not have lots of marginally productive employees; stocks were lean relative to sales; and few firms had much excess capacity. All this suggested that America was more likely to endure a gradual, even gentle, slowing of economic growth than a sharp contraction.

The one glaring imbalance was in housing: both house prices and construction had risen well above traditional norms by 2006. At that point the housing sector went bust, and by mid-2008 much of the imbalance had been worked off. Moody's Economy.com estimates that by the end of 2008 the ratio of house prices to income had returned to its long-run relationship, and the ratio of house prices to rents had corrected more than half its overvaluation. Construction of new homes for sale has fallen so low that, even at depressed sales levels, inventories of unsold homes have shrunk. A bottom to both construction and prices is likely within 12 months.

Unbalanced recessions

As home prices stabilise, mortgage delinquency rates will plateau (though remaining high), thanks in part to the federal government's purchases of tainted mortgage paper and its restructuring of some of that paper to keep homeowners out of foreclosure. That will put a ceiling on loan losses and help lending restart.

All the same, the nonpartisan National Bureau of Economic Research will almost certainly conclude in 2009 that a recession has occurred. Even if the economy grows, growth will be well below its long-run potential, and unemployment will rise to 7%, perhaps higher. With luck, the recession will be similar to those of 1990-91 and 2001, when output shrank only modestly and unemployment rose by between two and three percentage points.

A recovery will begin in 2009 but, as was the case after the past two recessions, it will be so weak as to be invisible to the naked eye. Post-1945 business cycles, until 1990, were v-shaped. Movements in stocks and interest-sensitive sectors such as home-building produced sharp contractions and sharp recoveries. But over time the stock cycle has been flattened by better management and the growth of services. Meanwhile, financial deregulation means it takes longer for the Federal Reserve to slow the economy with higher interest rates.

This has resulted in longer expansions with more growth in debt and asset prices. Once the cycle turns, these imbalances take a long time to correct. Redressing the imbalances of this cycle will be an especially drawn-out affair. Ridding the financial sector of its bad debt will take years. Lending standards will be permanently tighter and home construction will be subdued as the rate of home-ownership falls to a more sustainable level.

Couple this with an ageing population that can no longer depend on rising home and stock prices to finance its retirement, and Americans in coming years will consume less and save more (see box on next page). A weakened dollar and still-brisk growth in the emerging world will keep exports growing, so altering the orientation of the economy from domestic consumption to tradable goods.

The inflation that preoccupied the Federal Reserve in 2008 will evaporate in 2009 as oil prices slump and rising unemployment suppresses wage increases. Interest rates will not rise until the end of the year, and perhaps not even then. Indeed, further cuts are possible.

All this assumes that the fiscal and monetary authorities succeed in stemming the financial crisis. The aim is that lower interest rates, tax cuts and spending on public works will boost demand, the Fed's dramatic expansion of unconventional lending will get money markets functioning again, and the federal government's injection of equity into banks, purchases of mortgage securities, guarantees of bank debt and expanded deposit insurance will restore confidence in the financial system.

But if they don't, a second scenario will play out. More of the financial system, from banks to hedge funds, will be forced to shed assets and limit lending. This will undermine spending and investment. Stock and house

> A recovery will begin in 2009, but will be so weak as to be invisible to the naked eye

The boom-and-bust cycle
Change in employment numbers, '000
Sign of recession
*Estimate (Q3 2008)
Source: Bureau of Labour Statistics

Greg Ip: United States economics editor, *The Economist*

The bucks stop here

Leo Abruzzese NEW YORK

What happens when Americans start to save

Visit any American electronics retailer and it is hard to miss the gawkers crowded round the flat-panel televisions. Sales of these pricey toys climbed more than 50% in the first half of 2008—just as the American economy was shedding nearly 500,000 jobs. Another sign of the ever-resilient American consumer? Perhaps, but it could be one of the last. After decades of relentless spending, American wallets may snap shut in 2009. If they do, many of the world's merchants, from Chinese toymakers to Caribbean garment stitchers, will feel the pain.

China may now be a force in the global economy, but American households remain an even stronger one. Consumers in the European Union spend about as much as those in the United States, but Americans are more reliable: personal spending has risen every year for almost three decades and will top $10 trillion in 2009. Indeed, American consumer spending has not contracted for even a single quarter since 1991. But with mortgage delinquencies surging and the unemployment rate headed towards 7%, American consumers may have little choice but to start saving. That will mean less spending on computers from Taiwan and mobile phones from Finland.

Americans once saved as reliably as they now spend. In the 1980s American households salted away 9% of their income; this fell to around 5% in the 1990s and to barely 2% in the early years of this decade. Since the start of 2005, Americans have saved a mere 0.5% of what they earn. This may be changing. The saving rate jumped to 5% in May and averaged 2.4% in the following two months. The government stimulus cheques sent out during those months probably had something to do with this, as some of that windfall was saved. But this raises a question: what if Americans again started saving 5% of what they earn? What would it mean for America, and the world?

The answer, in a word, is recession, and probably a deep one. If the saving rate in 2009 rose to 5% from 0.5%, consumer spending would fall by about $500 billion a year. That is equal to around one-eighth of China's economy, and nearly five times the amount of the American government's stimulus payments. Industries that cater to discretionary purchases—clothing, furnishings, restaurants and, yes, flashy new televisions—would take the biggest blow. Most electronics sold in America come from Asia, so the effects would be particularly severe there.

How likely is this to happen? The saving rate rarely moves more than a couple of percentage points in a year, so a sudden pullback to 5% would be extraordinary. But these are extraordinary times: the worst housing crash since the Great Depression, an epic financial crisis, still-high energy prices. Household balance sheets in America are so stretched that a rise in the saving rate seems inevitable. Household debt is equal to 100% of GDP, twice what it was in 1980. Monthly debt payments as a share of income are around 14%, close to a record. And wages, adjusted for inflation, have been falling for the past year. Surely the American consumer, after a decade of splurging on over-priced homes, over-sized cars and over-engineered electronics, will take a breath.

However long it takes, a return to a 5% saving rate is hardly improbable. Households in the euro zone save 9% of their income on average. Americans do need to start saving more in order to boost investment and productivity. But if it happens too quickly, America, and the world, are in for a shock. ∎

Leo Abruzzese: editorial director, North America, Economist Intelligence Unit

surging and the unemployment rate headed towards 7%,
prices will fall steeply, depressing wealth and consumption and further crippling banks. The government will respond with more fiscal stimulus—despite the already gargantuan budget deficit—and expand its stakes in financial companies. The Fed will lower interest rates below 1% and lend in more once-unthinkable ways. Even so, the recession could be as severe as that of 1973-75 or 1981-82, when output shrank by 3% and unemployment rose by 4.4 and 3.6 percentage points, respectively.

There is a third scenario: the collapse in confidence reverses as rapidly as it occurred. As liquidity returns, investors conclude most banks are solvent. Opportunists pounce on undervalued mortgage paper and bank shares. Credit-spreads narrow, lending resumes and pent-up demand for homes is unleashed. Growth is sluggish for a few quarters before briskly resuming. Implausible? The American economy has repeatedly surprised itself with its resilience to shocks. Perhaps it will do so again. ∎

2009 IN BRIEF

Hollywood ignores the nation's economic woes with a wave of **new films**, previously delayed by the 2007 writers' strike.

National Association for the Alleviation of Credit Pandemonium

Yvonne Ryan WASHINGTON, DC

At 100, the NAACP still has a mission

Barack Obama's campaign for the White House raised many questions, for all Americans, about what it means to be black in America today—just in time for the centenary of the nation's oldest civil-rights organisation, the National Association for the Advancement of Coloured People.

The NAACP was formed on February 12th 1909 (itself a centenary, of Lincoln's birth) by a bi-racial group of reformers. It promised to fight for equal rights and opportunities for black Americans. Primarily using litigation and legislation, it has been fighting the good fight, with varying degrees of success, ever since.

Does the election of the first African-American as president mean the battle has at last been won? NAACP members gathering in New York in July 2009 for its 100th annual convention could be forgiven for wondering how much their organisation still matters. Mr Obama and other young black leaders, such as the Massachusetts governor, Deval Patrick, embody the successful black middle class; and for many 20-something African-Americans the NAACP's mission apparently means little when they feel overt discrimination is no longer an issue.

Hoping to make the NAACP relevant to that new generation is Benjamin Todd Jealous, a 36-year-old Californian who is the youngest chief executive in the NAACP's history. Mr Jealous has plenty to do.

When he took over the helm in September 2008, the NAACP had been in turmoil for several years. Never a mass organisation, its membership now languishes at around 300,000, from a high of around 600,000, the association claims, just after the second world war.

Mr Jealous launched his tenure with an ambitious online voter-registration programme aimed at young blacks. As priorities for the coming year the NAACP is also targeting discrimination in the criminal-justice system, improving public schools, increasing black political and economic empowerment and boosting African-American representation, for example as surgeons, in the upper reaches of the health sector.

African-Americans account for a disproportionate share of subprime loans

However, the credit crunch could prompt a shift in that strategy. African-Americans account for a disproportionate share of subprime loans, and tougher lending rules and tighter credit threaten to erode many of the gains made in recent years by black households.

The NAACP is suing 14 mortgage companies for discriminatory practices but it will need to do more, from expanding financial-literacy programmes to helping its constituents recover from financial crisis. In doing so, the NAACP might just find it matters once more. ∎

2009 IN BRIEF
Two hundred years after the birth of **Abraham Lincoln** in Washington, DC, Ford's Theatre (scene of the president's assassination) reopens after restoration.

Yvonne Ryan: currently researching a history of the NAACP

The struggle of the century

Crime, interrupted

Joel Budd LOS ANGELES

Treating violent crime as a disease

2009 IN BRIEF
To the annoyance of airlines and their foreign passengers, foreigners are to be **fingerprinted** before they leave American soil.

Crime will rise slightly in 2009, thanks largely to America's wobbly economy. Higher unemployment will drive more people to seek an illegitimate income, and budget shortfalls will force cities and counties to cut back on police officers, or at least fail to hire enough new ones to cope with their growing populations. The search will be on for a cheaper, smarter crime-fighting method—and one will be found.

For the past 15 years a single model of policing, developed in a single city, has dominated thinking about law and order in America. In the early 1990s New York hired thousands of extra police officers and told them to crack down on petty offenders in high-crime areas. Local commanders were held accountable for recorded crimes in their territory, which were tracked by means of a simple spreadsheet programme known as Compstat. The results were extraordinary. Murders fell from more than 2,200 in 1990 to fewer than 500 in 2007.

New York's "zero tolerance" methods seemed simple, and have been widely copied. Yet no other city in America or anywhere else has achieved quite such good results. This may be because most cities are poorer and less densely populated than New York, and so find it harder to flood the streets with cops. And New York had two big advantages in the early 1990s: its police chief, William Bratton, who now manages the cops of Los Angeles, and its mayor, Rudolph Giuliani, who was last seen running for the American presidency. Both men had a superb feel for police culture and knew how to motivate officers through a combination of praise and fear.

The approach that will come to prominence in 2009 is almost the exact opposite of zero tolerance. Rather than cracking down on petty offenders such as turnstile-jumpers and squeegee men, the authorities will focus on those who are most likely to kill or be killed. Some may be drug dealers recently released from prison. Others may be the associates of people recently wounded by gunfire. What makes the approach particularly novel is that it depends on local people. Rather than insisting on zero tolerance from the police, it tries to change what the residents of crime-infested areas will tolerate.

> The approach that will come to prominence in 2009 is almost the exact opposite of zero tolerance

The new method has been quietly honed for almost a decade in Chicago, where it is known as Operation Ceasefire. It has two main tools. The more conventional one is a team of outreach workers who try to mobilise communities to oppose violence, often in partnership with local clergy. Then, at night, "violence interrupters" hit the streets to sniff out trouble. Often former gang members and graduates of the prison system, the interrupters have a hard-nosed approach to law and order. They may, for example, encourage an aggrieved man to consider beating someone instead of shooting him, or try to convince rival drug-dealers that a turf war would be bad for business, as it would attract the police.

In May 2008 Operation Ceasefire was evaluated in a report for the Justice Department. The results were encouraging: in five out of seven areas examined, shootings dropped sharply. In four of these areas the decline was much steeper than in comparable parts of the city where Operation Ceasefire was not in place. But even these results do not explain why so many police forces are looking to Chicago for inspiration. The approach seems to offer a solution to what has become an intractable problem in inner cities from Los Angeles to London. Young people seem to be killing for inane reasons, such as somebody looking at their girlfriend the wrong way. And they appear to be unafraid of prison.

Operation Ceasefire's chief architect is Wesley Skogan. An epidemiologist, he likens shootings to a health crisis and insists that they can be tackled in a similar way to unsafe sex or needle-sharing. Zero tolerance's slogan was "take care of the small stuff and the big stuff will take care of itself". Mr Skogan's slogan is even snappier: "violent crime is a disease".

The approach may not travel perfectly. Chicago has relatively well-organised gangs and a strong tradition of community mobilisation. What has worked splendidly there may not work as well in, say, Phoenix. We will soon find out, because Operation Ceasefire is swiftly spreading. Baltimore, Newark and Kansas City have projects inspired by it. A further ten or so cities are in the planning stages. In 2009 one of the cities to roll out a trial programme will be New York. ∎

Try a dose of the new medicine

Joel Budd: West Coast correspondent, The Economist

MARTELL
COGNAC

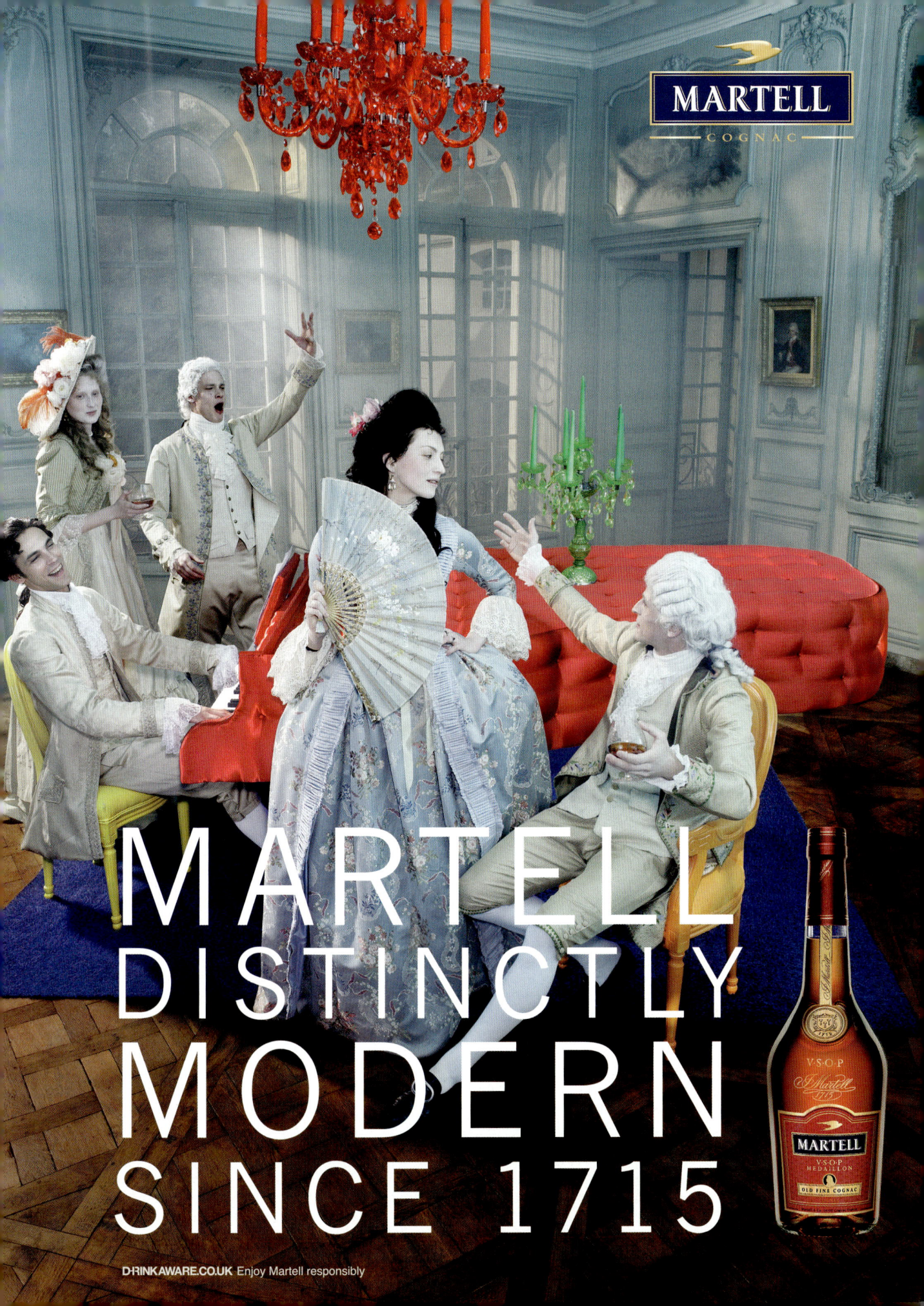

MARTELL
DISTINCTLY
MODERN
SINCE 1715

DRINKAWARE.CO.UK Enjoy Martell responsibly

An end of hubris

America will be less powerful, but still the essential nation in creating a new world order, argues **Henry Kissinger**, a former secretary of state and founder of Kissinger Associates

The most significant event of 2009 will be the transformation of the Washington consensus that market principles trumped national boundaries. The WTO, the IMF and the World Bank defended that system globally. Periodic financial crises were interpreted not as warning signals of what could befall the industrial nations but as aberrations of the developing world to be remedied by domestic stringency—a policy which the advanced countries were not, in the event, prepared to apply to themselves.

The absence of restraint encouraged a speculation whose growing sophistication matched its mounting lack of transparency. An unparalleled period of growth followed, but also the delusion that an economic system could sustain itself via debt indefinitely. In reality, a country could live in such a profligate manner only so long as the rest of the world retained confidence in its economic prescriptions. That period has now ended.

Any economic system, but especially a market economy, produces winners and losers. If the gap between them becomes too great, the losers will organise themselves politically and seek to recast the existing system—within nations and between them. This will be a major theme of 2009.

America's unique military and political power produced a comparable psychological distortion. The sudden collapse of the Soviet Union tempted the United States to proclaim universal political goals in a world of seeming unipolarity—but objectives were defined by slogans rather than strategic feasibility.

Now that the clay feet of the economic system have been exposed, the gap between a global system for economics and the global political system based on the state must be addressed as a dominant task in 2009. The economy must be put on a sound footing, entitlement programmes reviewed and the national dependence on debt overcome. Hopefully, in the process, past lessons of excessive state control will not be forgotten.

The debate will be over priorities, transcending the longstanding debate between idealism and realism. Economic constraints will oblige America to define its global objectives in terms of a mature concept of the national interest. Of course, a country that has always prided itself on its exceptionalism will not abandon the moral convictions by which it defined its greatness. But America needs to learn to discipline itself into a strategy of gradualism that seeks greatness in the accumulation of the attainable. By the same token, our allies must be prepared to face the necessary rather than confining foreign policy to so-called soft power.

Every major country will be driven by the constraints of the fiscal crisis to re-examine its relationship to America. All—and especially those holding American debt—will be assessing the decisions that brought them to this point. As America narrows its horizons, what is a plausible security system and aimed at what threats? What is the future of capitalism? How, in such circumstances, does the world deal with global challenges, such as nuclear proliferation or climate change?

America will remain the most powerful country, but will not retain the position of self-proclaimed tutor. As it learns the limits of hegemony, it should define implementing consultation beyond largely American conceptions. The G8 will need a new role to embrace China, India, Brazil and perhaps South Africa.

The immediate challenge

In Iraq, if the surge strategy holds, there must be a diplomatic conference in 2009 to establish principles of non-intervention and define the country's international responsibilities.

The dilatory diplomacy towards Iran must be brought to a focus. The time available to forestall an Iranian nuclear programme is shrinking and American involvement is essential in defining what we and our allies are prepared to seek and concede and, above all, the penalty to invoke if negotiations reach a stalemate. Failing that, we will have opted to live in a world of an accelerating nuclear arms race and altered parameters of security.

In 2009 the realities of Afghanistan will impose themselves. No outside power has ever prevailed by establishing central rule, as Britain learnt in the 19th century and the Soviet Union in the 20th. The collection of nearly autonomous provinces which define Afghanistan coalesce in opposition to outside attempts to impose central rule. Decentralisation of the current effort is essential.

All this requires a new dialogue between America and the rest of the world. Other countries, while asserting their growing roles, are likely to conclude that a less powerful America still remains indispensable. America will have to learn that world order depends on a structure that participants support because they helped bring it about. If progress is made on these enterprises, 2009 will mark the beginning of a new world order. ∎

America will have to learn that world order depends on a structure that participants support because they helped bring it about

The Americas

Also in this section:
Cuba's oily future 76
New strains in Canada 77
Luiz Inácio Lula da Silva: Building on the B in BRIC 78

Latin drift

Michael Reid

Sorting Latin America's pragmatists from its populists

After five years in which Latin America's economies have averaged 5% annual growth with generally low inflation, they face a severe test of their new-found resilience in 2009. Subdued consumption in the rich world will squeeze exports and commodity prices, and finance will be harder to find. Countries with diversified exports and sound policies will be better placed to ride out the storm than those, such as Venezuela and Argentina, that have squandered their commodity windfalls and spurned private enterprise. Politically, tougher times will coincide with, and contribute to, the start of a tentative shift away from the left.

Of the region's two big economies, Brazil will continue to do better than Mexico, but neither will do well. Softening commodity prices will erode Brazil's trade surplus (and cause further depreciation of the real), but the diversity of its export markets and the vigour of domestic consumption will keep growth below 3% (down by more than two percentage points from 2008). With a presidential election due in 2010, Brazilian politics will be dominated by preliminary jockeying over candidacies, with President Luiz Inácio Lula da Silva, the social-democratic president, seeking to transfer his own popularity to his chosen successor, probably Dilma Rousseff, his chief of staff.

The intertwining of Mexico's economy with United States' manufacturing will cut growth to under 1%. That will bring an increase in social tension: tighter border controls mean it has become harder to cross into the United States, and jobs are harder to find there, so the traditional safety valve of emigration will become blocked. The slowdown comes at an awkward moment for Felipe Calderón, Mexico's president. In a mid-term congressional election in July, Mr Calderón's conservative National Action Party is unlikely to win the majority it desperately needs to sweep away the vestiges of corporatism that still hobble the country's economy. The centrist Institutional Revolutionary Party, which ruled Mexico for seven decades until 2000, will make gains at the expense of the divided left. Whatever happens in the election, Mr Calderón will hope to make headway against powerful drug gangs.

Argentina's vigorous recovery from its financial collapse of 2001-02 will peter out in 2009, as commodity prices soften. Cristina Fernández de Kirchner, the populist president, will pay a political price for her failure—and that of her husband and predecessor, Néstor Kirchner—to persuade investors that Argentina is a safe place to do business. Despite the government's manipulation of the inflation index, Argentines know they are getting poorer. The Kirchners' hold over the Congress and the ruling Peronist party will vanish in a legislative election in October. Rather than the divided opposition parties, Peronist barons of the centre-right may be the big winners. Ms Fernández will govern at their pleasure for the rest of her term until 2012—if she lasts that long.

In Venezuela the cost of Hugo Chávez's rule will become clearer. Hitherto, a high and rising oil price has paid for ballooning imports and public spending, concealing the growing inefficiencies of the state-dominated economy. Unless oil, improbably, rises above $100 per barrel again, economic growth will slow to a crawl. Mr Chávez still has some room for manoeuvre: he has ▶

> *Mr Chávez may become more radical: expect him to unearth more fictitious coup plots*

2009 IN BRIEF
Chile hopes to join the **club of rich countries** by becoming a member of the OECD.

Michael Reid: Americas editor, *The Economist*; author of "Forgotten Continent: The Battle for Latin America's Soul" (Yale)

Old order, new oil

Michael Reid

Cuba's future will become a little clearer

The world will have several reasons to take notice of Cuba in 2009. The year will begin with the commemoration of the 50th anniversary of Fidel Castro's revolution on January 2nd. The man himself, mentally alert but physically frail since abdominal surgery in 2006, may not make a public appearance. But there will be much official self-congratulation at the revolution's survival in the face of an American trade embargo, CIA assassination attempts and the collapse of its former Soviet ally and patron.

For the long-suffering Cuban people there will be little to celebrate. Their privations have been increased by the devastation of housing and agriculture wrought by twin hurricanes in September 2008. This will make it difficult for Raúl Castro, who formally succeeded his brother as president in early 2008, to fulfil promises of higher wages. He is likely to accelerate steps to decentralise economic decision-making to state companies and co-operatives, and to lease idle state land to private farmers. Hurricane damage will also make Cuba even more dependent on aid from Venezuela's President Hugo Chávez.

Two other developments in 2009 should make the island's medium-term future a bit clearer. The first is a new American president. A change in the White House brings with it at least a chance that the United States will loosen its economic embargo and encourage some sort of political dialogue with the Cuban regime, rather than leave United States policy frozen in futility.

A second big question is oil. During 2009 a group of foreign oil companies will bring a drilling rig to the Cuban waters of the Gulf of Mexico to sink several exploratory wells. If they find oil, that will strengthen Mr Castro's position—and also reduce his dependence on Mr Chávez.

The year will end with a long-postponed congress of the ruling Communist Party. This will provide important pointers to a Cuba without the direction of the Castro brothers.

Raúl Castro has surrounded himself with veteran leaders, many of whom have been in power for decades. His government has a transitional flavour to it. The party congress, the first since 1997, may see the emergence of a much younger and more pragmatic leadership. Even so, change in Cuba will proceed slowly—at least while Fidel Castro remains alive. ■

Or perhaps not...

---

stashed away perhaps $15 billion in various development funds, and the central bank's reserves stand at some $30 billion. But as oil dollars become less abundant, the government will tighten import controls and a devaluation may be unavoidable. That will mean a downward spiral of inflation, stagnation and poverty.

Facing the unravelling of his regime, Mr Chávez may become more radical: expect him to unearth more fictitious coup plots and to curtail political freedoms.

Divided they fall

The most closely watched Latin American election in 2009 will be in Chile, where the Concertación, the moderate centre-left coalition that has governed the country since the end of General Augusto Pinochet's dictatorship in 1990, may lose power. For the first time, the Concertación will probably run two candidates. One would be from the Socialist Party—either Ricardo Lagos, a successful former president, or José Miguel Insulza, the secretary-general of the Organisation of American States. The Christian Democrats may run their own candidate, probably Eduardo Frei, another former president. That division would help Sebastián Piñera, a moderate conservative and successful businessman. He is likely to win the presidency narrowly in a run-off ballot.

Four smaller countries will also choose a new president in 2009. In Uruguay, the ruling centre-left Broad Front will win a second term, provided it unites around the candidacy of Danilo Astori, a moderate former finance minister. Similarly, in Panama the ruling centre-left Party of the Democratic Revolution should retain power. In El Salvador, the left-wing FMLN's attempts to dislodge the conservative Arena party may founder. In both El Salvador and Honduras the elections may be dominated by attempts by Venezuela's Mr Chávez to influence the result with money and offers of aid.

In Bolivia Evo Morales, the left-wing president, is likely to win a referendum to ratify a new constitution that "refounds" the country as an Amerindian socialist republic. But he will face continuing unrest in the more capitalist eastern provinces. Another of Latin America's radical socialists, Ecuador's Rafael Correa, will organise and win a fresh presidential election under a new constitution. In Colombia, the era of Álvaro Uribe will draw towards a close—assuming that he opts not to change the constitution to allow him to stand for a third consecutive term in 2010. The fastest growing of the larger economies in Latin America will once again be Peru, not least because its government will keep faith in free trade, rather than the socialism fashionable elsewhere. ■

2009 IN BRIEF

Portugal hosts a **summit of Iberian and Latin American states**, coinciding with the bicentennial celebrations of the independence of many Latin American countries from Spain and Portugal.

Canada's clashes

Jeffrey Simpson OTTAWA

New strains replace the old ones

Canada has often been described as "two solitudes": largely French-speaking Quebec and the rest of the country. Keeping the two groups united within the federation has always been the supreme test of Canadian political leadership. Quebec separatism is in deep slumber, and nothing suggests a wake-up any time soon. A nominally separatist party, the Bloc Québécois, won the largest number of seats in the province in the federal election of October 2008 by never mentioning separatism and by positioning itself as the best exponent of Quebec's "interests" in Canada.

> Something once unimaginable will happen: Ontario, the historic cash-cow of Canada, will begin to receive economic help from other provinces

Instead, the new strains in sprawling Canada are between three energy-rich western provinces—Saskatchewan, Alberta and British Columbia—and the economic laggards, Quebec and Ontario. These strains will not threaten Canadian unity, but they will make governing tougher.

In 2009, or perhaps in 2010, something once unimaginable will happen: Ontario, the historic cash-cow of Canada, will begin to receive economic help from other provinces. This is like Tuscany being overtaken by Sicily in Italy.

The Toronto-Dominion Bank's economic-forecasting team says Ontario's economy is slipping so fast relative to the three western provinces that it will soon be receiving payments through equalisation, a complicated scheme that transfers money from taxpayers in better-off provinces through the federal treasury to poorer regions. Ontario is set to join Quebec as a recipient.

Canada's growth in 2009 will limp along at below 1%, even with the boost of high-ish prices for energy, fertiliser and food, all of which western Canada exports in abundance. Ontario and Quebec are the country's manufacturing heartland. Their manufacturing sectors will take a beating in 2009, with growth rates potentially low enough to qualify as being in recession. Ontario, in particular, will be affected. High energy prices are terrific for western Canadian producers, but bad news for Ontario, which imports almost all its oil and gas.

Ontario's manufacturing sector is led by the car industry, whose North American producers are being hammered. An American recession will drag down the central Canadian regions that depend on exports to their south. Some of the country's large banks, headquartered in Ontario's capital, Toronto, have already suffered from America's housing and credit meltdowns.

Ontario manufacturers can no longer ride the magic carpet of a cheap Canadian dollar. In 2008 the Canadian dollar hit parity with the American dollar, then slid a bit, and will nestle in the low 80-cent range in 2009—but this is merely the gap needed to make up for a productivity level some 20% lower than in the United States.

Quebec enjoys plenty of cheap hydroelectric power. Ontario is less fortunate. Huge problems with its nuclear reactors—cost over-runs and expensive reactor refits—mean surcharges on all hydro bills. The provincial government is committed to building more reactors, but these will take years to provide power. In the meantime, Ontario's energy costs will remain high, and go higher.

Ontario's premier, Dalton McGuinty, has been complaining about his province's plight—and his protests have been ignored. Indeed, in the October election that produced another minority national government, the federal Conservatives improved their standing, suggesting that the prime minister, Stephen Harper, was unhurt by the premier's complaints. But Mr McGuinty has a point. Through equalisation and many other federal programmes, about C$20 billion ($16.9 billion) a year gets sent out of Ontario to other parts of Canada. The country's cash-cow cannot afford that drain any more.

Western Canada's growth and central Canada's slump will cause tensions in 2009. Central Canada will press the Bank of Canada to keep interest rates low, but the bank will have to contend with inflationary pressures from western growth. The central government that finances the equalisation scheme will find its budget distended by having to fork over money to Ontario.

You can't have it both ways

A clash looms, too, between the federal government and Alberta and Saskatchewan. These provinces will want to do nothing that slows growth in the oil-sands, natural-gas and coal industries. Alberta, the biggest per head polluter, is prepared to allow greenhouse-gas emissions to rise by 20% by 2020. Yet the federal government says that Canada will cut its emissions by 20% by 2020.

A national 20% reduction is impossible if Alberta's emissions rise by 20%. Canada will either negotiate hypocritically in international climate-change talks in 2009 by committing to a target it cannot meet, or Ottawa will somehow force more rigorous measures on Alberta. ■

Jeffrey Simpson: national affairs columnist, the Globe and Mail

---

2009 IN BRIEF

Peru and the United States implement a **free-trade agreement**, one of several promoted by the US to counter rival proposals by Venezuela's President Hugo Chávez.

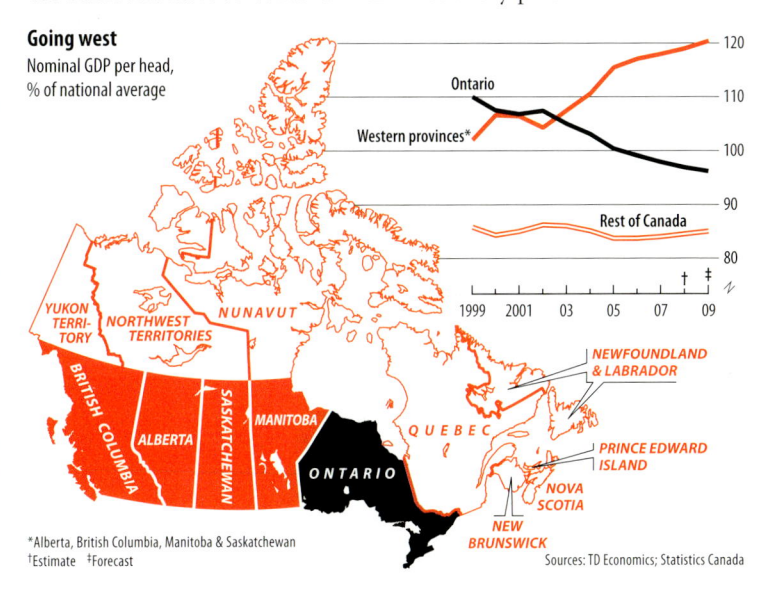

Going west
Nominal GDP per head, % of national average

*Alberta, British Columbia, Manitoba & Saskatchewan
†Estimate ‡Forecast

Sources: TD Economics; Statistics Canada

Building on the B in BRIC

Luiz Inácio Lula da Silva, president of Brazil, sees a growing global role for big emerging economies

Upon first taking office in 2003, I pledged to end hunger in my country. Under the "Zero Hunger" banner, I put poverty-eradication and the alleviation of inequality at the forefront of government action. I was convinced that without dealing squarely with these two evils, it would be impossible to overcome centuries of economic backwardness and political unrest.

After nearly six years, much progress has been made. The number of very poor in Brazil has been slashed in half. The middle class is now in a majority, 52% of the population.

There is no cause for complacency. Many Brazilians are still unable to support themselves with dignity. Yet Brazilian society's response to eliminating social and economic deprivation is an indication of the profound changes the country is undergoing. Brazil has never been in a better position to meet the challenges ahead and is fully aware of its growing global responsibilities.

A global agenda

Brazil's ethanol and biodiesel programmes are a benchmark for alternative and renewable fuel sources. Partnerships are being established with developing countries seeking to follow Brazil's achievements—a 675m-tonne reduction of greenhouse-gas emissions, a million new jobs and a drastic reduction in dependence on imported fossil fuels coming from a dangerously small number of producer countries. All of this has been accomplished without compromising food security, which, on the contrary, has benefited from rising agricultural output.

Food scarcity threatens to undermine our achievements in reducing world poverty. Brazil is expanding agricultural production, reinforcing the country's position as the world's second-largest food exporter. At the same time, the pace of deforestation in the Amazon has been reduced by half, an indication that Brazil's modern agro-industry poses no threat to the rainforest. We are setting up offices in developing countries interested in benefiting from Brazilian know-how in this field.

The replication in Latin America and Africa of many Brazilian social initiatives, including the Zero Hunger and HIV-AIDS programmes, is proof that the Millennium Development Goals are attainable at a relatively low cost. The antiretroviral manufacturing plant Brazil is set to open in Mozambique in 2009, for example, will help Africa to fight the HIV-AIDS epidemic.

In tackling climate change, collective action is the only way forward. The question-mark around the relevance of the G8 and the unreformed Security Council—not to mention the Bretton Woods institutions—highlights that it is no longer possible to exclude major emerging economies from the debate on issues of paramount importance to the global agenda. Greater democracy in international decision-making is essential if truly effective answers to global challenges are to be found. The magnitude of the current financial crisis, for instance, requires a vigorous response from the multilateral institutions.

Brazil remains committed to the successful conclusion of the Doha round. We wish to eliminate all barriers to international trade that strangle the productive potential of countless countries in Asia, Africa and Latin America. I have been in direct contact with leaders from some of the main players—the United States, India, China, Indonesia, Britain—and believe we still have a real chance to achieve a breakthrough on the relatively minor outstanding issues.

The industrialised world should take the lead in reducing greenhouse-gas emissions and provide support for developing nations to follow, but without having to compromise on domestic growth. Similarly, intellectual-property protection cannot take precedence over the ethical imperative of ensuring that poor populations have access to life-saving drugs.

Implementing this agenda requires a new, more transparent and rule-based international system. To this end, Brazil has joined India and South Africa in establishing IBSA, an association of the three major democracies of the global South focusing on co-operation and development issues. Within the framework of the BRIC countries (Brazil, Russia, India and China) and of the expanded G8, Brazil seeks to help identify the role of these emerging players in the unfolding multipolar order.

We have also joined our neighbours in setting up the Union of South American Nations (UNASUL), which aims to enhance regional integration and to ensure a stronger international presence for our block. UNASUL is setting up an energy plan, a defence council and a development bank.

Through such initiatives we will enhance dialogue and improve the mechanisms required to reinvigorate multilateralism. Most of all, we will strengthen our capacity to join hands in building a more peaceful, just and prosperous future for all. ■

Greater democracy in international decision-making is essential if truly effective answers to global challenges are to be found

THE WORLD IN 2009

Asia

Also in this section:

NATO forces in Afghanistan 80
India's election season 81
Post-Olympics China 82
Chinese bird-watchers 83
An upheaval in Japanese politics 83
Australia's drought 84
Indonesia votes 85
Kevin Rudd:
The role of medium powers 86

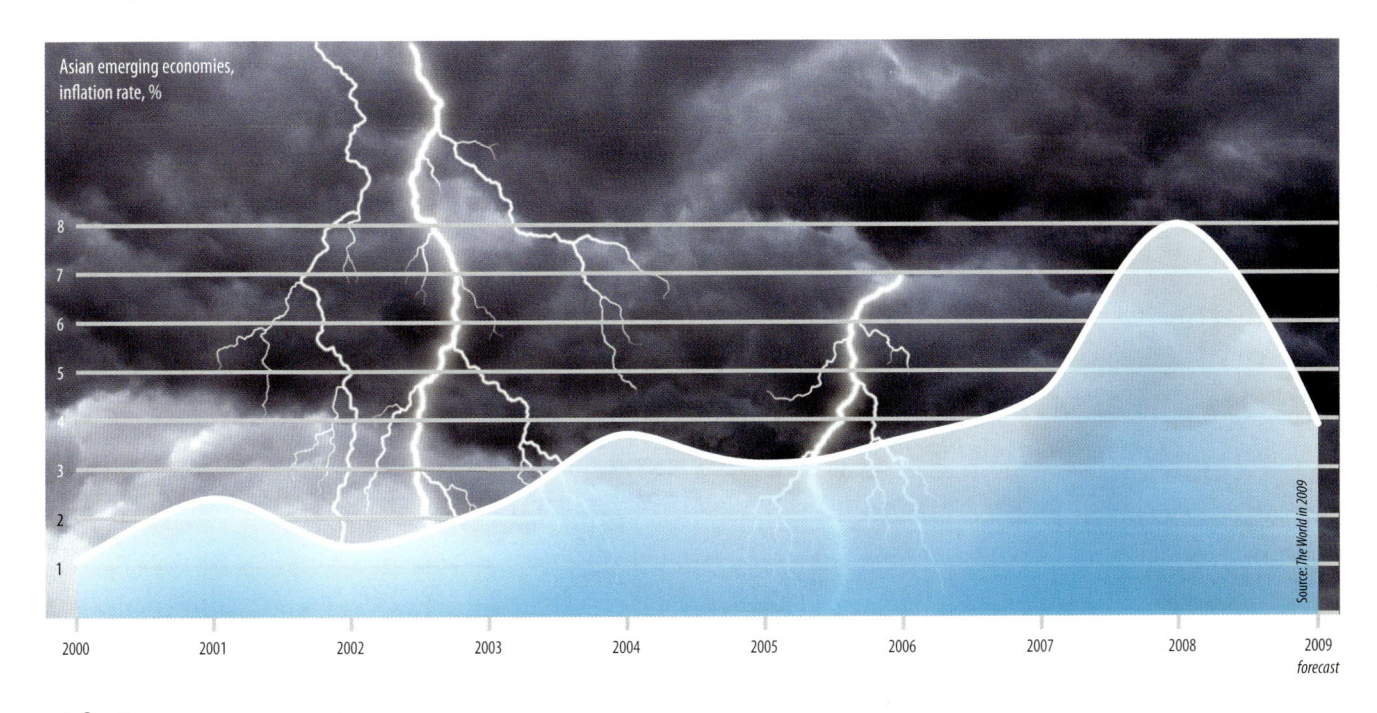

Asian emerging economies, inflation rate, %

Source: The World in 2009

2000 2001 2002 2003 2004 2005 2006 2007 2008 2009 forecast

Riders on the storm

Pam Woodall HONG KONG

Asia will enjoy moderate growth and lower inflation in 2009

Asia's emerging economies have long been the world's most dynamic, with GDP growing at an annual rate of 7.5% over the past decade, two-and-a-half times as fast as in the rest of the world. Over the past year, however, Asia has been hit by a series of typhoons: an economic downturn and credit crunch in the rich world, dearer energy and a surge in inflation. These are particularly troublesome for the world's most export- and energy-dependent economies, and many people worry that they will badly damage Asia's growth prospects. In 2009 the pessimists will prove to be wrong.

Asia's export-driven economies had benefited more than any other region from America's consumer boom. Its manufacturers have therefore been hit hard by the slump in American demand. Exports to America will weaken further in 2009, and European markets will also be squeezed. But America and western Europe together buy less than 30% of emerging Asia's total exports. Over half of China's exports go to other emerging economies, where demand remains stronger.

Some of the smaller economies, such as Singapore and Hong Kong, are more vulnerable, with exports to America amounting to 20-30% of GDP (compared with only 8% for China) and will therefore slow more sharply. Almost everywhere, however, consumer spending and infrastructure investment will remain robust and so help to offset weaker exports. China's retail-sales volume, for example, could increase by around 15% in 2009.

Stockmarkets in the region have tumbled recently, yet Asian countries have largely avoided the financial excesses undermining so many Western economies. Private-sector debts are low, banks' holdings of risky assets are small, and economies are less dependent on foreign capital than they used to be. The main exception is South Korea, where banks borrowed heavily abroad to fund a surge in lending to households and firms. Unlike most other Asian economies, it also has a current-account deficit. As a result, its economy will be hit harder by the global credit crunch.

In general, however, the Asian economies are not only in much better shape than a decade ago, but also when compared with other emerging economies in eastern Europe or Latin America. China, which has accounted for about one-third of global growth in 2008, will continue to support the region.

Growth in emerging Asia as a whole will slow, but not slump, in 2009, with GDP increasing by an average of just under 7%. That is well below growth of over 9% in 2007, but that was unsustainable. Slower growth, more dependent on domestic demand rather than exports, will be the pause that refreshes. If the global downturn forces Asian governments to shift the mix of growth from exports to consumption, this will help to ▶

The good news is that inflation will ease in 2009

2009 IN BRIEF
China invites the world's aerospace and defence industry in September to the biennial **Beijing Aviation Expo**.

Pam Woodall: Asia economics editor, *The Economist*

2009 IN BRIEF

After just two years in service, Taiwan's first **bullet train** turns a net profit—or so the operators predict.

make future growth more sustainable.

If domestic demand falters, several countries, including China, Hong Kong and Singapore, have budget surpluses which will allow them to support their economies with higher spending or lower taxes. However, India's budget deficit of 8% of GDP (including off-budget subsidies) leaves it with no such cushion.

Emerging Asia's inflation rate reached 8% in mid-2008, up from an average of only 2.8% since 2000. China hit its highest rate for 12 years, Singapore and Malaysia their highest for around 25 years. But the good news is that inflation will ease in 2009.

Most of the jump in inflation was caused by a surge in the price of food, and to a lesser extent oil. Food makes up a much bigger slice of consumer spending in these countries than in the rich world. Inflation has also been fuelled by over-rapid growth in some economies, which pushed up wages.

Two forces will therefore help to reduce inflation in 2009. First, if food and energy prices stabilise at their current lower levels, this will produce a sharp fall in the year-on-year rate of inflation. Second, slower growth will also help to dampen wage demands. Emerging Asia's average inflation rate will drop below 4% in 2009, which will give central banks more room to cut interest rates. And since Asia uses more energy to generate a dollar of GDP than other parts of the world, it will also enjoy the biggest boost from lower oil prices.

A longer-term concern is whether more expensive labour could wipe out Asia's competitive edge. Labour costs are rising much faster than in the developed world, forcing some Chinese firms to close down. But Chinese manufacturing wages are still less than 10% of those in America.

More factories in southern China will go bust in 2009 because the country is starting to lose its competitiveness in some low-value products, such as toys, shoes and textiles. This is forcing Chinese manufacturers to move up the value chain, just as those in South Korea and Taiwan did years ago. But this is evidence of success as countries grow richer, not a sign of dwindling competitiveness. ∎

A rocky and a hard place

Anton La Guardia

Afghan woes are NATO's too

With the end of the surge in Iraq in 2008, Afghanistan will see its own military surge in 2009. How big it will be and, crucially, whether it will succeed will be determined by events elsewhere. The ability to reinforce NATO forces in the Hindu Kush will depend on how soon American troops can be shifted out of Mesopotamia. And whether they manage to reverse Afghanistan's downward spiral will depend, in part, on the degree to which Pakistan is able and willing to get a grip on its lawless tribal belt.

Compared with the blood and treasure expended in Iraq, Afghanistan has been an "economy of force" mission—military-speak for "starved of money, soldiers and equipment". Afghanistan is bigger than Iraq in both size and population, but it has less than half the number of Western and local troops to fight its war.

European countries, short of will and resources, are unlikely to provide many more fighting soldiers. Indeed, the Dutch are expected to stop operations in 2009. And the Canadians will largely withdraw by 2011.

So the military effort will depend ever more on America. General David McKiernan, the (American) NATO commander in Afghanistan, has asked for four more American combat brigades—about 15,000 troops—to add to NATO's current 50,700-strong force and the 12,000 soldiers of America's separate but parallel Operation Enduring Freedom. So far, he has been promised only one extra brigade in early 2009, though more are likely.

That said, increases in troop levels in the past two years, and the use of counter-insurgency tactics of the kind successfully employed in Iraq, have so far failed to stop the Taliban from becoming stronger. Reliable data are hard to come by, but the number of Western troops killed in Afghanistan makes the point: only 12 were killed in 2001, when the Taliban were toppled, whereas more than 230 died in the first nine months of 2008.

America wants the Afghan army to be expanded from the planned 80,000 men to about 130,000. That may still be too few, if Iraq's 260,000-strong army is anything to judge by. The Afghan police, corrupt and poorly equipped, are often part of the problem rather than the solution.

Military force can help only up to a point. Economic development, and curbing the government corruption that accompanies the opium-fuelled economy, are as important. But a weakened President Hamid Karzai, facing re-election in 2009, is unlikely to embark on radical reform.

The task for NATO is to extend government authority over a country that has rarely known it, and to prod Pakistan to do the same in its lawless borderlands. It will be very difficult. ∎

Anton La Guardia: defence and security correspondent, *The Economist*

Mission impossible?

A subcontinent votes

James Astill DELHI

India enters an uncertain election season

It has been an Indian summer in the world's biggest democracy. Since coming to power in 2004, India's coalition government, which is led by the Congress party, has presided over a splendid run of around 9% annual economic growth—despite failing to introduce almost any of the liberal reforms that India needs. But 2009 will bring a new season. Hit by a global slump, the economy will slow down enough to erode confidence in the government. A general election, due by May, will cause uncertainty, and perhaps even unrest.

Poor Indian voters have a habit of anti-incumbency. Yet this is complicated by two factors. One is a separate electoral cycle in the states. In 2009 this will work to Congress's advantage: three big states governed by its main rival, the Hindu-nationalist Bharatiya Janata Party (BJP), are due to hold elections shortly before the national poll.

The second factor is the rise of regional parties, at the expense of both Congress and the BJP. This trend will continue in 2009, with Congress and the BJP liable to shrink within their coalitions. It is even conceivable that India's two main parties will win less than half the available seats—opening the way for a coalition government that includes neither. This might be led by the Bahujan Samaj Party (BSP), which is dedicated to *dalits*, formerly called "untouchables", and governs populous Uttar Pradesh (UP) state. The BSP's tough leader, Mayawati, a former primary-school teacher with a fondness for diamonds, would become India's first *dalit* prime minister.

Her time may come; but probably not in 2009. More likely, India will have another fractious coalition led by Congress or the BJP—depending on which makes the better alliances. Here, too, Congress will have an edge. Its allies in Tamil Nadu and Bihar will do badly. But it will hope to do better in UP, thanks to a possible alliance with the state's former rulers, the Samajwadi Party. The BJP's hopes rest upon its ability to re-engage three former allies, in Tamil Nadu, West Bengal and Andhra Pradesh. But its choice of L.K. Advani, an octogenarian bruiser, for its prime ministerial candidate makes this difficult. Mr Advani is a Hindu chauvinist, accused of inciting communal violence, and all three former allies have sizeable Muslim support.

For its part, Congress would like to name as its prime ministerial candidate Rahul Gandhi, the 38-year-old son of its leader, Sonia Gandhi, and her murdered husband, Rajiv, a former prime minister. But it will not do so. Mr Gandhi is well-educated (Harvard and Cambridge), and has tried hard to endear himself to Indians. But he is an awkward politician, whom they are as likely to deride for his spoiled existence as love for his ancestry. Alas, while waiting for Mr Gandhi to shine, Congress has failed to bring order to its chaotic state-level leadership. Its prime ministerial candidate in 2009 will be Manmohan Singh, India's elderly leader, whom Mrs Gandhi rates highly, not least because he is no long-term rival to her son.

Business as usual

Whatever government emerges, Indians and foreign investors should expect no big new policies in 2009. But the next government will maintain the broad commitment to reform that all Indian governments have shared, albeit fitfully, since the early 1990s. A BJP-led government would show more reformist zeal, for example in banking and insurance. But a fresh Congress-led government may be more effective than its predecessor: it would probably not be shackled with that government's erstwhile ally, a gang of Communist parties which blocked much reform before quitting the government in mid-2008.

The Communists took umbrage at India's nuclear co-operation agreement with America. In 2009 this deal will open the way for big investments in India's civilian nuclear programme. Yet the deal, making nuclear-armed India an exception to the usual counter-proliferation rules, has extra significance: as proof of the new stature that India has won from its economic rise.

Even with a shrinking availability of credit, and economic troubles in America and Europe, the main markets for India's IT firms, the economy will grow by between 6% and 7%. It is a mark of India's recent achievements that this will be considered less than impressive. ■

> The next government will maintain broad commitment to reform

2009 IN BRIEF
The number of Indians who **suffer from diabetes** reaches 30m.

James Astill: South Asia correspondent, *The Economist*

Destination unknown

After the Olympics

James Miles BEIJING

A new agenda for China

2009 IN BRIEF
Cambodia celebrates 30 years of freedom from the Khmer Rouge.

With its main objectives achieved at the Olympic games—the most gold medals, a good attendance by foreign leaders, and much praise for the facilities and organisation—China's leadership is relieved at last to be able to focus on other matters. Much attention will be needed in the coming year as policymakers strive to prevent economic growth from slowing too fast while curbing inflation. They are under pressure too from a nascent middle class troubled in 2008 by a stockmarket slump and gathering gloom in the property market. Twenty years after the crushing of the Tiananmen Square democracy movement, demands for political change will also be a challenge.

On the external front there will be some relief that the election of a new American president has not involved much wrangling between candidates over America's relations with China. Calmer relations with Taiwan will also be a blessing. For the first time this decade, a new year begins with little sign of anxiety in Beijing over political developments on the island. Taiwan's President Ma Ying-jeou will continue the efforts he has been making since his inauguration in May 2008 to defuse tensions with the mainland.

Years to remember

At home the conclusion of the Olympics will mean a loosening of political fetters. No longer will officials and the public feel so constrained by a need to demonstrate a unity of purpose. The result could be a year of greater social turbulence. Street protests directed explicitly at one-party rule remain unlikely, but there are numerous potential catalysts for unrest, ranging from inflation to the environment. Even in the build-up to the games, with security forces on heightened alert, riots over local grievances erupted in several parts of China.

James Miles: Beijing bureau chief, *The Economist*

Yin and yawn

Political activists will use the 20th anniversary of the June 4th 1989 crackdown in Tiananmen Square to step up demands for political change. Such petitions are commonly circulated around this date and are greeted with silence by the Communist Party. But in 2009 debate about political reform will intensify within the party itself. This will be fuelled by official commemorations of the 30th anniversary in December 2008 of China's "reform and opening" policy, which put the country on the path to capitalism. Even in the official media there have been suggestions that the next stage of reform should focus more on politics (though no one has dared propose a proper multi-party system). Such questions will surface again around October 1st, when China celebrates the 60th anniversary of its founding as a communist state. Sixtieth birthdays are hugely important in Confucian cultures such as China's, but amid the hoopla many will be asking about the revolution's unfinished business—giving power to the people.

> Political activists will use the 20th anniversary of the crackdown in Tiananmen Square

China's ethnic-minority regions will be particularly restless. The huge security contingent used to suppress the turmoil that swept Tibet and ethnic Tibetan areas of neighbouring provinces in March 2008 will remain largely in place. It is likely to be strengthened in the approach to the 50th anniversary, on March 10th 2009, of the rebellion that led to the flight of the region's spiritual leader, the Dalai Lama, into exile. March is always a sensitive time in the Tibetan calendar because of this date. There will be another outbreak of recriminations between China and the West (and a headache for America's new president) should the authorities respond heavy-handedly to any attempt by Tibetans to mark it.

China will certainly find itself at loggerheads with the West over the environment. The country has been trying hard to present itself as pro-green, with a slew of measures in the build-up to the Olympics aimed at curbing air pollution and ensuring "carbon-neutral" games. On January 1st 2009 a new law will take effect requiring industries to cut water consumption, use more clean energy and recycle waste. But China will be very reluctant to pledge any specific targets for cuts in carbon emissions when negotiators meet in Copenhagen at the end of November 2009 to discuss a successor to the Kyoto treaty on climate change.

The country's climate-changing potential will become all the more conspicuous in the coming year as China's manufacturing output continues to climb rapidly. Global Insight, an economic research company, says that in nominal dollar terms China should surpass America as the world's biggest manufacturer in 2009. In real terms (adjusting for inflation and exchange rates) this will not occur until 2017, it says. But the earlier milestone will be the one that grabs attention.

For all its insistence that it is still a developing country and ought to be treated as one, China in 2009 will make a clear demonstration that it has (in scientific terms at least) the ambitions of a great power. With Russia's help, it will send its first probe to Mars late in 2009. ■

Twitching China

Dominic Ziegler

Discovered: a new species whose numbers are actually soaring

Mere amateurs in 2009 will make ornithological history in China by discovering birds unknown to science. Notch up another of the country's transformations: the arrival of the home-grown twitcher.

Until recently local bird-watchers were unknown. Professionals studied China's "signature" birds—pheasants, cranes and swans—and foreigners were responsible for much of the knowledge about the remaining 1,200-odd bird species.

The number of twitchers has exploded in the past few years, with a few thousand members in two dozen clubs. Most are in the affluent areas along China's seaboard. You need free time to watch birds, and money. Yet the physical changes that go with affluence destroy the habitats of migratory shorebirds and seabirds, wreaking havoc on their numbers along the crucial East Asian-Australasian flyway. The rediscovery earlier this decade of the Chinese crested tern, long thought extinct, was cause for celebration. But with a population of only 30, and only two breeding pairs in 2008, its fate hangs by a thread.

Another surprise discovery along the coast is unlikely. But China's mountain forests of the south-west are nearly virgin territory for ornithologists. This is where amateur bird-watchers will drag their scopes and cameras, and cause the world's professionals to admit they've been out-twitched. ■

Shock and aftershock

Dominic Ziegler TOKYO

An upheaval in Japanese politics is on the way

One consequence of the global financial storm, though far from its eye in the United States and Europe, will be the *bouleversement* of Japan's post-1945 political system. For in attempting to deal with recession in the coming year, the ruling Liberal Democratic Party (LDP) will only hasten its own unravelling, after a half-century of nearly unbroken rule.

The system has outlived its sell-by date. The LDP was forged in 1955 as a pro-American bulwark against the Soviet Union in East Asia and its leftist sympathisers at home. The party and its junior partners were always a very big tent. Factional squabblings were glossed over for as long as the Soviet Union existed, and economic growth allowed the LDP machine to spew favours about. Both enemy and growth disappeared at about the same time. So the internal fights—between those who argued for painful change to the structure of the political system as well as the economy, and those whose baronies would be threatened—broke into the open.

Some modernisers stormed out of the party to form the germ of a viable opposition. One of them, Ichiro Ozawa, a former party secretary-general, in 1993 declared that his goal was to bring down the LDP, however long it took. Yet the ruling party gained a fresh lease on life, thanks to Junichiro Koizumi, reformist prime minister from 2001 to 2006. A showman, he told the country he could destroy from the inside all that voters hated about the party. In a 2005 general election, the LDP won overwhelmingly. But two years later the opposition Democratic Party of Japan (DPJ), led by Mr Ozawa, wrested control of the upper house of the Diet (parliament) from the LDP, a first. And in 2008 Mr Koizumi announced his retirement from politics. His going leaves a wandering band of followers, like samurai who have lost their lord, to cause no end of trouble for the LDP.

The man who will try to save the party, but who will be blamed for its demise as we know it, is blue-blooded Taro Aso. His grandfather was Shigeru Yoshida, a prime minister who laid the foundations for Japan's post-war recovery. Mr Aso, by contrast, will prove to be the third short-lived prime minister in as many years.

He will not lack spirit, taking the fight into the camp of that bruiser, Mr Ozawa, unlike Mr Aso's two morose predecessors. He will also attempt to respond swiftly to the baneful effects of the global slowdown. But his cabinet, packed with the favoured offspring of political dynasties, will prove underwhelming, and reform will remain off the agenda. Fresh cases of bureaucratic incompetence, for instance in managing the national pension system, will surface.

Prepare for the earthquake

Mr Aso must call a general election before September 2009. Then ordinary Japanese, sick of political gridlock and increasingly worried about pocketbook issues, will hear the opposition's siren call and vote for the DPJ in large numbers.

This will be the upheaval in Japanese politics that Mr Ozawa has long promised to bring about. Yet the tremors will last for an uncomfortably long time.

For a start, the DPJ may become the Diet's biggest party without winning an absolute majority. A grand coalition will be attempted between the LDP and the DPJ, though that will disgust voters. The stage will be set for all sorts of horse-trading and treachery, and reformists in the LDP will leave in droves. But disenchantment with the DPJ will soon set in. Its lack of managerial experience will become very clear, with ideological differences within the party proving far greater than differences with the LDP. The mercurial Mr Ozawa, if he agrees to be prime minister, will not last long in the role. A *bouleversement*, then, but as much political confusion at the end of the year as at the beginning of it. ■

2009 IN BRIEF

Macau marks the tenth anniversary of its return to China from Portuguese rule.

Dominic Ziegler: Tokyo bureau chief, *The Economist*

Hurry, Murray-Darling

Robert Milliken GOOLWA

The world's second-dryest continent is running out of surface water

2009 IN BRIEF
The world's first **underwater hotel**, complete with transparent walls, off the coast of Fiji, starts to take bookings.

Kevin Rudd's first year as Australia's Labor prime minister proved a hit with voters. But in 2009 the road ahead will not be so smooth. Mr Rudd spent 2008 calmly dismantling the conservative social legacy of John Howard, his predecessor. He apologised to aboriginal Australians for past injustices. He pushed climate change to the forefront of public policy. He closed Mr Howard's offshore "detention centres" for asylum-seekers and abolished his workplace laws that had shifted power to bosses.

Symbolic changes are one thing. Mr Rudd will now be dealing with a country whose implacable faith in both the economy and nature to deliver abundance is starting to fray. On both fronts, his government will face its biggest challenge over Australia's water shortage.

After 220 years of European settlement, the world's second-dryest continent (after Antarctica) is running out of surface water. The Murray river and its main tributary, the Darling (known as the Murray-Darling basin), drain one-seventh of Australia, a region about the size of France and Spain combined. They irrigate farms and supply towns and cities in the big eastern states where most Australians live. Mark Twain once likened the Murray, and its old trading network of paddle steamers, to the Mississippi. But the romance has long gone.

A crunch has come from drought, climate change and decades of state governments' reckless water allocation for farming irrigation. Volumes flowing into the Murray from its main tributaries over the past two years were the lowest since records began in 1892. From its source as a fresh stream in the Snowy Mountains of New South Wales (NSW), the river ends 2,530km (1,580 miles) away at Goolwa, in South Australia, where its silted, salty mouth is now below sea level. Half of Goolwa's boat moorings are now on dry land.

So in 2009 there will be mounting pressure on governments from people like Jock Veenstra, a Goolwa tour-boat operator, and thousands of others whose livelihoods depend on the Murray. The year will be a crucial test for two initiatives the Rudd government has launched to get the river flowing to sustainable levels again. The first is the Murray-Darling Basin Authority, a new body with power to set limits on water extraction across the entire river system, in a bid to end the four basin states' bickering. The second is the federal government's plan to spend at least A$400m ($330m) buying water entitlements from crop and livestock farmers in Queensland and NSW and releasing them back to the river itself.

Lucky for some

The Murray's future will also depend partly on the Rudd government's plans for legislation in 2009 to start an emissions-trading scheme in 2010. Some climate-change models predict that rainwater volumes running into the basin could fall by as much as 70% by 2030. Unless the various schemes to tackle climate change, over-use and other causes of Australia's water shortage start bearing fruit, a decline of this scale would be enough to kill the Murray dead.

There is a cruel irony to all this. On the other side of the country the Pilbara region, in the north of Western Australia, will be a driving force of Australia's economy in 2009 and beyond. China's steel mills are demanding its vast reserves of iron ore faster than mining companies can dig the stuff out of the ground. In this red desert, water is the least of their problems: the Pilbara's ancient aquifers under the desert floor allow the mining companies to spray their dirt roads and precious stockpiles with water day and night to stop them blowing away—a luxury the Murray river's farmers and townsfolk in the east can only imagine. ■

> Some climate-change models predict that rainwater volumes running into the basin could fall by as much as 70% by 2030

Strewth, you'd better have a beer, Bruce

Robert Milliken: Australia correspondent, *The Economist*

Indonesia sets an example

Peter Collins BANGKOK

The largest Muslim country will stage a remarkable feat of democracy

In 2009 Indonesia will mount an impressive spectacle of popular choice, in which around 174m voters across 14,000 tropical islands will choose a president and vice-president and 560 parliamentarians. The chances are good that, as in the previous national elections in 2004, polling will be mostly peaceful and that the overwhelming majority of successful candidates will be committed to a pluralistic Indonesia with freedom of both speech and religion. Once again, the world's most populous Muslim country will demonstrate that there is nothing incompatible between practising Islam and being democratic.

This achievement will be all the more remarkable considering where Indonesia was just ten years ago: in chaos. After three decades in power, the authoritarian regime of President Suharto had collapsed amid rioting and no one knew what might take its place. Could such a huge, diverse and impoverished archipelago, with hundreds of ethnic groups, possibly hold together, given the weakness and corruption of its national institutions?

Since then the country has consistently surprised on the upside, even if the pace of reform has been ploddingly slow. Indonesia's shattered finances have been repaired. It has developed a free press. The army's hands have been prised from the levers of power. And, above all, Indonesia has become a democracy in which the voters can chuck out their government. Freedom House, an American think-tank, now rates Indonesia as the only completely free country in South-East Asia—putting its richer neighbours, Malaysia, Singapore and Thailand, to shame.

Popular wisdom

The 2004 elections allowed Indonesians, for the first time, to choose their president directly. The man they selected, Susilo Bambang Yudhoyono, a liberal ex-general, was deemed by international observers to have been the wisest choice from those on offer. Though the speculation about possible presidential candidates and governing coalitions has already begun, the parties will wait and see how they do in the legislative elections in April before entering into serious talks about the presidential vote (whose first round will be in July with a run-off, if needed, a few months later).

Even so, it is quite likely that the two main presidential contenders will be the same as last time: Mr Yudhoyono and his immediate predecessor, Megawati Sukarnoputri. Mr Yudhoyono's popularity has been dented by decisions to cut fuel and electricity subsidies, so as to avert financial ruin and redirect state spending towards the poorest. Miss Megawati has been on a meet-the-people comeback tour since early 2008 and has benefited from discontent over rising living costs. Yet the election is Mr Yudhoyono's to lose.

A few other candidates will run, probably including Wiranto, a former army chief indicted by a UN-backed tribunal over the violence that accompanied the breakaway of the former East Timor in 1999. Mr Wiranto will argue that an old-fashioned strongman is what the country needs but it will be surprising if he does any better than the third place he got in 2004. Golkar, the party that used to support Suharto, is now led by Vice-President Jusuf Kalla but his opinion-poll ratings are probably too weak for him to win the presidency. Thus Golkar may, as in the second round in 2004, offer him for the vice-presidential slot on Mr Yudhoyono's ticket.

Whereas the presidential race will feature some very familiar personalities, the parliamentary contests will also introduce fresher faces. In recent elections for provincial governors, voters have spurned established figures. This has convinced the main parties that they will need an infusion of new blood to do well in the parliamentary races: Miss Megawati's Indonesian Democratic Party of Struggle (PDI-P) says up to 70% of its candidates will be newcomers.

At first sight the parliamentary elections look like a recipe for confusion. There will be something like 12,000 candidates from 38 parties battling for the 560 seats. This is a big increase on the numbers in 2004 but the next parliament will in fact be less fragmented than the current one. This is mainly because a new rule requires parties to get at least 2.5% of the national vote to win any seats. Of the 17 parties that won seats in 2004 only eight would have met that test.

Furthermore, several mid-sized parties, such as the National Awakening Party of Abdurrahman Wahid (president in 1999-2001), are riven by splits. So the new parliament will be dominated by Golkar, the PDI-P and Mr Yudhoyono's Democrats—all of which are staunchly secularist—plus the mildly Islamist Prosperous Justice Party (PKS). The PKS, like the smaller Islamist parties, has found that moderating its calls for *sharia* and embracing pluralism is the only way to win new votes. It will be the cost of living that dominates the campaign, not theology. ■

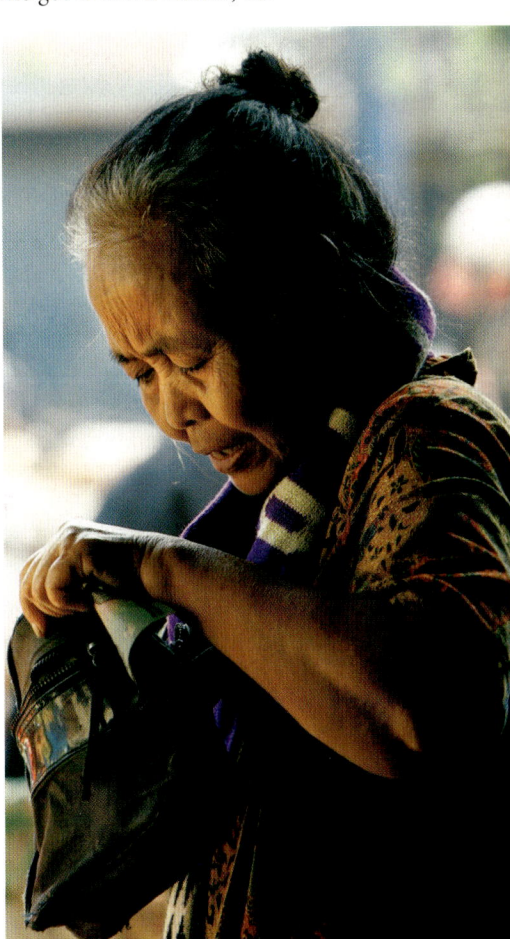

> The country has consistently surprised on the upside

Now where did I put my vote?

Peter Collins: South-East Asia correspondent, *The Economist*

Large issues and medium powers

The greatest challenges facing the world in 2009 require nations to work together in new ways—on matters ranging from the global financial system and world trade to climate change, terrorism and the spread of weapons of mass destruction. We struggle to address these problems effectively, in part because we often wrongly assume that only great-power leadership can solve threats to global security and prosperity.

Medium-sized powers are under no illusion: they understand that their influence relies on the power of their ideas and the effectiveness of their coalition-building—not the headcount of their population, the size of their GDP or the force of their military arsenal. They have a history of creativity, establishing multilateral institutions and bridging the gap between opposing parties. They can also sustain a long-term focus on specific problems in a way that great powers, juggling competing priorities, often find difficult.

Australia has used its status as a medium-sized power to positive ends for years. We established the Cairns Group (of agricultural exporters) and the Canberra Commission on the Elimination of Nuclear Weapons. We were one of the main drivers behind APEC (Asia Pacific Economic Co-operation), and we have helped resolve several regional conflicts.

We have a proud tradition of leading by example—such as our unilateral tariff reductions, beginning in the late 1980s, which contributed to the global progress on free trade in the years that followed. In 2009 Australia will revive this tradition with targeted measures on global financial stability, climate change, nuclear proliferation and development.

A mid-sized helping

The spiralling global financial crisis during 2008 highlights the importance in an interdependent global economy of nations collaborating in confronting common threats. The medium-sized powers that comprise much of the G20 (the world's largest economies) can harness their experience of different regulatory models to play a leading role in ensuring sustained financial stability.

Like other medium-sized powers with experience of a range of disclosure regimes, Australia will work for stronger global disclosure standards for systemically important financial institutions, as well as stronger supervisory frameworks to provide incentives for more responsible corporate conduct. Australia will also advocate accounting reforms that will foster a more medium-term perspective on underlying asset values. And it will urge a strengthening of the International Monetary Fund's mandate for prudential analysis and early-warning systems for institutional vulnerabilities.

No problem more underscores the interdependence between nations than climate change. It asks our global system to do something it has never done before. We must achieve global agreement on an economic transformation to a low-carbon economy. Making that happen will require, above all, political determination—and that must be evident at Copenhagen in December 2009.

In 2009 the Australian government will legislate for the world's most comprehensive emissions-trading scheme, covering three-quarters of our emissions. By 2009 we will be the first nation with a comprehensive legal framework for large-scale carbon capture and storage technology. Relying on coal for 80% of our power generation, Australia recognises this is essential to achieve immediate reductions in greenhouse-gas emissions.

Medium-sized powers are among the most active contributors to collective security and peacekeeping efforts, and preventing the proliferation of nuclear weapons has been a priority of Australian diplomacy for many years. We recently joined with Japan to establish the International Commission on Nuclear Non-Proliferation and Disarmament. The task in 2009 is to build an international consensus on action ahead of the 2010 review conference of the Nuclear Non-Proliferation Treaty.

Australia also believes our commitment to giving every person a "fair go" must extend beyond our shores. Australia will increase official development assistance to 0.5% of national income by 2015—with a focus on new partnerships with Pacific island neighbours to fight poverty in our own region.

In 2009 the APEC forum marks its 20th anniversary. As the world's centre of gravity is shifting to the Asia-Pacific region, I believe we must look beyond APEC to the best regional economic, political and security architecture for 2020 and beyond. On the wider global-trade agenda, Australia will continue to press for a successful conclusion to the Doha round—an outcome that is critical to building a stronger and fairer global economy.

The fruits of the progress that we make in 2009 will not be borne immediately. But harnessing the energies and initiatives of medium-sized powers will accelerate the process. ∎

Kevin Rudd, prime minister of Australia, outlines the part his country and other medium-sized powers will play in tackling global issues

By 2009 we will be the first nation with a comprehensive legal framework for large-scale carbon capture and storage technology

Middle East and Africa

Also in this section:
Going nuclear in Iran 88
A disillusioned Israel 89
What will happen to the Gulf's spending spree? 90
The future for the sub-Saharan economies 91
Mapping Africa 92
Queen Rania of Jordan: Closing the knowledge gap 93

Iraq wants its sovereignty back

Xan Smiley

Arguments over the pace of America's withdrawal will persist

Barack Obama's election-time promise to remove all American troops within 16 months of his inauguration—by May 2010—is going to be hard to keep. For sure, he has since given himself a bit of wiggle-room. He has talked of keeping a "residual force" that would help the Iraqis stand on their own feet. His people have said that if things got really bad, an Obama administration would "reserve the right to intervene, with the international community" to create safe havens, as happened after the first Gulf war in 1991. But if all goes well, not least with an improving economy attracting foreign investment, expect the 140,000-plus American troops in Iraq at the end of 2008 to fall to 80,000 or so by the end of 2009.

Though the new president will reiterate his desire to withdraw all American troops as soon as possible, he will almost certainly concede that a rigid timetable cannot be adhered to. Much will depend on the situation on the ground. Even so, there will be strong pressures on Mr Obama to fulfil his promise. If the security situation continues to improve, as it did in 2008, he will argue that the Iraqis have less need for help—so the Americans can withdraw faster. And if it worsens, as it may, he could revert to his original argument that the Iraqis will sort themselves out once they are forced to—without outsiders holding the ring.

Much will also depend on the attitude of the Iraqis themselves. The biggest political events in 2009 will be provincial elections (originally scheduled for October 2008), with luck early in the year, and a general election at the year's end. The provincial ones should mark a first big step towards empowering the Sunni Arabs, most of whom boycotted the contest last time round and thus relegated themselves to the sidelines or pushed themselves into the arms of the insurgents. This time they are likely to elect representatives of the Sahwa (the Awakening), a movement led largely by tribal sheikhs who have turned against the radical Islamist insurgents, especially the fanatics known as al-Qaeda in Mesopotamia.

Both sets of elections will be fraught with danger. The new Iraqi establishment, led by the Shia Arab majority, who number at least 55% of Iraq's total population against some 20% for the Sunni Arabs and another 20% for the Kurds, has done too little to embrace the "Sons of Iraq", the militias that have emerged out of the Sahwa. These militias, 100,000-plus strong, have been responsible, together with the American "surge" of troops since 2007, for pacifying western Baghdad and the once-bloody western province of Anbar. At first paid for by the Americans, they were expecting to be inducted into the Iraqi security forces, but the Shia-led government has balked at letting them in. The Sahwa's representatives will be elected in droves to the provincial councils, so the Sunni Arabs should benefit from

> The elections will force the contestants to stress their dedication to full Iraqi sovereignty

2009 IN BRIEF
Iraq will choose a **new flag**, to replace the temporary one that superseded the Saddam-era banner.

Xan Smiley: Middle East and Africa editor, *The Economist*

Going nuclear in Iran

Xan Smiley

Ever closer to getting the bomb

The Iranian government's first and biggest hope for 2009 is, unsurprisingly, that its country will not be bombed—either by Israel or by an American administration, especially the outgoing one in its dying weeks. So it will try to spin out talks with the six-country negotiating group (China, Russia, the United States and the European trio of Britain, France and Germany) for as long as possible, as before. It will carry on playing cat and mouse with the increasingly frustrated International Atomic Energy Agency, the UN's nuclear watchdog. Meanwhile, it will continue to enrich uranium, getting ever closer to the point where it will be able to make a nuclear bomb. Indeed, it is likely, within a few years, to achieve that aim.

Thanks to Russia's falling-out with America, Iran should also be safe from wider or tighter UN sanctions. The Russians will probably veto another round of them in the UN Security Council.

Even so, Iran's economy is in dire straits, despite its oil. If the price of oil keeps dropping, popular dissatisfaction will rise. As it is, Iranian living standards will go on falling. But there is virtually no mass opposition to the regime, and little likelihood of it brewing up in 2009. So the regime, though pained by sanctions, will reckon on surviving them.

The biggest political event in Iran's calendar will be the presidential election. Mahmoud Ahmadinejad, the incumbent, is widely considered to have messed up the economy, so more pragmatic leaders will bid to oust him. Akbar Hashemi Rafsanjani, a former president who opposes Mr Ahmadinejad, is ineligible to run, because he will turn 75 in February, but Mehdi Karroubi, a former speaker of parliament, and Muhammad Khatami, another former president, may stand for the pragmatists' wing. As before, out-and-out reformers will be barred by vetting councils of conservative clerics.

The final say in all policy, including nuclear issues, will remain with Ayatollah Ali Khamenei, the supreme leader. Despite rumours that he is annoyed with Mr Ahmadinejad, Mr Khamenei has broadly backed him. A few pragmatists have suggested a wider election for the supreme leader and fixed seven-year terms of office; Mr Khamenei has held power since succeeding the revolution's founding father, Ayatollah Ruhollah Khomeini, on his death in 1989. He will be 70 in July, and is said to be in good health.

Whether or not Mr Ahmadinejad hangs on, Mr Khamenei is likely to stay in ultimate power for a good many years yet. Especially if Iran manages not to be bombed in 2009, he will continue the campaign to achieve nuclear capability—and will ensure that Iran remains a thorn in America's side in the region. ■

Mr Khamenei takes aim

2009 IN BRIEF

Libya abolishes most of its government ministries so that the people—given a share of oil revenue each month—can supposedly run the country.

---

an increase in funds and power. But if their militias are rebuffed, they could well become insurgents again.

The general election may well be bitter, not just because the sectarian division of Iraq into three main blocks—Sunni and Shia Arabs and Kurds—will be as stark as ever but because, this time, the fiercest contest will be between rival Shia parties. The prime minister, Nuri al-Maliki, will become increasingly authoritarian and increasingly determined to hold on to power. He may get some votes from Sunnis who think he should be rewarded for stabilising the country after the sectarian bloodbath of 2006. But his Dawa party is very small. The second party in government, the Islamic Supreme Council of Iraq, heavily backed by Iran, may also fare badly. Both parties are determined to keep from power the populists loyal to a fiery nationalist cleric, Muqtada al-Sadr. The Sadrists may even be banned from running as a party. But many people known to be loyal to Mr Sadr may run as individuals—and do very well.

That is one reason why Mr Maliki will insist—at any rate before the elections—on a rapid American withdrawal. For the canny Mr Sadr has long played the anti-American card, always calling for the Americans to leave forthwith. As 2009 begins, Mr Maliki will hope to have nailed down a Status of Forces Agreement (known as SOFA) with the Americans, persuading them to agree to withdraw their troops to a dozen or so bases outside the main city centres and to declare that none will be permanent; to let Americans working for private security companies be liable to Iraqi law; and to promise that all military operations within Iraq and against other countries nearby (that is, Iran) will be subject to prior Iraqi government approval. In other words, the elections will force the contestants to stress their dedication to full Iraqi sovereignty on all fronts.

However, that may prove to be rhetorical. Mr Maliki, for one, knows that the Iraqi forces will need American logistical support, especially from the air, and American firepower. Besides, the SOFA is likely to name the end of 2011 as the deadline for America's withdrawal—more than a year later than Mr Obama's original promise. But calling for a rapid American exit will be a powerful Iraqi election slogan, even though most Iraqis, according to opinion polls, are pragmatic about dates, and would reluctantly prefer foreign forces to stay until the situation seems stable rather than leave in haste while chaos prevails. All the same, 2009 will be the year when Iraq gets back a lot of its sovereignty. ■

Full of angst

David Landau JERUSALEM

A disillusioned Israel on the political slide

Almost the only certainty in Israel as 2008 drew to an end was that 2009 would be a year of domestic political uncertainty, with an election looming early in the new year and the probability of a stable government even after that election low. It was fairly certain, too, that thoughtful Israelis would increasingly fret over the instability of their politics, while more and more others, not necessarily less caring or less patriotic, would switch off in apathy, in effect opting out of the democratic process.

Perhaps the mounting disaffection will trigger the kind of massive crisis that engenders radical reform. That would be a painful but hopeful prospect, were it not for two other massive crises on Israel's horizon. Iran threatens to reach, or dangerously approach, nuclear-weapons capacity in 2009. And the Palestinian civil war, between fundamentalist Hamas and moderate Fatah, threatens to reignite, possibly spreading from Gaza to engulf the West Bank too. Israelis will have their heads full of existential angst, as usual, and their disaffection will fester.

Falling turnout in elections has become a steady trend, as has a decrease in party membership and in other forms of political activism. Even attendance at demonstrations, whatever their stripe, is down. This is not an apathy of comfortable indifference. It is born of distrust and frustration. Pollsters register a steep decline in public confidence in the institutions of state: the government, the Knesset, the courts, the police, even the army (which long enjoyed uncritical admiration).

The people who staff these institutions hurl blame at each other. "The rule of law gang", a loose alliance of prosecutors, policemen and civil servants, points to corrupt politicians as the source of the rot. Ehud Olmert, deposed as prime minister, is likely to stand trial during 2009 on a slew of bribery and fraud charges. His minister of finance, Avraham Hirschson, is on trial for theft and another minister, Tzachi Hanegbi, for illicit appointments in his ministry.

A former army chief of staff ousted under Ariel Sharon, Moshe Yaalon, and an accountant-general at the treasury ousted under Mr Olmert, Yaron Zelicha, have written books full of dark accusations. These will fuel the gang's campaign. But they will fuel the growing backlash, too. Some politicians and pundits, braving obloquy by association, say the splurge of purported whistle-blowing is paralysing the work of government by deterring decision-making, stifling initiative and rewarding politicians and civil servants who do nothing, and hence do no wrong. Mr Olmert was the fourth prime minister in a row to entertain police interrogators at his official residence—a coincidence, say the gang's critics, too implausible to be credible. Mr Sharon successfully fobbed them off onto his son, who served time for election-finance fraud. Ehud Barak and Binyamin Netanyahu were grilled on lesser allegations, not eventually proven.

> The root of the political malaise lies in the electoral system

The root of the political malaise, which has been recognised for years, lies in the electoral system, a form of proportional representation run riot. It makes for a plethora of amoeba-like parties frequently splitting and regrouping, and for fragmented coalitions and short-lived governments that serve at the mercy of a few fickle politicians. It needs to be reformed. But reform (short of revolution) requires a majority, and the parties in the Knesset refuse to provide one.

Live and let Livni?

It is into this sour atmosphere that Tzipi Livni, the newly elected leader of the ruling Kadima party, will be trying to inject her agenda of "new politics". She enjoys an unsullied reputation for probity, which after ten years in Israeli politics is noteworthy. But she is not naive. She hired Mr Sharon's former aides to help her win her party primary and they will be advising her on how to become prime minister after an election.

The politics she must deal with, moreover, are not new. Ms Livni's main rivals are Mr Barak and Mr Netanyahu, both back at the helms of their parties, respectively

In the mood, but not for politics

2009 IN BRIEF

Qatar's population grows by more than 14%, to 1.8m, mainly because of the world's **highest rate of immigration**.

David Landau: Israel correspondent, *The Economist*

Labour and Likud, after intervals on the outside making money. Both admit to past failings. Both claim to have changed for the better.

But both remind Israelis that political reform is not a panacea. They were each elected in the 1990s under a reformed system which they enthusiastically supported. It was supposed to strengthen the prime minister vis-à-vis the Knesset, and to shore up his position at the head of the ruling party. But they each emerged weakened, at the head of shrunken parties, and served only truncated terms at the helm of government. After they left, the system was changed back.

Beyond the déjà-vu effect of watching Messrs Netanyahu and Barak jostling for another chance, their separate sparring with Ms Livni thwarts any hope of a return to broadly bipolar politics of the left and right. Kadima, founded by Mr Sharon after his disengagement from Gaza, straddles the centre, sucking strength from both sides. Unless Labour completely implodes, this triangular pattern, with no one party leader able to rule without the help of at least one of the other two, will harden the parliamentary gridlock that precludes real stability, and suffocate the chance of change in Israel's seriously sick system of democracy. ∎

Buying the world

Max Rodenbeck DUBAI

The Gulf's plans for its petrodollars

2009 IN BRIEF
The Abraj al-Bait Towers, one of the tallest and biggest hotel complexes in the world, nears completion in Saudi Arabia's **holy city of Mecca**.

As most countries tighten their belts, the Arab monarchies along the Persian Gulf face a different problem: what to do with the $4.7 trillion-$8.8 trillion that their oil sales are expected to garner by 2020 (based on an oil price of $50-$100 a barrel). Whatever the actual sum—and cheaper oil will mean some belt-tightening even in the Gulf—that is a great deal of cash, and even more so considering that the six-nation Gulf Co-operation Council is home to fewer than 40m people.

One option is to spend it, and increasingly Gulf governments and investors are doing this at home. By one estimate, the share of Gulf savings invested locally has risen from 15% to 25% since 2002. McKinsey, a consulting firm, estimates that spending on local projects may top $3 trillion by 2020.

Already, the region has gained fame for superlative-scale trinkets. The brash city-state of Dubai, one of the seven statelets that make up the United Arab Emirates, expects to inaugurate the world's tallest building, the 160-storey Burj Dubai, in 2009. In addition to the world's biggest airport, largest man-made islands, longest indoor ski slope and some of the biggest shopping malls and hotels anywhere, it is also building a mega theme park, Dubailand, which consists of some 45 separate projects, including such brand-name attractions as Legoland, a Tiger Woods golf course, a Six Flags fun fair, a Formula One park, and themed attractions from Dream-Works (a Hollywood film studio) and Marvel Comics.

Not all the region's spending is so frivolous. The neighbouring emirate of Abu Dhabi is bringing branches of the Louvre and Guggenheim museums to adorn a new island suburb. Qatar, an independent state whose per head income in 2008 of $64,350 makes it one of the world's richest countries, and whose economy is projected to outpace all others in 2009, with a growth rate of 13.4%, has invested in branch campuses for half a dozen of the finest universities in the West.

Saudi Arabia plans to turn itself into an industrial powerhouse. It is building no fewer than six new "economic cities" and a giant industrial zone, at a combined cost of some $150 billion, which will incorporate aluminium smelters, refineries and car-assembly plants. For its part, Kuwait plans to spend half that sum on just one new town, Silk City, which is meant to be a free-trade zone linking Asia and Europe, with a projected population of 700,000 people by 2030.

Shopping abroad

That still leaves plenty of cash to spend abroad. Until recently, much of the region's savings went into such stately investments as United States Treasury securities, or shares in Daimler, Sony, Citicorp and Deutsche Bank. But the region's investment portfolio, led by sovereign-wealth funds whose current assets are estimated at $1 trillion, has grown far more diversified. It now includes big stakes in Las Vegas casinos, Australian gold mines, Chinese refineries, Indian luxury developments, Mexican resorts, Dutch petrochemicals, England's Manchester City football club, and yacht manufacturers in Turkey, Egypt and Italy.

Gulf money-men have also expanded in an industry they know all too well. Taqa, a majority state-owned energy company in Abu Dhabi, has busily bought up oil and gas concessions in the North Sea, Canada and the United States. The ambition is straightforward: to have a global presence, and $60 billion in assets, by 2012. ∎

Max Rodenbeck: Middle East correspondent, *The Economist*

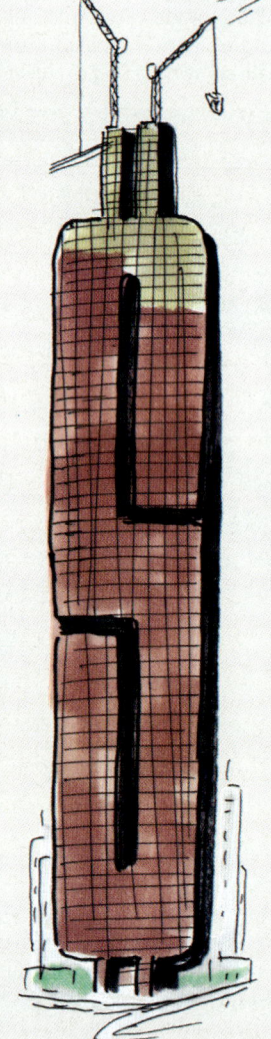

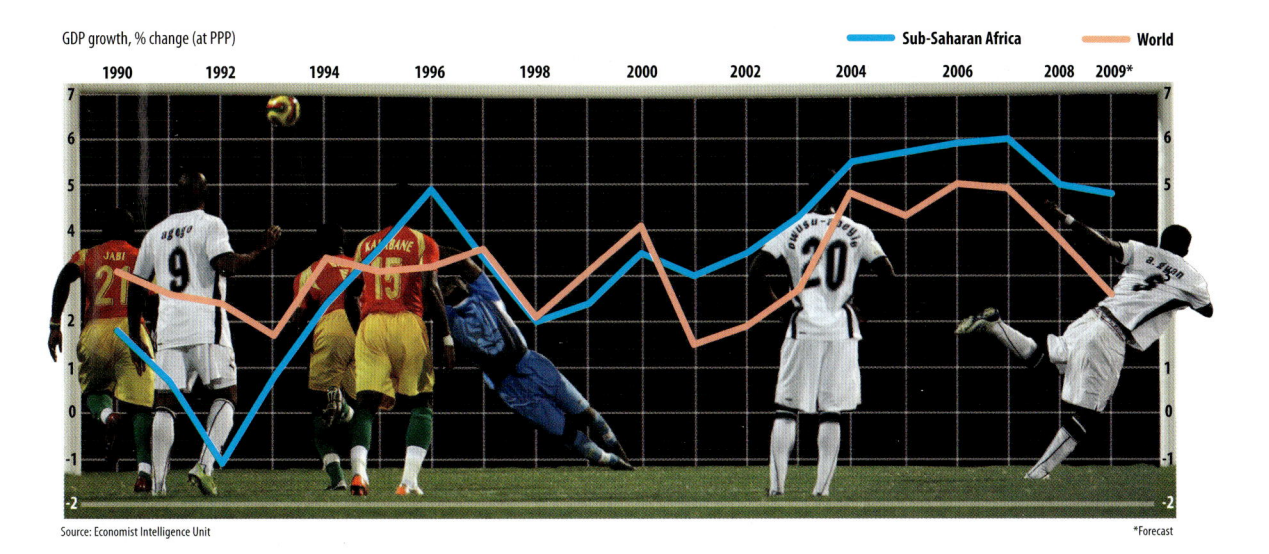

Middle East and Africa

GDP growth, % change (at PPP) — Sub-Saharan Africa — World

Source: Economist Intelligence Unit   *Forecast

Everything to play for

Pratibha Thaker

A better future for sub-Saharan Africa depends on better policies

It is the "final frontier" for emerging-market investors, and it has enjoyed record-breaking growth in recent years. After a generation in the doldrums, sub-Saharan Africa (SSA) grew by an average 6.5% a year in 2003-07, reversing the long-term decline in income per head. But is this sustainable, or simply another false dawn? Opinion is divided, with doubters ranged against relative optimists (including the donor industry, which would like to think its policies are working).

Perennial problems, such as self-serving governments, weak institutions, inadequate infrastructure and a shortage of skills, will not be remedied overnight, but there are some grounds to hope that the boom will not peter out entirely: trade barriers are slowly being dismantled, the concept of public-private partnership is taking root and democracy is spreading. With proper policies and implementation—and a dose of luck—sub-Saharan Africa could leapfrog some rungs on the development ladder.

The year ahead will be both pivotal and challenging. Although food and fuel prices dropped in 2008, they will stay fairly high, but other commodity prices look vulnerable. A swathe of SSA economies—especially oil and mineral exporters, and coffee, cocoa and tea producers—should enjoy robust growth. But the probability is that most commodity prices will falter in 2009, with adverse consequences for many SSA countries.

Food, power and phones

The consequences of a two-thirds rise in food prices over the past two years have been food riots, strikes, price controls, export bans and a massive increase in subsidy costs. All this is reversing recent gains in the fight against poverty. The International Monetary Fund pinpoints 18 SSA countries that will need additional balance-of-payments and budgetary support in 2009. Some good may come out of this, however, as several governments (Kenya and Uganda among them) urgently rethink their farm policies, aiming to boost food production.

Not before time: farming may be the dominant sector in sub-Saharan Africa, but productivity is the lowest in the world. The green revolution that helped drive development in Asia is not happening. The region as a whole has enormous farm potential, but fulfilling it will require better institutions and infrastructure. Meanwhile, the role of small-scale farmers is controversial: some experts contend that they have no place in a modern economy; others think that they can be productive with appropriate support.

Development is also impeded by a serious electricity shortage. At least 30 out of the 47 SSA countries have suffered severe energy troubles in recent years. Booming domestic demand and a lack of new investment (including in South Africa, the local "powerhouse") are to blame. If all the countries raised their power infrastructure to the standard of the continent's best performers (such as Mauritius), GDP growth per head could rise by an additional two percentage points annually. Significant investment in new plant and power-lines that cross national borders is under way—often drawing in the private sector—but many projects remain on the drawing board, and shortages will persist.

> Armed conflict and political instability have become less frequent

Even so, there will be opportunities in 2009 as well as problems. The surge in Asian investment in the region, especially from China and India (which are competing for influence and resources in the continent), will continue. Even though Asian economies will not be spared the impact of the global downturn, they take a long-term view of investment, and competition among them will work to sub-Saharan Africa's advantage. The main challenge, as ever, will be to channel the gains into productive purposes, rather than allowing them to line a few pockets.

Another bright spot will be the telecoms sector, especially mobile phones. Africans have as much appetite for communicating as the rest of the world and mobile ▶

2009 IN BRIEF
Work starts on the **Saudi Landbridge**, a 1,000-kilometre (620-mile) railway linking the Red Sea with the Gulf.

Pratibha Thaker: regional director, Africa, Economist Intelligence Unit

Putting Africa on the map

Jonathan Ledgard NAIROBI

An information revolution in the making

It will be the year of the map in Africa. Not just street directions uploaded to mobile phones for the befuddled, although that will be a blessing on a continent where often the only address is a post-office box, but internet maps galore, most of them available to the public. This will do more than any political initiative in 2009 to determine exactly where money should best be spent in Africa.

It is hard to overestimate how important a shift this is for Africa, says Oxford University's Bob Snow, who heads the Wellcome Trust's anti-malaria initiative in Kenya. Back in 1989, when the programme was set up in Kilifi on the Kenyan coast, it took Mr Snow 12 letters and several months to get a map of Kilifi district. A request had to be filed with the ministry of health to go to the ministry of planning, which would then request the mapping division to allow release of a map—if the army approved.

Digital mapping is nothing new, says Tim Robinson of the United Nations Food and Agriculture Organisation. But its possibilities have grown with satellite data, and new technology for storage. "No more tapes and dodgy optical disks—you simply buy a new stack of hard drives."

The kind of maps which in the past had been held to ransom by secretive African governments will pop up in an African internet café in less than a minute in 2009. Many will be annotated "wiki" style, with layers of information added and verified by an online community: street names for all, distribution of infant deaths for development workers, livestock density for agricultural officials, Catholic primary schools for a local bishop, and YouTube videos on the best snorkelling spots for tourists. The head of the East Africa office of Google, Joseph Mucheru, says these maps will lead a push for more local information in Africa and "will allow you to see parts of your own country you haven't seen before".

It won't stop there. Africa harbours many of the planet's most infectious diseases. Urban migration within Africa and air travel from Africa to the rest of the world have increased the risk of them spreading, but detection has been limited. Mark Smolinski, a "disease threat detective" at Google.org, the philanthropic arm of the internet company, points out that the first clinical case of HIV-AIDS can now be traced back to Africa in 1959, but was not identified until 1981. By using digital maps of Africa and overlaying them with information of interest to researchers, such as local consumption of bush meat, Mr Smolinski believes teams of epidemiologists working together with medical workers texting in information from their mobile phones will do a better job of tracking exotic pathogens before they become mass killers. Similarly, aid workers in 2009 will use digital maps for real-time information on famines and conflict, starting with an acute famine in Ethiopia.

The maps on Google and other sites are too general to produce new data for scientific research, but they will serve to disseminate the findings of scientists to African policymakers and the public, changing the way money is spent. Mr Snow cites a map of malaria incidence in Somalia, a country too dangerous for epidemiologists to visit. A glance at the map shows that much of the money to treat the disease goes to the north of Somalia, where the incidence of malaria is lower. Expect more embarrassing maps to be pushed by activists, published in newspapers and waved around in government meetings across Africa. ■

Patchy knowledge: red marks the spots of epidemiological data on malaria

J.M. Ledgard: eastern Africa correspondent, *The Economist*, and novelist

▶ telephony has enabled them to bypass the old-style telecoms infrastructure. The trend will be reinforced by the addition of eastern Africa to the global fibre-optic system in 2009-10 and the opening of new links up the west coast. Speedier and cheaper connections will boost internal trade and encourage global ties.

Much will depend on politics. Armed conflict and political instability have become less frequent. There were 21 coups on the continent in the 1960s and 18 in the 1980s, but no more than five since the turn of the century. Some 25 years ago there were only four African democracies—Botswana, Senegal, Zimbabwe and Mauritius. Today, 32 African countries have governments elected in multi-party polls, which include flawed and imperfect democracies, such as Kenya and Uganda. They also include authoritarian Zimbabwe, where another dire agricultural season in 2009 will make Robert Mugabe's rule increasingly untenable.

Elections are, of course, no guarantee of effective leadership—as several countries south of the Sahara have shown—and they can stoke fears of unwelcome policy shifts. The near-certain victory of the African National Congress's populists in South Africa's April 2009 election is already alarming some investors. But over time free voting remains the best hope for a better future for the whole region. ■

Closing the knowledge gap

The first day of school. Waleed trudges through the gates, head down and shoulders slumped. But as he enters the school yard, he notices something has changed. The building's cracked walls have been fixed and painted. The concrete yard has become a playground. In a few moments, he will enter a renovated classroom. Over the next few weeks, he will take part in computer labs, be mentored by volunteers from some of Jordan's biggest companies and join in extra-curricular music and sports with students from a private school that is "twinning" with his. In 2009, for the first time, Waleed will look forward to going to school.

The transformation has been wrought by Madrasati ("My School" in Arabic), a national programme I launched in 2008 which links businesses, local leaders and communities in support of Jordan's neediest public schools. Collaborative planning helps to turn dilapidated neighbourhoods into vibrant community hubs. Madrasati is based on the simple idea that every citizen has a stake in our children's education.

Regrettably, this spirit of shared responsibility is still nascent in my part of the world. Despite our significant investments in education and our successes in boosting enrolment and gender parity, Arab educational systems lag behind those of many other regions. The result is a knowledge gap that holds the Arab world back. I believe that closing this gap must be among the Arab region's top priorities—not only for 2009, but for years to come.

Across the Arab states, almost 57m adults are illiterate, two-thirds of them women. More than 6m children are not enrolled in primary school, the majority of them girls. Too many Arab school systems are based on rote learning, instead of encouraging our children to question, explore and create. We've also failed to build strong bridges between schools and the private sector—with the paradox that even as we produce more graduates than ever, unemployment among the young is especially high, and many of our brightest students end up pursuing careers abroad.

Clearly, we cannot afford to keep squandering so much of our talent. With more than half our region's population under the age of 25, the next 15 years give the Arab world a promising demographic edge: we will have the highest ratio of potential workers to dependants of any region in the world. But in order to make the most of this, we must create real opportunity for our youth.

That is why I believe the Arab world must embrace what I'll call "the three Rs 2.0"—not simply ensuring the fundamentals of reading, writing and arithmetic, but revamping our curricula, rewarding our best teachers and reinforcing the link between our classrooms of today and the workplaces of tomorrow.

It's a daunting agenda, but Jordan has shown that real change can take root in desert soil—and that innovative educational practices can be exported region-wide.

The lamp of learning

In 2003, for example, we launched the Jordan Education Initiative (JEI), combining public-sector commitment with private-sector creativity to bring internet-enabled learning to our schools. Today, JEI technology is in more than 100 schools nationwide—allowing science teachers to bring virtual experiments to the classroom, and humanities teachers to draw on innovative e-curricula. More than just wiring schools, JEI is sparking new ways of teaching, and the model is now being replicated in Egypt, Palestine and India.

INJAZ, another example of dynamic partnership for learning, connects students with private-sector volunteers who offer seminars on topics from economics to ethics to entrepreneurship—as well as on practical skills like public speaking or writing résumés. Founded in Jordan in 1999, INJAZ has spread to 12 other Arab countries and aims to reach 1m Arab youths a year by 2018.

At the same time, we're investing in the people who bring the Arab world's classrooms to life. In collaboration with Columbia University's Teachers College, a new Jordanian teaching academy will soon train teachers from across the region.

Other Arab nations are taking important and innovative steps of their own, from Yemen waiving tuition fees for young girls and Egypt creating more girl-friendly schools to Morocco targeting literacy programmes at disadvantaged populations. In Dubai, the Mohammed bin Rashid al Maktoum Foundation aims to invest $10 billion towards building Arab knowledge capital through teacher training, scholarships, research grants, youth leadership development, and more. In Qatar, a 2,500-acre Education City is home to branch campuses of some of the world's top academic and research institutions.

In 2009 such initiatives must gather momentum, reigniting the lamp of learning and discovery that lights the Arab world's way ahead. We in Jordan will do our part. ■

Queen Rania of Jordan urges the Arab world to embrace innovation in education

With more than half our region's population under the age of 25, the next 15 years give the Arab world a promising demographic edge

SARAH ELLNER | T: +44 (0)1865 422888 | EXECED@SBS.OX.AC.UK

ECLIPSED OR ILLUMINATED?

THE UNIVERSITY OF OXFORD: EDUCATING LEADERS FOR 800 YEARS

Combining the resources of the business school and the wider university, Executive Development at Oxford University's Saïd Business School shapes the 21st century leadership agenda by working with individuals and organisations to create and meet new opportunities.

OXFORD EXECUTIVE EDUCATION

LEADERSHIP & GENERAL MANAGEMENT

THE OXFORD ADVANCED MANAGEMENT PROGRAMME

NEW! THE OXFORD DIPLOMA IN ORGANISATIONAL LEADERSHIP

THE OXFORD STRATEGIC LEADERSHIP PROGRAMME

THE OXFORD HIGH PERFORMANCE LEADERSHIP PROGRAMME

WHAT NEXT? FOR LEADERS WITH MORE TO OFFER

THE OXFORD-HKU SENIOR PROGRAMME IN CORPORATE LEADERSHIP

STRATEGY & CHANGE

THE OXFORD PROGRAMME ON NEGOTIATION

THE OXFORD SCENARIOS PROGRAMME

NEW! THE OXFORD PRICING STRATEGY PROGRAMME

CONSULTING AND COACHING FOR CHANGE

THE CIO ACADEMY

FINANCE

THE OXFORD DIPLOMA IN FINANCIAL STRATEGY

THE OXFORD FINANCE FOR EXECUTIVES PROGRAMME

THE OXFORD PRIVATE EQUITY PROGRAMME

CUSTOM PROGRAMMES to suit your organisation's strategic needs

WWW.SBS.OXFORD.EDU/EXECED

oxford SAID BUSINESS SCHOOL

DEUTSCHE WELLE GLOBAL MEDIA FORUM

CONFLICT
PREVENTION IN THE
MULTIMEDIA
AGE

INTERNATIONAL CONFERENCE
3-5 JUNE 2009 · BONN, GERMANY

...the multimedia revolution and its impact on conventional media YouTube & Co.: Generating new audiences or excluding even more people? Blogging for peace or use as a way to bypass censorship. A tale of two worlds: Is the "digital divide" overrated? Mobbing or civic participation: Are users' contributions a blessing or a curse? IPTV and its worldwide cross-cultural impact Community media and TV in conflict resolution: A model for countries in crisis? The young generation: Is anyone watching, is anyone listening? Digital natives: Under the spell of mobile phones and social networking? Viral...

WWW.DW-WORLD.DE/ GLOBALMEDIAFORUM

International

Also in this section:
What we failed to predict in *The World in 2008* 96
Long shots for 2009 97
War of the Ferris wheels 98
The scramble for the seabed 99
Iconic museums 100
A rethink on ageing 101
Public intellectuals 102

A bad year for diplomats

Gideon Rachman

Multilateralists of the world, despair!

President George Bush has had many insults hurled at him during his time in office. One of the politer accusations is that he is a "unilateralist". Believers in global governance hope that a new occupant of the White House will get the United States to "re-engage" with the rest of the world—and that this will bring progress on a range of vexing international issues, from climate change to trade.

But 2009 will bring disappointment. It will become evident that it will take more than a new American president to breathe new life into multilateral diplomacy and international institutions.

In 2009 efforts to revive the Doha round at the World Trade Organisation (WTO) will fail. The European Union—the foremost champion of international governance—will be unable to revive its moribund Lisbon treaty. The Nuclear Non-Proliferation Treaty will come under further pressure. The International Criminal Court will fail to make progress with its most high-profile prosecutions. The United Nations will continue to lose prestige, as it suffers from the combination of a weak secretary-general and a deadlocked Security Council. And to round the year off, the attempt to achieve a global climate-change agreement will fail at a mega-summit in Copenhagen.

By the end of the year, therefore, it will be evident that the system of global governance is gummed up for reasons that extend well beyond the intransigence of the Bush administration.

The collapse of the Doha round of trade negotiations at the WTO in 2008 sets an ominous precedent for the coming year. The WTO is the single most successful example of international co-operation. It is an international organisation with binding procedures for settling disputes. Even superpowers like America and China are prepared to accept its rulings.

The Doha round ultimately broke down because of a stand-off between the United States, India, China and the European Union over agricultural trade. This turn of events has gloomy implications for the global negotiations on climate change—which replicate the WTO by pitting the interests of rich, developed areas like America and the EU against faster-growing developing economies like China and India.

The issues involved in Doha were relatively narrow and easily defined—and an agreement at the WTO offered the prospect of real economic benefits. By contrast, the global climate-change negotiations are tackling an issue that presents dazzling political and technical difficulties (see the special section on the environment). They are also mainly about sharing pain with little prospect of compensatory gains, at least in the short term.

Climate-change experts agree that any viable international agreement is going to have to involve America and Europe cutting carbon-emissions much faster than the Chinese and other developing nations. But it will probably be politically impossible to sell any such deal in the United States—particularly with the American economy sputtering.

The new world disorder

International negotiations over trade or climate change or nuclear non-proliferation always run into trouble for very specific reasons. But their collective difficulties show that the whole business of international governance is getting harder. There seem to be three big rea-

> Global governance is gummed up for reasons that extend well beyond the intransigence of the Bush administration

2009 IN BRIEF
NATO turns 60, but is busier than ever.

Gideon Rachman: chief foreign-affairs columnist, *Financial Times*

International

2009 IN BRIEF

The UN launches the **International Year of Natural Fibres**, hoping to make progress towards the Millennium Development Goals, supposedly to be achieved by 2015.

sons for this.

First, globalisation means that there are more powerful international actors whose interests need to be taken into account. The days when a deal on trade or climate change could be cooked up by the Western nations (and Japan) represented at the G8 are over. India, China, Brazil and other developing nations have to be part of it.

Second, talk of a new cold war with Russia makes it even harder to find agreements at the United Nations in 2009. And torpor and deadlock at the UN will cast a shadow over all other international negotiations—for example over nuclear non-proliferation.

Lastly, global governance may be the victim of its own success. It is easier to sell international agreements when they appear to be technical, boring, nuts-and-bolts issues best left to experts. But when they advance into areas that obviously affect living standards, or touch upon sensitive issues of national identity, then agreements are much harder to push through.

For example, successive EU treaties have meant that the big issues left on the table in Brussels are highly political ones, such as collective defence and foreign policy. Similarly, earlier successful trade rounds largely left agriculture to one side, precisely because it is so politically sensitive. The Doha round had to contend with powerful farm lobbies in India, Europe and the United States.

Diplomats have run smack up against one of the paradoxes of globalisation. In an inter-connected global economy, an increasing number of issues demand international agreements. But those agreements have to be sold in individual nations—where conceptions of identity and interests remain stubbornly local. Do not count on the diplomats to crack this problem in 2009. ■

About 2008: sorry

Daniel Franklin

Telling it how it wasn't

The past year has been full of big surprises, particularly for banks. One minute it was 85-year-old Bear Stearns that collapsed, the next it was 158-year-old Lehman Brothers, and then the whole financial system needed bailing out as confidence in free-market capitalism itself all but evaporated. Who would have thought, at the start of 2008, that the year would see crisis engulf once-sturdy names from Freddie Mac and Fannie Mae to AIG, Merrill Lynch, HBOS, Wachovia and Washington Mutual (WaMu)?

Not us. *The World in 2008* failed to predict any of this. We also failed to foresee Russia's invasion of Georgia (though our Moscow correspondent swears it was in his first draft). We said the OPEC cartel would aim to keep oil prices in the lofty range of $60-80 a barrel (the price peaked at $147 in July). We thought that Romano Prodi would probably see out the year as prime minister of Italy (his government collapsed and Silvio Berlusconi triumphed in an election); that Canada would pull its troops out of Afghanistan's Kandahar province (it didn't); that Ken Livingstone would be re-elected as mayor of London (he was defeated by his Conservative rival, Boris Johnson). Oh, and we expected that by now Hillary Clinton would be heading for the White House.

Why then, with such a dismal record last year, should anyone bother to read our current batch of predictions? For two-and-a-half reasons.

First, although we missed the once-in-a-lifetime global financial crisis, we had better luck in other areas.

Our economic outlook, for example, proved reasonably accurate. In America, we expected slumping house prices and a battle to resist recession through government spending, interest-rate cuts and surging exports (indeed, growth held up for longer than many expected). In the wider world, we forecast a striking gap between surging emerging markets and sluggish rich economies. We gave warning of the storm facing London and the British economy, at a time when the government was still issuing bright forecasts. In Asia, we highlighted the froth of the Shanghai Stock Exchange—which fell by two-thirds over the next 12 months.

In politics, as expected, José Luis Rodríguez Zapatero won a second term in Spain. Vladimir Putin duly retained real power in Russia despite stepping down from the presidency. And, as we suggested might happen, the Kuomintang's victory in Taiwan's presidential election opened the way for a resumption of direct flights to and from mainland China.

We had a pretty good Olympics, too. We expected the games to be well-run but politically contentious, with China doing its utmost to stifle dissent, including over Tibet. And we forecast that China would for the first time overtake the United States in the gold-medal table, with Russia in third place.

Win some, lose some

The second reason to carry on reading is that, oddly enough, getting predictions right or wrong is not all that matters. The point is also to capture a broad range of issues and events that will shape the coming year, to give a sense of the global agenda.

As for the predictions themselves, many of them were in fact cunningly nuanced. That's the half-reason—or, if you like, our semi-excuse: many of our mistakes were subtly hedged.

Yes, we thought Mrs Clinton would be president, but we also said it was a "golden rule" of American politics that every election season brings at least one big surprise. We did not think oil prices would surge as dramatically as they did, but they have since come back to earth, in line with our claim that OPEC's latest ascendancy contained the seeds of its own destruction. We missed 2008's extreme financial panic, but expected banks like JPMorgan Chase to expand by acquiring stricken competitors (it snapped up Bear Stearns and WaMu's banking operations).

The world is, of course, wonderfully unpredictable. Our biggest hedge a year ago was to stress that some of the most important events of 2008 would be entirely off our radar screen. How true. ■

Daniel Franklin: editor, *The World in 2009*

Long shots for 2009

John Andrews

The unlikely, but possible, turn of events

As the world's bankers have proved so catastrophically, assessing risk may be best left to bookmakers and casino bosses. Still, in our modest way we try our hardest, predicting election results, forecasting economic progress (or its lack), even delving deep into the mysteries of science. But what do we miss? Our practice is to look for the shortest odds. Yet, as any gambler will tell you, it is the long odds that can ruin a bookmaker's day. So let's play a "5%-to-20% game", searching for those events that no one thinks are likely in 2009—but which could just plausibly happen: the kind of things that can upset the apple-cart.

Some long shots in our 5%-20% range are hardy perennials. A natural disaster, for example, could well afflict the world in 2009—but just what, when and where defy our crystal ball. Every year brings such things, on a grand scale: the SARS panic of 2003, Asia's 2004 tsunami, the hurricanes and the great Pakistan earthquake of 2005, the Java quake of 2007, the floods in Bangladesh in 2007, Myanmar's cyclone Nargis in 2008. One scary thought for 2009 is that a huge Polar ice-shelf will collapse and turn ocean currents cold—but, fingers crossed, the odds are still below our 5% hurdle.

Similarly, there could be man-made disasters. Nuclear energy has an excellent safety record, but there are now over 430 commercial nuclear-power plants in the world, in some 30 countries, and over 200 nuclear-powered ships and submarines. When and where will be the next Three Mile Island near-tragedy or the Chernobyl actual one? Or will carelessness or corruption allow the theft of a nuclear device to terrify us all?

Meanwhile, the world of politics will be as fraught with risk, and as determined by chance, as the roulette wheel. The thought of assassination haunts politicians from Pakistan and Afghanistan to Africa and America, with the odds determined largely by their security men. If the CIA is wrong, Iran could conceivably be nuclear-ready in 2009—and (nudging the 20% upper limit of our probability range) Israel might act with military might to forestall the possibility. Iran could also frighten the neighbourhood by putting a satellite into orbit, which would mean its having the capability to launch an intercontinental ballistic missile.

Optimists may still hope for a peace deal to be signed by Israelis and Palestinians, but pessimists will fear another war between Israel and Lebanon's Hizbullah, with the "Party of God" acting as Iran's proxy. More comfortingly, though nothing comes easily in Middle East politics, perhaps 2009 will mark the long-sought peace between Israel and Syria—in which case, the geopolitics of the whole region will shift, not least by weakening the traditional alliance between Syria and Iran.

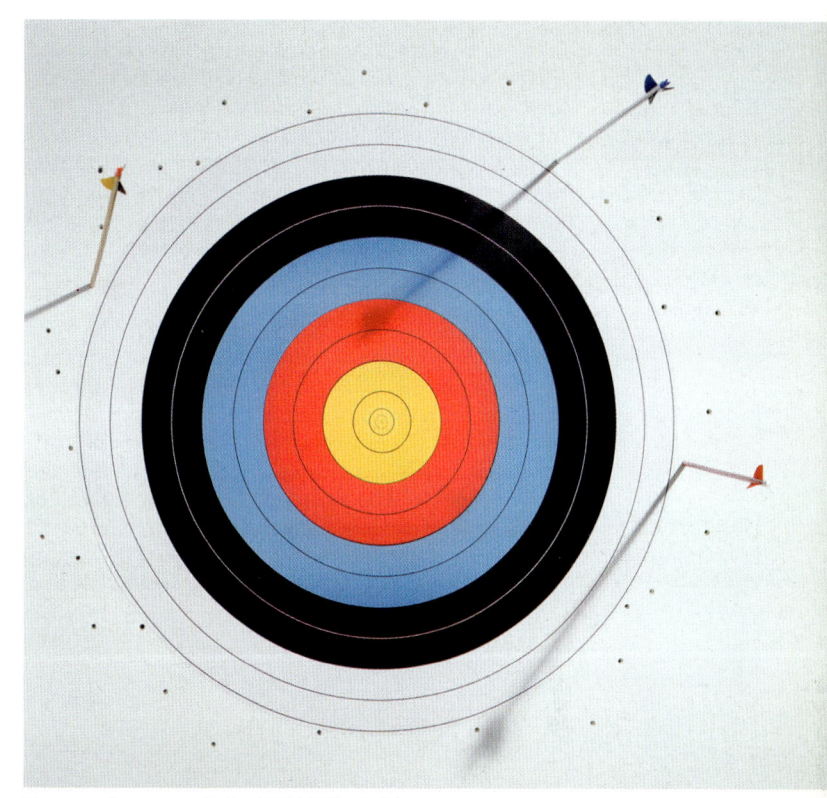

> Will carelessness or corruption allow the theft of a nuclear device?

You never know, one just might hit the bull's-eye

The Middle East is not the only region with tempting or troubling long shots. Will a settlement, for example, at last be reached for the conflict, now more than three decades long, between Morocco and the Algeria-backed Polisario in the Western Sahara? With good luck, and continued good will by Pakistan's President Asif Ali Zardari, India and Pakistan will be fully reconciled. With bad luck, of which there is always plenty in the region, Mr Zardari is ousted (perhaps by military men sympathetic to Afghanistan's Taliban) and the two countries clash violently yet again over Kashmir. As unlikely, yet plausible, would be a settlement between Sri Lanka and its Tamil separatists. In South Africa, most think the ANC's Jacob Zuma is a shoo-in at the 2009 presidential election—but they could be wrong if the interim president, Kgalema Motlanthe, proves wildly popular.

One long shot for East Asia would be the collapse of North Korea, leading to a hugely challenging—and costly—reunification of the peninsula. Another would be a successful military coup in the Philippines, after so many failed ones.

Disturbing the peace

Problems are certain enough in the Caucasus. What is uncertain is their result. The attempted secession of Ingushetia from the Russian Federation? Or the same with Dagestan? Meanwhile, will Russia, having surprised us with 2008's brief war with Georgia, continue to flex its muscles, conceivably by annexing Crimea?

Or could the UN Security Council expand its permanent membership? Most analysts think not, just as they doubt that Sudan's president, Omar al-Bashir, will appear before the International Criminal Court on charges of genocide. Yet such surprises are not impossible.

2009 IN BRIEF

The **Inter-Parliamentary Union** meets in Addis Ababa to discuss freedom—and climate change.

John Andrews: deputy editor, *The World in 2009*

International

2009 IN BRIEF

Litigation permitting, yachting billionaires will begin a protracted competition for the 33rd **America's Cup**, the oldest trophy in the sporting world.

As the memory of September 11th 2001 fades, the odds of a terrorist atrocity in America may seem to have lengthened—but the risk remains real. Capturing or killing Osama bin Laden has become a long shot (in 2002 the odds were much shorter). Following cyber-attacks on Estonian websites in 2007, the odds on cyber-terrorism—perhaps by governments—are shortening. One nasty thought is that the internet will clog up, unable to cope with the increased traffic of a wired world.

The rich world is risky, too

Risk does not, of course, confine itself only to the troubled bits of the globe. In peaceful Britain, for example, might Queen Elizabeth, after 57 years on the throne, abdicate? And if so, in favour of her eldest son, or elder grandson? As for America, though sceptics will scoff, campaigners will cling to an outside chance that the death penalty will be abandoned, either by the will of a succession of states or possibly by the Supreme Court ruling it "cruel and unusual".

In the world of business, it is now a good bet that Detroit's "Big 3" carmakers will become the "Big 2"—but some pundits will even bet on a General Motors "Big 1", while Main Street's fury at Wall Street's excesses could lead to prominent bankers being hauled into court. Futurists always emphasise technology breakthroughs, and many will predict a commercially viable "tipping-point" for electronic books such as Amazon's Kindle. A braver bet would be early success for a hand-held electronic newspaper. Meanwhile, most companies will continue to put terrorism low on their risk-list, but business around the world will suffer if the oil price soars thanks to a spectacular terrorist attack in Saudi Arabia.

But let us end on an optimistic note, by happily taking long odds on medical breakthroughs: a vaccination against HIV; a cure for Parkinson's disease; even a cure for the common cold. None is likely in 2009; all are conceivable. Long-suffering British tennis fans might say the same of a Briton to win Wimbledon, some 73 years after Fred Perry. But in 2008 Scotland's Andy Murray reached the final of the United States Open, so the odds are shortening fast. ■

The great wheel of China

Nicola Bartlett

Mine's bigger than yours

Originally designed to last for a year, the London Eye, like that other "temporary" attraction, the Eiffel Tower, is not going anywhere. Instead, with over 3.5m visitors a year London's Ferris wheel has paved the way for other cities hoping to cash in on the effect. In 2009 Chicago, the original home of the Ferris, will upgrade its Navy Pier wheel to double its original size, to over 91 metres (300ft), and Berlin's wheel, around 50 metres higher than its 135-metre London rival, will be the tallest in Europe at almost 185 metres.

But China will set the world record with its 208-metre Beijing wheel. It will take over from Singapore's 165-metre wheel. Beijing's Great Observation Wheel, as it is formally known, is a government-sponsored project set in Chaoyang park. With 48 air-conditioned capsules, each weighing 18 tonnes and containing 40 people, its maximum capacity of 1,920 people per rotation will dwarf the London Eye's 800.

Dubai, if its spending spree lasts, launches its 185-metre wheel as part of the Dubailand theme park. But things won't stop there. World Tourist Attractions, the company behind wheels in York, Manchester and Brisbane, will open its first Indian wheel in the southern city of Bangalore in April, and in 2010 the Great Wheel Corporation (responsible for the ones in Singapore, Berlin and Beijing) plans to open the Orlando wheel in Florida, standing at 122 metres and with panoramic views stretching 25 miles (40km).

With violence seemingly on the wane, Baghdad's authorities are beginning the tough sell of tourism in the Iraqi capital, having recently launched a design competition for a Baghdad wheel. Although details of the wheel, even its location, are sketchy, a municipal spokesman has confirmed that it will reach 198 metres into the sky and carry some 30 capsules. It may be just over a century since G.W. Ferris designed his attraction, but it seems no modern city skyline can be complete without a wheel—and the bigger the better. ■

The Great Observation Wheel, Beijing
Capacity: 1,920 people — 208 metres

The London Eye
Capacity: 800 people — 135 metres

The original Ferris Wheel in Chicago, 1893 Capacity: 2,160 people — 80 metres

Nicola Bartlett: editorial assistant, *The World in 2009*

Scramble for the seabed

John Grimond

A looming deadline for claims to underwater riches

May 13th 2009 looks like one of those dates used to name boulevards in coup-prone republics. In fact it is the deadline by which countries wishing to lay claim to extensions of their continental shelf must make their submissions to the United Nations. For long largely unnoticed by the bureaucracies of many poor countries, especially some island states with a lot to gain or forfeit, the need to register is causing a belated dash to assemble the necessary geological and other scientific information. The months leading up to May 13th will see a host of new claims to vast expanses of the seabed.

The deadline applies to all countries that ratified the 1982 UN Convention on the Law of the Sea before May 13th 1999. Any other coastal state has ten years from the date the convention entered into force for that state. In all, as many as 80 countries may be able to substantiate a claim to an extension of the continental shelf.

Measuring up

What does that mean? In law, all coastal states can exploit the natural resources on and below the seabed up to 200 nautical miles (370km) from shore. To lawyers, this is the limit of the continental shelf, a juridical concept that carries rights regardless of geography. But the shelf is also a geographical term, used to describe the physical prolongation of land below the sea. Where this extends beyond 200 nautical miles, as it does in several places, the adjacent state can claim the extra margin, up to 350 nautical miles from land (and so long as it is not more than 100 nautical miles from the point at which the water depth reaches 2.5km). If its claim is approved—quantities of geophysical data are necessary—it gains the right to exploit the mineral resources.

Back in the 1970s, when the law of the sea was being debated at the UN, the resources on the seabed aroused enormous excitement. Parts of the ocean floor, it was pointed out, were littered with manganese nodules containing nickel, copper and cobalt, and deposits of other metals abounded, not to mention oil and gas. Two obstacles killed the excitement. First, the United States was intensely hostile to the sharing of technology with the new International Seabed Authority (and hence other countries) that the convention made mandatory. This turned America against the entire convention and at the same time put an end to investment in seabed mining by big American and multinational companies. Second, the cost of extracting minerals from several kilometres below the surface of the sea was prohibitive.

Much has changed. In 1994 the convention's provisions on deep-seabed mining were altered, making the treaty much more appealing to the United States (which will undoubtedly soon ratify it, with Senate and presidential approval). Higher prices of almost all metals, as well as oil and gas, have transformed the economics of mining the deeps. Over the past five years China, France, Germany, India, Japan, Russia, South Korea and a consortium of east European countries have all been given licences by the International Seabed Authority to explore mining possibilities on the deep-ocean seabed, and Russia has sent a submarine to plant a corrosion-resistant metal flag on the floor of the Arctic Ocean and thus stake a symbolic claim to the resources four kilometres below the North Pole.

Another change is a clutch of new deep-sea discoveries. Some concern minerals: manganese crusts, rich in cobalt, have been found in various places, for example, and American government scientists now believe the Arctic may contain 90 billion barrels of oil and vast amounts of gas. Even more exciting to the energy industry are the gas hydrates that lie on the seabed all over the world. Together these are thought to hold about twice as much energy as all the fossil fuels in existence—though they are immensely awkward to extract and the methane they contain is a pernicious greenhouse gas.

Other discoveries are more exotic. Among them are "black smokers", the towering rock chimneys along some mid-ocean ridges that send forth from hot vents dark plumes of polymetallic sulphides and other chemicals. Some of these support strange creatures with baffling properties—sulphur-eating bacteria, for instance, and blind shrimps that may be highly irradiated by the vents yet can repair their DNA. Scientists hope that some of these creatures, which are among the few to derive their energy from a source other than sunlight, may hold the clues to anti-carcinogens or tumour-reducing drugs.

Most of the new discoveries lie in deep waters that will remain beyond national jurisdiction. But there will still be rich pickings in the extended continental shelf that is up for grabs by May 13th. Hence the scramble—not quite the scramble for Africa, an area of 30m square kilometres, but a scramble for half as much. And with two-thirds of the 460 maritime boundaries between coastal states either disputed or unresolved, this latest land grab may prove nearly as controversial, as well as profitable, as its 19th-century predecessor. ■

> The Arctic may contain 90 billion barrels of oil

2009 IN BRIEF

The International Atomic Energy Agency appoints a successor to Mohamed ElBaradei as director-general of the **nuclear-energy watchdog**.

John Grimond: writer at large, *The Economist*

The museum-building binge

Emily Bobrow NEW YORK

Starchitecture, civic pride and the race to become the next Bilbao

Like religious pilgrims, tourists have flocked to Bilbao in record numbers ever since the Guggenheim anointed the rusty Spanish city with a glorious, shimmering outpost. Frank Gehry's museum, opened in 1997, inspired a speculative building boom in the museum world. New iconic structures have sprouted up all over—more than two dozen in the United States alone—in a trend dubbed the "Bilbao effect". The recipe seemed simple: choose a "starchitect", raise tens of millions of dollars, add a pinch of buzz (did you say "titanium wings"?) and voilà: you have a tourist-luring, economy-fuelling, shrine-like source of civic pride.

But it is not so simple to replicate Bilbao's success—as several grand museum projects may discover in 2009.

In Chicago, Renzo Piano's $370m addition to the city's landmark Art Institute is slated to open in May 2009. His Modern Wing is designed to harmonise with the original Beaux Arts building yet evoke an airy lightness. Made from glass, steel, aluminium and limestone, it looks a little as if it is floating. Its most distinctive element is the "flying carpet" canopy roof, with aluminium blades designed to diffuse natural light inside. A footbridge connects the wing to the Millennium Park next door, where there is already a concert pavilion designed by Mr Gehry and an enormous sculpture by Anish Kapoor. "It's like defying gravity," Mr Piano has said.

Blair Kamin, the architecture critic for the *Chicago Tribune*, predicts that the extension's third-floor galleries overlook-

> Museums often enjoy high visitor numbers in the first year or two, but then attendance tends to taper off

ing the park will be hailed as "some of the most beautiful rooms in Chicago". Yet this hardly means that James Cuno, the institute's director, can sit back, relax and observe the coming throngs. Museums often enjoy cheeringly high visitor numbers in the first year or two, but then attendance tends to taper off.

"Sustainability is the new buzzword," explains Javier Pes, editor of *Museum Practice*, a journal published by the Museums Association. Wealthy private donors have been happy enough to contribute large sums in exchange for a glamorous new wing named after them. But donations tend to ebb after the museum reopens, and directors need to find other ways to pull in tourists after the initial excitement wears off, such as pricey blockbuster shows. Operating costs go up.

In Denver, for example, where Daniel Libeskind designed a new $110m building for the art museum, an initial boom of visitors in 2006 has waned, and budget constraints have forced the museum to cut staff. The remarkable new structure—an explosion of angles and intersecting shapes—is the centrepiece of Denver's nascent culture district. Yet some visitors complain of feeling disoriented inside.

The coming year will usher in several other glamorous new museums. François Pinault, a French luxury-goods magnate, beat the Guggenheim for the chance to transform a 17th-century customs house into a contemporary-arts centre in Venice. The Punta della Dogana building is timed to reopen with the Venice Biennale, after a minimalist renovation from Tadao Ando, a Japanese architect.

The eternal building site in Rome

In Rome, Zaha Hadid's ambitious vision for Italy's national museum for contemporary art—the Museo Nazionale delle Arti del XXI Secolo, or MAXXI—should at last open its doors more than a decade after she won an international competition to design it. (Funding hiccups and the peculiarities of Italian politics caused the building to be dubbed the "eternal building site".) The building features long, curving, windowless cast-concrete walls and a glass roof.

Such investments are clearly unsafe bets for urban renewal. That, plus the economic downturn, may dampen enthusiasm for the "Bilbao effect" in some places. But the Gehrys and the Hadids need not worry about finding future work. As long as there are cash-rich and asset-poor parts of the world, such as China and the Gulf (Abu Dhabi has ambitious plans for a Louvre and a Guggenheim), grand cultural cathedrals will continue to rise. ■

Emily Bobrow: editor, moreintelligentlife.com

Another blockbuster

International

2009 IN BRIEF
The world's **Protestants** (or some of them) mark the 500th anniversary of the birth of Calvin.

Farewell to youth

Adam Roberts

The rich world reaches middle age in 2009. It is time to think afresh about ageing

Cate Blanchett, Jennifer Lopez, Renée Zellweger, Catherine Zeta-Jones and Jennifer Aniston might prefer you not to mention it. Each marks her 40th birthday in 2009. As they blow out their candles they might consider this demographic detail: the median age in the seven big, rich democracies (the G7) will also pass 40 in the coming year.

The rich world is greying fast. Germans, Italians and Japanese are already, on average, well into their 40s. In 2009 the British, French and Canadians will join them. By one estimate the median age of west Europeans is rising by an average of two days with each passing week. It will carry on doing so for at least another couple of dec-

> Our workforces will shrivel, almost certainly beginning in 2009

ades. In the G7 only Americans remain relatively young, with a median age in 2009 of just 36.4 years, thanks to a steady influx of sprightly Mexicans.

Does this matter? Ms Blanchett and co will claim that their best work lies ahead of them, darlings. And there is plenty of advice for individuals on how to age gracefully. As long ago as the 1930s an American, Walter B. Pitkin, wrote a bestselling self-help guide that coined a familiar phrase: "Life Begins at Forty". He decried "the cynical youth who looks upon forty as a living death".

So much for individuals. For societies there are some benefits of ageing: longer life and better health are fine in themselves, and they are linked with faster economic growth. One study suggests that for every extra year of average life expectancy in a population there is a 7% rise in GDP per person. Social gains are likely, too: fewer young people usually means lower rates of crime.

But demographers, economists and politicians are right to fret about our greying. In the rich world babies are vanishing and the ranks of the retired are swelling. In 2008, for the first time, there were more British pensioners than children. By the middle of this century the average Japanese will be 55 years old. Nor will this trend reverse. Despite a tiny uptick in fertility rates in some European countries, the birth dearth continues. And although migration is the only thing which prevents many European populations from shrinking, an influx of outsiders will not change age-structures by much.

The downhill slope

As a result, our workforces will shrivel, almost certainly beginning in 2009. According to a World Bank study, the European labour force peaked in 2008 and will start to decline, as more elderly workers retire than there are young workers to take their places. In the rich world the labour force as it has traditionally been understood (those between 15 and 65) is expected to peak in 2010, at about half a billion people. From then on it is downhill, with some 25m workers shed in the following 15 years.

In Europe, from 2009 onwards, the numbers of non-workers depending on the wealth created by others will grow—bad news for funding health care and pensions. Today in western Europe there are 3.8 people working for every pensioner. In a little more than two decades it will be just 2.4 people working to support each greybeard.

The obvious response is to postpone, gradually, retirement. Economies, especially European ones, could make more use of experienced, skilled and generally healthy old populations. In America, Japan and South Korea, many more people in their 50s remain in employment than in western Europe, where rules on the provision of pensions and other benefits deter older people from staying at work.

And here is a suggestion for where some of the elderly might find jobs: in the burgeoning "age industry"—the think-tanks, agencies and activist groups that develop bright ideas about how to make the most of ageing. Big gatherings will look at the issue. Melbourne, Australia, hosts the tenth global conference on ageing, in 2010. And an international forum will take place in Japan. The great and the good will attend, though Ms Blanchett and friends may be busy elsewhere. ■

Adam Roberts: news editor, Economist.com

Isaiah, chapter 100

Robert Cottrell RIGA

And what it says about the role of public intellectuals

"Public intellectuals" have been in business since Plato and Aristotle at least, but they had to wait for television to bring them popular fame. One of the first and best of this modern era, Isaiah Berlin, was born 100 years ago in Riga, Latvia. His centenary will be celebrated there, and in Oxford, on June 6th. Like A.J.P. Taylor, Berlin was a consummate telly-don, always available for a word-perfect interview in grainy black-and-white with Bernard Levin or Bryan Magee on the meaning of life or the way of the world. He knew how power worked, too. His wartime job as a British diplomat in America won him Winston Churchill's admiration—though Churchill, intending to invite Berlin to lunch in Downing Street, ended up with Irving Berlin by mistake. Asking about his guest's proudest achievement, Churchill was surprised to receive the answer, "White Christmas".

Most of all, Isaiah Berlin was a serious scholar, probably the past century's greatest historian of ideas. He thought the task of any intellectual was to make ideas as interesting as possible, and in this he succeeded to a fault. Just as a skilled conversationalist brings alive the least promising interlocutor, so Berlin could conjure a fascinating essay from the most forbidding pages of Fichte, or Vico, or De Maistre. In "Russian Thinkers", Berlin tackled a clique of 19th-century talkers considered heavy going even by Russia's exacting standards—and his critique became not merely a popular paperback but even, in the hands of Sir Tom Stoppard, a sparkling trilogy of plays, "The Coast of Utopia".

The term "public intellectual" gained currency 20 years ago, describing a writer or academic who commanded public notice, especially when accepted as an authority in many fields. There was nothing new about such "brand-extension" in the humanities. Like Plato, Goethe or Berlin, writers and philosophers had long drifted in and out of public view, holding forth on life in general. But when nuclear weapons, environmentalism and genetics began to perturb Western public opinion in the 1960s, so more scientists followed Albert Einstein out of the academy and into the public arena. Richard Feynman, James Watson and Jacob Bronowski produced bestselling books without diluting their reputations. Freeman Dyson and Steven Weinberg wrote regularly for the

Dreaming of a white Christmas card

New York Review of Books. Noam Chomsky's left-wing politics eclipsed his scholarly work in linguistics.

The top tier of public intellectuals has come to speak mainly through upmarket news media such as the *New York Times*, *Foreign Affairs*, the *New York Review of Books* and the BBC. But the rise of blogs has greatly enlarged and confused the market. A disparager would say that anybody can be a blogger, and anything can be a blog: is this not proof of low standards? And yet, top bloggers include academics and commentators whose work would qualify them as public intellectuals by any traditional measure—for example, Tyler Cowen, Daniel Drezner, James Fallows, Steven Levitt, Lawrence Lessig and Andrew Sullivan. Indeed, it seems fair to say that if you have the quick wit and the pithy turn of phrase traditionally needed to succeed as a public intellectual, then you are one of nature's bloggers. If you cannot quite imagine Berlin posting to Twitter, then think how well he would put, say, Hannah Arendt in her place, on bloggingheads.tv.

New leaders in America and elsewhere will bring with them new advisers and gurus—new intellectuals with proximity to power. Good luck to them. Public intellectuals tend to perform best in opposition, where their ideas go untested. Where dissent does have an impact, it tends also to be dangerous: think Alexander Solzhenitsyn or Vaclav Havel.

The fusing of religious and political spheres under Islam has produced a hybrid species of faith-based public intellectual scarcely seen in America, where faith speaks the vernacular of populism. Thinkers from the Islamic countries took all top ten spots in the 2008 *Prospect/Foreign Policy* internet poll of the world's "top 100" public intellectuals. But this was a sign of mass voting from Turkey, not of a freethinking boom.

Minds of the moment

Whatever their provenance, the public intellectuals of 2009 will want to be fluent in the obvious issues of the moment: environment and energy, market turmoil, China, Russia, Islam. On that basis it looks like another good year for established stars such as Thomas Friedman, Martin Wolf, Bjorn Lomborg and Minxin Pei. But a rising generation of bloggers is terrifyingly young and bright: expect to hear more from Ezra Klein, Megan McArdle, Will Wilkinson and Matthew Yglesias.

And, if public intellectuals are allowed to perform posthumously, try to hear more of Isaiah Berlin. He spent much of the 20th century arguing that different people would always want different things out of life, that this was part of the human condition, and that we had better get used to it. He meant this as an argument against totalitarianism. But as an approach to world problems in general, it bears another look. ∎

Robert Cottrell: co-founder, thebrowser.com

Forget about the tortoise and the hare. The winner is a frog.

HEC Paris has been ranked the number 1 business school in Europe by the Financial Times in 2006 and 2007.

HEC
PARIS

The more you know, the more you dare

www.hec.edu

affiliated to **Chambre de commerce et d'industrie de Paris**

THE FLETCHER SCHOOL
TUFTS UNIVERSITY

Study from afar.
Get closer to your international goals.

The Global Master of Arts Program (GMAP) delivers the innovation and excellence of a Fletcher international affairs degree without interrupting your career. GMAP brings 35 international professionals together—through residencies and Internet-mediated learning—to examine how legal, economic, social, and political forces alter an increasingly complex world. Together with professors and classmates, you join a global network of leaders seeking meaningful solutions to today's pressing issues. Apply today.

Courses Include:

International Politics	Leadership and Management	Transnational Social Issues
International Negotiation	Security Studies	International Trade
International Finance	International Business and Economic Law	International Organizations

CLASSES BEGIN IN MARCH AND JULY.

GLOBAL MASTER OF ARTS PROGRAM

Visit fletcher.tufts.edu/GMAP or call 617.627.2429.

«I dream of the day that cars leave no more of a trace on our planet than a yacht on the ocean...»

Ellen MacArthur, sailor.

Leaving as small a trace as possible is the commitment of Renault eco²

RENAULT eco²

PRINCIPAL PARTNER TO BT Team Ellen

For over 15 years, Renault has been working to reduce the environmental impact of its activities. With Renault eco², Renault is committed to manufacturing, in more environmentally friendly plants (ISO 14001 certified), vehicles which consume less energy, emit less CO_2 (emissions below 140g/km) and which are manufactured from as much as 17% recycled plastics.

Visit us at www.renault-eco2.com

RENAULT

THE WORLD IN 2009

The environment

Also in this section:
Alternative energy 106
A carbon-neutral city 107
Green politics 108
How IT can help clean up 109
Disaster relief 110
Driving the green way 111
Sport and sustainability 111
Peter Brabeck-Letmathe:
A water warning 112

Wonderful, wonderful Copenhagen?

Emma Duncan

Don't count on a climate-change deal

The most important year for climate change since 2001, when the Kyoto protocol (which set targets for cutting carbon-dioxide emissions) was agreed, will be 2009. The first period of the protocol runs out in 2012. The deal to replace it is supposed to be done at the United Nations' Climate Change Conference in Copenhagen, which starts on November 30th 2009 and is due to end on December 11th. No deal means that mankind gives up on trying to save the planet.

The accord needs to be a substantial one, not just a face-saving agreement to declare that the issue must be tackled. The rich world (especially America) needs to commit itself to legally enforceable carbon-emissions reductions for the second period of Kyoto, from 2012 to 2016 and beyond. The big emitters from the developing world, such as China, need to commit themselves to something substantive—not economy-wide emissions-reductions, but, for instance, carbon-intensity targets (cuts in carbon emissions per unit of GDP) or measures directed at the power sector in particular.

The rich world, which has been responsible for most emissions so far and recognises that it needs to pay up because of that, also needs to find a way of transferring money to the developing world to help it pay for cutting carbon. The Clean Development Mechanism, which was set up under Kyoto to allow rich countries to buy carbon credits from poor countries that have cut their emissions, does that already, but is probably not robust enough to do the job on the scale needed. There needs to be some new vehicle, such as the Superfund proposed by Jagdish Bhagwati, professor of economics at Columbia. He thinks the world should copy America's approach to other forms of pollution: make polluters contribute to a fund which pays for the costs of cleaning up.

So will we get a deal in Copenhagen? That depends on what happens beforehand in three places: Washington, Brussels and Beijing.

What happens in Washington is most important. Progress on climate change is much likelier under the new administration than the old, for the new one is committed to introducing mandatory federal carbon-emissions cuts through a cap-and-trade scheme of the sort that operates in Europe. What is not clear, though, are the answers to the crucial subsidiary questions. Where do the cuts come from? And how big will they be?

Emma Duncan: deputy editor, The Economist

The amount of political capital the new president is prepared to spend on climate change will determine the answers to those questions. Plenty will be needed to overcome opposition from organised labour, which fears possible job losses resulting from the higher costs that carbon constraints are bound to impose, and from dirty industries, such as aluminium, cement, oil and carmaking, which fear the impact on profitability. The administration is likely to reach for "border adjustments" (tariffs on carbon-intensive goods from countries that America thinks are not doing enough to cut emissions) to help overcome objections from those quarters. It may disappoint greens by going for a system that includes a cap on the carbon price, and by setting the cap on emissions higher than environmentalists would like. And even with those compromises, getting legislation through Congress in time for Copenhagen will be exceedingly difficult.

The strength of Europe

The European Union has led the fight against climate change. As part of its implementation of the Kyoto protocol, it set up its ground-breaking Emissions-Trading Scheme which allows companies in EU member-states' dirty industries to trade carbon-emissions permits and has thus put a price on carbon. And in 2007 the European Commission produced the "20/20/20 by 2020" plan: emissions cuts of ▶

The environment

2009 IN BRIEF

ITER, a consortium of the EU, Japan, China, India, South Korea, Russia and America, continues slow preparations for a **nuclear fusion reactor** at Cadarache in France, aiming to create safe and environmentally friendly energy.

20% below 1990 levels (plus a 20% gain in energy efficiency and 20% of energy from renewables) by 2020. But the plan must be approved by the Council of Ministers and the European Parliament in 2009, and it is meeting hefty opposition—from heavy industry, and coal-dependent countries such as Poland. Getting the package through will be hard; but any backtracking in Europe will undermine America's efforts.

A change of attitude in Beijing is also crucial to a deal in Copenhagen. It was China's refusal to agree to any form of constraint that led America to walk away from Kyoto in 2001. These days China, now the world's

> The Chinese government resists the idea that it should give ground to get America to move

biggest emitter of carbon dioxide, accepts the need to take action against climate change; it argues that, through energy-efficiency and renewable-energy targets, it is doing as much as can reasonably be expected. But the American Congress will want China to take on extra commitments—perhaps in the form of targets for particular industries—if it is to legislate cuts. And the Chinese government resists the idea that it should have to give ground in order to get America to move.

Getting progress on climate change in these three places would be tough at the best of times, and the year ahead looks like being one of the worst of times. A substantive deal in Copenhagen therefore looks unlikely; but the world's leaders are not likely to give up trying to save the planet there and then. Perhaps the likeliest outcome in Copenhagen in 2009 is a repetition of what happened in Kyoto in 2000—a big bust-up, another meeting called and a deal done the following year. ■

Actually, there is an alternative

Geoffrey Carr

Expect shifts in the way energy is produced and used

It has come to something when an oilman as dyed in the wool as T. Boone Pickens starts to harangue his fellow Americans about the need to convert the country to wind power. Surely that is for namby-pamby, quiche-eating greens? But Mr Pickens has even addressed Congress on the matter, and he is backing his opinion with several billion dollars of his own money and attempting to sign up the governors of America's states to a plan to run the United States on wind and natural gas.

Wind power in America grew 45% in 2007. Around 1% of America's electricity is already generated by the wind. That is expected to rise to 15% by 2020. So all Mr Pickens is really achieving is to hurry the process along a little faster. His motive has little connection with greenery (he wants to substitute electricity now generated from natural gas with wind power, and then use the gas for cars and lorries to reduce America's dependence on imported oil), but his plan is one indication that alternative-energy technologies are starting to become mainstream.

Another such sign is the rise of the electric car (see "Want to drive green?" in this section). More and more electric models are becoming available. Most of these vehicles, though fitted with back-up petrol-powered generators, are driven by battery-powered electric motors. Israel, meanwhile, will in 2009 begin fitting itself out in earnest with a network of vehicle-charging points and battery-exchange stations that will eliminate the need for back-up generators and allow it, if the demand is there, to become the most electro-motivated country in the world.

Like Mr Pickens, Israel's desire is to end dependency on imported oil. But if the extra electricity crucial to both ideas is generated from zero-carbon sources (and there is plenty of potential for solar

Geoffrey Carr: science and technology editor, *The Economist*

Building ecotopia

Natasha Loder

The world's first carbon-neutral city

Although most cities seem to form by accident, for thousands of years some of them have been designed. Whether for defence, beauty or practicality, urban designers have imposed their ideas of what a city should be about. But ideas are subject to changing needs and fashions. Centuries ago, a moat or a castellated wall would have been *de rigueur*. Now, greenery is in vogue. While existing cities look for ways of becoming more environmentally friendly, a number of new ones are planned that intend to be totally green.

China is planning several eco-cities, including Dongtan—built on behalf of the Shanghai Industrial Investment Corporation by a British construction firm, Arup. By 2010 the first stage of this carbon-neutral city will supposedly be ready to accommodate 10,000 people. But Dongtan will be pipped at the green post by Masdar City in Abu Dhabi, designed by Foster + Partners. It will also run on renewable energy sources and with a zero-carbon and zero-waste design. It is due to complete the first phase of its design in 2009.

Masdar, which means "the source", is a 1,500-acre (six-square-km) project including housing, commercial and manufacturing space for eco-friendly products and a university. In 2009 the Masdar Institute of Science and Technology (MIST), which will be dedicated to renewable energy, will open its doors. In the coming year, says Khaled Awad, director of property development at Masdar, the city will also have a 10MW photo-voltaic farm.

By 2010 Masdar will be able to accommodate 2,000 people but ultimately it will be home to 50,000. Most of the city's electricity will come through solar power. Renewables will also support a desalination plant that will provide fresh water.

Creating the city is a feat of integration, says Mr Awad, requiring a fusion of technologies, systems and policies. Finding ways of using less energy and water has been a crucial part of the planning. Through a smart metering system, at any given moment a citizen of Masdar will be aware of how much energy, water and carbon he or she is consuming compared with the average citizen.

Down town

There is, though, more to this picture of ecotopia than meets the eye. A huge degree of central planning, control and even restrictions on individual freedoms is needed to make Masdar work. The city will make many decisions that residents elsewhere would take for themselves. Cars will not be permitted (the city provides electric pods to transport people and goods), and starting a business is not straightforward. Commercial activities will be restricted to those that "add value" to the city. To keep Masdar carbon-neutral, businesses that use lots of hydrocarbons will not be welcome. (But they presumably have to continue to exist somewhere, even if they are not on Masdar's carbon balance sheet.) Will such a paternalistic city work well? Social factors are crucial in getting cities to hum.

Masdar's advertising states that "one day, all cities will be built like this." This is not the case. For one thing, Masdar is experimental and a work in progress. What emerges will not necessarily translate well elsewhere. Courtyards and corridors that channel breezes and are cooled by photo-voltaic panels are not right for northern Europe. Each green city, says Arup, is unique, and getting it to work depends on its location and economy.

Every aspect of Masdar has been designed. That will appeal to some people, and deter others. One surprising feature is that it has walls. The walls are to protect the city from the harsh, hot winds of the desert. As all fashionistas know, if you wait long enough certain designs, whether it is flares or mini-skirts, come around again. So this trendy green city will be wearing walls. ■

Natasha Loder: science and technology correspondent, *The Economist*

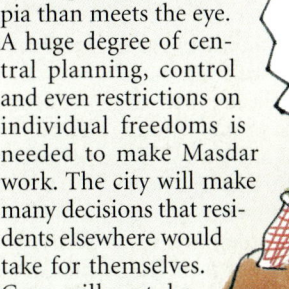

---

power in Israel), then there will be environmental benefits, too.

These benefits mean that solar power will grow in importance elsewhere, as well. Algeria, another country with abundant sunshine, will open a plant that works by employing heat from the sun to make steam and thus drive a generator, rather than using expensive solar cells to produce electricity directly—the most common method at the moment. The long-term aim is to export power across the Mediterranean to Europe. But solar cells are not going away. In fact, they are being deployed faster than wind turbines and the amount of electricity they generate is growing by 60% a year. What will be the world's largest solar-power plant, at Moura in Portugal, uses traditional solar cells.

Biofuels, the other green alternative to petrol and diesel, are also made ultimately from sunlight, via the plant-building process of photosynthesis. At the moment ethanol fermented from Brazilian sugar cane, the cheapest biofuel in the world, is kept out of the American market by high tariffs. However, in 2009 a pilot plant intended to make hydrocarbon vehicle fuels from sugar will open in Campinas. This is a joint venture between Crystalsev, a Brazilian firm, and Amyris, an American one, and is an important breakthrough for America's biotechnology industry. Tariffs in this case, therefore, are unlikely.

Whether Mr Pickens would approve of swapping America's dependence on Saudi Arabia for dependence on Brazil is doubtful. What is not in doubt, though, is that 2009 will see some interesting changes in the world of energy. ■

> *Alternative-energy technologies are starting to become mainstream*

2009 IN BRIEF

Abu Dhabi awards the first **Zayed Future Energy Prize** to three individuals, companies or organisations that have contributed to the future of energy conservation.

Fighting for the planet

Edward McBride

So much to argue about in green politics

The giddy price of oil subsumed most talk of the environment in 2008; in 2009 the price of carbon will be the most pressing question. In America, the new president has pledged to cut emissions by instituting a cap-and-trade scheme: expect a drawn-out battle in Congress. Meanwhile, the European Union will be fine-tuning the rules for the next phase of its carbon-trading scheme. New Zealand is launching one too. And all around the world politicians will be debating how to update the Kyoto protocol, the United Nations' treaty on climate change, a successor to which is supposed to be agreed upon at a summit in Copenhagen in December.

As with free-trade deals, the proliferation of regional and local carbon-trading schemes is likely both to spur efforts to reach a global accord and to complicate them. In America, ten north-eastern states have grouped together to form the Regional Greenhouse Gas Initiative, a cap-and-trade scheme among utilities that starts running on January 1st. Opponents of emissions-trading will hold up every glitch as an example of how misguided the whole concept is; proponents will insist it proves emissions-trading is viable, whatever its flaws.

Western states plan another, more ambitious programme, while Midwestern states are working on a third. To make matters even more complicated, several Canadian provinces plan to participate in the various American initiatives, in protest at the relative modesty of Canada's own national scheme. Australia and New Zealand will try to link up their respective systems. And there will be a row, complete with legal battles, over the EU's plan to levy a carbon tax on flights to or from Europe. As a negotiating stance, the regions and countries with more stringent policies will insist that national and global arrangements must not pander to the lowest common denominator. But they will also be quick to scale back their green ambitions if efforts to set up broader trading schemes founder.

All this uncertainty will not be good for the carbon markets. Prices will be volatile, providing more ammunition to those who dislike the idea of emissions-trading. In particular, the market for the sort of offset sanctioned by the Kyoto protocol will dry up, as buyers wait to see what the future holds. That will make life difficult for the firms that have sprung up to take advantage of the Clean Development Mechanism, as the offset provision is known, and so hamper the launch of a future global carbon market, if one is set in motion at Copenhagen.

What price virtue?

The bickering about emissions-trading will also focus attention on the expense of fighting global warming. Some of the more lavish incentives for biofuels, windmills, nuclear plants and the like will come under fierce scrutiny. More governments will follow Spain and Germany and cut subsidies for solar power. Increased parsimony will drive a wedge between greenery and other fashionable but expensive causes, such as "energy independence", "fair trade" and organic farming. Spectacular bust-ups will break out among pressure groups and politicians on the many sides of this debate.

Low-carbon technologies will boom, however, as more countries put a price on carbon emissions. The shortage of silicon that has bedevilled the solar-panel industry will ease, only to be replaced by bottlenecks in other areas, such as turning the silicon into wafers and ingots. As ever more firms spring up to convert organic waste into diesel, gas and power, a shortage of trash and slurry will afflict some countries. Financing for more speculative renewable-energy start-ups will be harder to come by, thanks to the credit crunch.

Meanwhile, the clamour that global warming is already under way, and that more needs to be done to adapt to it, as well as forestall it, will grow even louder. Renegade ecologists will be caught transporting threatened species from one habitat to another, in a last-ditch attempt to save them from extinction. Leaders of low-lying islands, along with drought-ridden states in Africa and flood-prone spots such as Bangladesh, will denounce the aid they have been given to cope with the ill effects of climate change as grossly inadequate, causing a row about priorities.

In short, the politics of global warming will not get any simpler in 2009, despite the change of heart at the White House. ■

> Renegade ecologists will be caught transporting threatened species from one habitat to another

I'm out of here

2009 IN BRIEF
Algeria and Spain complete the Medgaz **natural-gas pipeline**, bringing another 8 billion cubic metres a year of Algerian gas to Europe.

Edward McBride: energy and environment correspondent, *The Economist*

THE WORLD IN 2009   The environment   109

More silicon, less carbon

Tom Standage

In fighting climate change, are computers part of the problem or part of the solution?

"Please consider the environment before printing this message." Those words, appearing at the bottom of many e-mails, are a visible manifestation of a trend that will gather momentum in 2009: the move towards more environmentally friendly information technology, or "green IT". Advertisements for PCs already tout their meagre energy consumption just as prominently as their number-crunching prowess.

Overall, computing and telecommunications today produce 2% of global emissions, according to the Global e-Sustainability Initiative (GeSI), an industry group. Of these, 49% come from PCs and printers, 37% from telecoms networks and devices, and 14% from data centres—the large warehouses full of computers operated by companies.

The overall volume of emissions is comparable with that from aviation. But the IT industry, unlike aviation, has not provoked the wrath of environmental campaigners. Perhaps that is because computers are less visibly polluting, or their use is not deemed, like air travel, to be frivolous and unnecessary.

The aviation industry has found itself on the defensive, emphasising its efforts to switch to less fuel-hungry aircraft in the coming years. Makers of computer and telecoms gear, by contrast, have chosen to highlight the volume of emissions their machines produce, because they already have newer, greener products to sell today. New processing chips, clever software that lets one machine do the work of many, and smarter cooling systems can all reduce energy consumption and thus carbon-dioxide emissions.

For vendors, in other words, the large environmental footprint of computing presents a sales opportunity. That is one reason why the hubbub about green IT will increase in 2009.

A second reason is that companies like to tell everyone about their efforts to reduce their own carbon emissions, and technology is a relatively easy place to start. Hardly a week goes by without a large company announcing that it has just installed fancy new videoconferencing suites to reduce its carbon footprint. BSkyB, a British satellite-television and telecoms operator, was one of the first companies to go carbon-neutral by reducing its emissions as much as possible (by programming its set-top boxes to switch themselves to standby when not in use, for example), and offsetting the rest. Vodafone, a mobile-telecoms giant, has been turning down the air-conditioning in its base-stations, which accounts for a quarter of its carbon footprint. Allowing the base-stations to operate at 25°C instead of 21°C can cut energy use by 10% in some cases, and newer base-stations can happily run at 35°C.

This will, the company says, help it to meet its target of cutting its emissions by 50% between 2006 and 2020. Expect more such announcements, in particular from telecoms and financial-services firms, since a large part of their carbon footprints is associated with computers and networks.

Green IT is also being pushed for a third reason: the computer industry's desire to stay in the limelight. It has become apparent that clean technology will be the "next big thing" as the internet becomes pervasive and, correspondingly, less exciting. Venture capitalists and executives have been jumping from computing to clean-tech companies. Promoting computing itself as a clean technology may help those left behind to convince themselves that their field is still at the cutting edge.

However, the GeSI report forecasts that even if whizzy energy-saving technologies are widely adopted in PCs, telecoms networks and data centres, their combined carbon footprint will still nearly double by 2020 simply because so many more people will be using them.

But the good news, according to GeSI, is that there is vast scope to use computers in indirect ways to cut carbon emissions in other industries. Indeed, the savings made possible by computing's "enabling effects" could amount to five times computing's own footprint. The examples that spring to mind are the use of videoconferencing and teleworking as low-carbon alternatives to business travel and commuting. In fact, far bigger savings could come from using computers to improve logistics (say, by planning the routes of delivery vehicles more efficiently); using data networking in electrical grids to manage demand and reduce unnecessary energy consumption; and computer-enabled "smart buildings", in which lighting and ventilation systems turn themselves off if nobody is around.

So computing does indeed have a role in fighting climate change, but that role mainly involves using computers in new ways, rather than making the machines themselves more efficient. It is time for the industry to start thinking outside the box, as it were. ■

> There is vast scope to use computers in indirect ways to reduce carbon emissions

IT footprints
Emissions by sub-sector, 2020

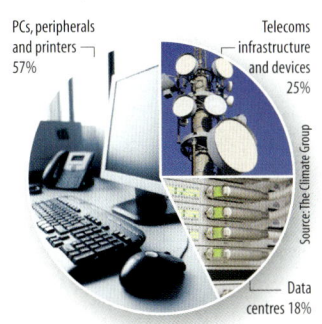

PCs, peripherals and printers 57%
Telecoms infrastructure and devices 25%
Data centres 18%

Total emissions: 1.43bn tonnes CO₂ equivalent
Source: The Climate Group

How IT can help
Global emissions and possible reductions, tonnes CO₂ equivalent

- Emissions
- of which from ICT*
- Possible ICT*-enabled reductions
- Other possible reductions

*Information and communications technology

2002 | 2020 business as usual | 2020 minus reductions

Source: The Climate Group

2009 IN BRIEF
The Stockholm International Water Institute marks the UN **World Water Day** with a $150,000 prize for achievement in water conservation.

Tom Standage: business editor, *The Economist* and editor, *Technology Quarterly*

More help now, please

John Holmes NEW YORK

How to tackle tomorrow's disasters

Timing is everything. Nowhere is this truer than in humanitarian relief. When disaster strikes, delays can mean the difference between life and death. Timing, however, involves more than a stopwatch approach to emergencies. It also means looking forward—not only to identify the trends that will reshape the humanitarian landscape, but to harness the forces necessary to respond to them.

Any credible vision of the future must recognise that humanitarian needs are increasing. Climate change will be the main driver. Nine out of every ten disasters are now climate-related. Recorded disasters have doubled in number from 200 a year to more than 400 over the past two decades. In 2007 my office at the UN issued an unprecedented 15 funding appeals for sudden natural disasters, five more than the previous annual record; all but one resulted from climatic events.

So welcome to the "new normal" of extreme weather. Climate change may well exacerbate chronic hunger and malnutrition across much of the developing world. And it will almost certainly precipitate battles over resources.

No nation, rich or poor, is exempt from nature's destructive potential. But nature is not the real problem. We are. Be it through dangerously high emissions of greenhouse gases, depletion of essential resources or reckless urbanisation, we are creating a house of cards that could mean humanitarian catastrophe for millions. Too often we do not take the simple precautions that can reduce loss of life and livelihoods. Natural hazards need not automatically result in human calamity or erode years of development gains. From planting back mangrove trees to bicycle-and-bullhorn early-warning systems, many of the most effective tools are about mobilising people, not expensive technology. Bangladesh has cut dramatically its disaster death-toll using such simple, cost-effective methods.

From planning and preparedness to financing, we need to act now if we are to reduce our vulnerability to hazards. And we need to act together. As we saw in Myanmar during cyclone Nargis, isolation is not an option when the scale of a disaster exceeds a government's ability to cope.

If climate change is the most fundamental factor, the global food crisis is the immediate problem. The knock-on effects extend far beyond hunger to include child malnutrition, lower primary-school attendance and, not least, increased political instability. I fear that today's food crisis is but the opening act in a larger drama in which swathes of the developing world will suffer acutely. Within our children's lifetimes, how will we feed 50% more people while using 50% less carbon energy, which the Intergovernmental Panel on Climate Change says is imperative to avoid environmental chaos?

We must address the problem at its roots. A vital first step is to bolster the yields of subsistence farmers by providing them with seed and fertiliser. In the longer term, we need a green revolution in every sense of the term: agriculturally productive, environmentally sustainable and economically profitable. Scaled-up financing for African agriculture, including investments in crop adaptation, topsoil preservation, drip irrigation—all this and more is urgently required.

Meanwhile, human conflicts will, like the poor, always be with us. Whereas wars between states are less frequent, internal conflicts—and the humanitarian consequences—show little sign of disappearing. In every global hotspot, humanitarians come armed only with principles, not guns. Unfortunately, respect for international humanitarian law, especially the responsibility to protect civilians, is in scarce supply. Humanitarians are being deliberately targeted. The ability to maintain a neutral humanitarian space, in which aid workers can operate safely and impartially, independent of political and military objectives, is under tremendous pressure.

In a post-September-11th world, this independence is a practical, life-saving necessity, not a naive humanitarian longing. Of course, humanitarian action is a necessary but insufficient response to suffering during conflicts. It cannot be a substitute for political solutions and should not serve as an excuse for their absence.

What is to be done? First, states must expend more effort and resources on these solutions. Second, politicians must respect humanitarian principles, while humanitarians themselves need to build more bridges with local actors to engender trust, the cornerstone of any aid effort. Third, we must create innovative partnerships with regional organisations, the private sector and the Islamic world to broaden the base for humanitarian support.

Above all, whether for conflicts or natural disasters, we need to mobilise more resources to meet rising demands and (legitimately) rising expectations. Our principles will be of little use without the money to back them up. ■

> Nine out of every ten disasters are now climate-related

2009 IN BRIEF
Oil-rich Abu Dhabi hosts a conference in January to discuss **alternatives to oil**.

Sir John Holmes: UN under-secretary-general for humanitarian affairs and emergency-relief co-ordinator

Want to drive green?

Paul Markillie

Your choice will widen

One way to save fuel and be kinder to the environment is to drive a smaller car. Or you can buy a hybrid, which is also cleaner and meaner with petrol by using a combination of an internal-combustion engine and an electric motor. Then there are all-electric cars that don't use any petrol at all, and hydrogen-powered ones, some of them using fuel cells. And increasingly there will be variations in between. Picking a new green drive in 2009 will not be an easy decision.

For a start, the choice will be much bigger. Plug-in versions of Toyota's Prius hybrid will allow that groundbreaking vehicle to be charged from a mains socket. But it will face tough competition from a new Honda Insight hybrid capable of 80mpg or more. Watch out too for a new six-seater Renault hybrid and a four-wheel drive Citroën with a diesel engine powering the front wheels and an electric motor operating the rear ones.

Other fuel-saving cars will appear at motor shows. General Motors will also start road testing the Chevy Volt before it goes into mass production. The Volt is a compact plug-in hybrid able to travel on a full charge for about 40 miles (64km)—a typical daily commute—but with a small petrol engine kicking in as a range-extending generator thereafter. It will cost around $30,000.

Better batteries will give electric cars a boost. Some already leave petrol ones in the dust—at a price. The Tesla Roadster, based on a British Lotus, uses a power-pack of more than 6,000 beefed-up versions of the lithium-ion batteries found in laptop computers. It can accelerate from 0-60mph in under four seconds and reach around 125mph. It is already on sale in California; Europeans will be able to get their hands on one in 2009—at around €100,000 ($140,000). If you do not mind 0-60mph in eight seconds and one less wheel, then ZAP, a Californian maker of electric vehicles, will offer a sleek three-wheeler called Alias for around $32,000. Classed as a motorcycle, it resembles a souped-up Reliant Robin.

More hydrogen-powered vehicles will arrive, but remain constrained by a lack of refuelling stations. Not so for petrol and diesel cars, which will be getting better too. Fiat's new Multiair engine will start appearing in its cars. These engines use hydraulics and electronics to optimise valve settings. When combined with a turbocharger, this will allow tiny two-cylinder engines to perform like four-cylinder ones, but use 20% less fuel.

With such tricks, some small petrol and diesel cars will be able to achieve around 80mpg—and, with a light foot on the accelerator, break 100mpg. But big cars will become more frugal too. A new Daimler engine will operate as a petrol engine when power is needed and like a diesel when economy is required. Daimler has called it the DiesOtto after two German engineers, Rudolf Diesel and Nicolaus Otto. The internal-combustion engines they helped to pioneer may be more than 100 years old, but they have yet to reach the end of the road. ∎

2009 IN BRIEF
From January 1st **no sulphur** is allowed in petrol and diesel sold in the Netherlands.

Paul Markillie: innovation editor, *The Economist*

Green games

Matthew Glendinning

Sports compete to save the planet

Sustainability is now enshrined as one of the three pillars of the Olympic movement (together with sport and culture). On October 2nd 2009 the belief of the International Olympic Committee (IOC) in these principles will again be tested when IOC members choose the city to host the 2016 Summer Olympic games.

The four in the frame for 2016—Chicago, Madrid, Tokyo and Rio de Janeiro—have all declared an interest in hosting the greenest of games. Tokyo promises to undergo what it calls the "greatest urban and environmental transformation ever". Chicago's mayor, Richard Daley, has re-imagined the Windy City as a green champion. Although the IOC admits that "air quality remains a challenge", it has acknowledged that Chicago is committed to a carbon-neutral event. That should do the trick: the IOC will award the games to Chicago.

The wider world of sport is following the green fashion too—whether out of conviction, to please sponsors or to appease public authorities. This is happening in increasingly inventive ways.

Take the NBA's New Jersey Nets. The basketball franchise has bought "carbon credits" that support four small hydro-power stations in China, as part of a programme to offset its own carbon emissions in America. The Nets claim to be the first major professional sports team to achieve carbon-neutral status.

But everyone can play. The Washington Nationals' baseball stadium became the first to receive a Leadership in Energy and Environment Design certificate, in 2008. Denver's Pepsi Centre became the first American arena to offset 100% of its electricity demands through purchases of wind power. More than 500 National Hockey League players have promised to offset their travel emissions by buying carbon credits.

Even those gas-guzzlers from Formula One motor racing are getting in on the act. From 2009, F1 will begin its first big green push with the introduction of the "Kinetic Energy Recovery System", which will enable each car to store energy created when braking for use on acceleration. The theory is that this green technology will filter down to passenger cars. ∎

Matthew Glendinning: sports and business writer

A water warning

Peter Brabeck-Letmathe, chairman of Nestlé, argues that water shortage is an even more urgent problem than climate change

I am convinced that, under present conditions and with the way water is being managed, we will run out of water long before we run out of fuel

The rise in the price of basic food has had devastating effects on the most vulnerable—the poor who spend up to two-thirds of their income on food. Some of the measures taken in response, such as export restrictions, have been highly counter-productive. In 2009 the world needs to reflect on the underlying causes of the food crisis and start addressing structural factors, in particular the link to biofuels and water.

Frank Rijsberman, from the Sri Lanka-based International Water Management Institute, gave warning in 2003 that if current trends continued, the livelihoods of one-third of the world's population could be affected by water scarcity by 2025: "We could be facing annual losses equivalent to the entire grain crops of India and the United States combined." Normally, when people hear about water scarcity they think of tap water; he talked about crops. And the dimension of the problem ahead is vast: America and India combined produce about 30% of globally consumed cereals.

It was a very hot summer that year. In Paris the heatwave left old people dying in their apartments. The big issue in the media was climate change. Mr Rijsberman's warnings remained unnoticed.

So what has happened since to the relevant trends? They have indeed changed, but not for the better. New factors—in particular the craze for biofuels—have added to the urgency of the water issue.

Let me quickly illustrate some of the links between food and water. It takes about one litre of water to produce one calorie from food crops. The actual water requirements differ according to plant, climate (most of the water withdrawn by plants is for cooling through evaporation) and the efficiency of irrigation.

Diets are another variable. Europeans and Americans have for years had high proportions of meat in their diets, but now this trend is catching on in emerging markets as incomes rise. Meat requires ten times the water withdrawn per calorie by plants. So the average daily diet in California requires some 6,000 litres of water in agriculture, compared with 3,000 litres in countries such as Tunisia and Egypt.

Compare these 3,000-6,000 daily litres withdrawn per head of world population for farming the food we eat with the three to four litres we drink or the 300-600 litres of water needed for other purposes, such as hygiene, or manufacturing (about 100 litres).

Water withdrawals for agriculture continue to increase rapidly. In some of the most fertile regions of the world (America, southern Europe, northern India, north-eastern China) overuse of water, mainly for agriculture, is leading to sinking water tables. Groundwater is being withdrawn, no longer as a buffer over the year, but in a structural way, mainly because water is seen as a free good.

As if this were not enough, politicians have added another drain—biofuels. It takes up to 9,100 litres of water to grow the soy for one litre of biodiesel, and up to 4,000 litres for the corn to be transformed into bioethanol. What is meant to alleviate a serious environmental problem (climate change) is making another, even more serious problem (water shortage) worse. Whatever the scenarios for climate change, we must reduce the consumption of fossil energy. But biofuels from crops specifically planted to be transformed into energy are clearly the wrong answer. I am convinced that, under present conditions and with the way water is being managed, we will run out of water long before we run out of fuel.

How to avoid running dry

There are solutions. They start in politics—for example, stopping subsidies for biofuels. Even more important, look for ways to use water in agriculture more efficiently. There is enough land and water to supply more meat to people in emerging economies. Efficient irrigation, for instance, would reduce fresh-water withdrawals almost by half.

And more can be done at international level. Some crops are better grown in water-rich countries, others grow well with relatively little water. If water had a price (such as from locally tradable water rights, though of course not for basic human needs), and if farm products could be traded freely and without subsidies across borders, a water-efficient allocation of production would follow.

What is business doing? At Nestlé, we have brought down freshwater withdrawals for our production from five litres per dollar of sales ten years ago to less than 1.8 litres. We actively participate in the public-policy dialogue on water, and together with other companies we have initiated the UN Global Compact CEO Water Mandate, aiming at a more efficient water use in industry.

We must all take the water issue seriously, better understand the link to food security and stop the trend towards overuse of freshwater. The decisions of the coming years will determine whether a major global crisis of water and food shortage can be avoided. ■

# The world in figures: Countries

Europe
Austria 113
Belgium 113
Bulgaria 113
Croatia 113
Czech Republic 113
Denmark 114
Estonia 114
Finland 114
France 114
Germany 114
Greece 114
Hungary 114
Ireland 114
Italy 114
Latvia 114
Lithuania 114
Netherlands 115
Norway 115
Poland 115
Portugal 115
Romania 115
Russia 115
Slovakia 115
Slovenia 115
Spain 115
Sweden 116
Switzerland 116
Turkey 116
Ukraine 116
United Kingdom 116

Asia
Australia 116
China 116
Hong Kong 116
India 116
Indonesia 117
Japan 117
Kazakhstan 117
Malaysia 117
New Zealand 117
Pakistan 117
Philippines 117
Singapore 117
South Korea 117
Sri Lanka 118
Taiwan 118
Thailand 118
Uzbekistan 118
Vietnam 118

North America
Canada 118
Mexico 118
United States 118

Latin America
Argentina 119
Bolivia 119
Brazil 119
Chile 119
Colombia 119
Cuba 119
Ecuador 119
Paraguay 119
Peru 119
Uruguay 119
Venezuela 119

Middle East and Africa
Algeria 120
Angola 120
Cameroon 120
Egypt 120
Ethiopia 120
Iran 120
Iraq 120
Israel 120
Jordan 120
Kenya 122
Lebanon 122
Libya 122
Morocco 122
Nigeria 122
Saudi Arabia 122
South Africa 122
Tanzania 122
Zimbabwe 122

For an interactive version of these pages, go to: www.economist.com/theworldin

TOP GROWERS

As the world's richest countries struggle economically, the fastest growth will be concentrated among the minnows—though mainly, as in the past, with producers of sought-after commodities. In fact, take out China and the combined economic output of those on the list is about equal to Thailand's. China, 16 times bigger, manages only fifth place, though 8% growth is nothing to sniff at: it will add $250bn to real global GDP in 2009.

Oil wealth explains the strong performance of the top three, and of Turkmenistan; other commodities underpin a further five (Uzbekistan's gold, Malawi's uranium, Mozambique's steel, Madagascar's nickel, Armenia's base metals). But with the 2008 reversal in commodities prices, the natural-resources boom may be over.

Strong Western investment will help Georgia recover from Russia's territorial incursion in 2008.

Rank	Country	GDP growth, %
1	Qatar	13.4
2	Angola	9.8
3	Congo (Brazzaville)	8.5
4	Malawi	8.3
5	China	8.0
5	Georgia	8.0
5	Uzbekistan	8.0
8	Madagascar	7.2
9	Mozambique	7.1
10	Turkmenistan	7.0
10	Azerbaijan	7.0
10	Armenia	7.0

2009 forecasts unless otherwise indicated.
Inflation: year-on-year annual average.
Dollar GDPs calculated using 2009 forecasts for dollar exchange rates (GDP at PPP, or purchasing-power parity, shown in brackets). All figures simplified by rounding.
Source: **Economist Intelligence Unit**
london@eiu.com

Sustained effort
Energy source as % of total
■ Renewables ■ Nuclear ■ Gas ■ Oil ■ Solid fuels

	1990	2000	2010	2020	2030
Renewables	4.5	5.9	8.2	10.0	11.8
Nuclear	12.3	14.2	13.2	11.3	10.3
Gas	17.9	23.0	24.9	25.7	25.7
Oil	37.9	38.0	36.4	35.7	35.3
Solid fuels	27.3	18.8	17.2	17.4	16.7

Source: European Commission

EUROPE

Main event: Rebuilding the shattered banking system **Euro-zone growth:** 0%
EU-27 growth: 0.1% **Eastern and central Europe:** 4.4% **Russia and CIS:** 4.5%

AUSTRIA
GDP growth:	0.8%
GDP:	$399bn (PPP: $343bn)
Inflation:	2.3%
Population:	8.4m
GDP per head:	$47,600 (PPP: $40,860)

An alliance between the centre-right Austrian People's Party and the centre-left Social Democrats seemed a likely outcome of snap elections in September 2008. The death of Jörg Haider, former leader of the right-wing Freedom Party, will make it easier for the party and the breakaway faction Mr Haider headed to consider reuniting. Weaker investment will hold back the economy.

BELGIUM
GDP growth:	0.5%
GDP:	$492bn (PPP: $404bn)
Inflation:	3.6%
Population:	10.6m
GDP per head:	$46,370 (PPP: $38,040)

Yves Leterme's government, comprising the Flemish and francophone Christian Democrats and Liberals and the francophone Socialists, will probably call an early national election in June to coincide with regional and European contests, having failed to satisfy the demands by the country's Flemish majority for devolution. At an anaemic 0.5%, economic growth will be much slower than in 2008, with scarcer credit and weak business confidence bringing investment nearly to a halt.

BULGARIA
GDP growth:	4.1%
GDP:	$52bn (PPP: $102bn)
Inflation:	8.0%
Population:	7.5m
GDP per head:	$6,990 (PPP: $13,650)

Good news and bad
■ % change ■ % of GDP ■ % of GDP
(chart showing Consumer prices, Budget balance, Current-account balance from 2000 to 2009)

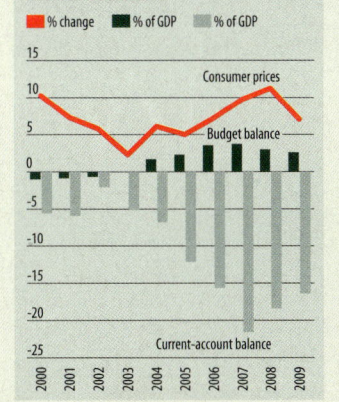

The severe reprimand delivered by the EU for misuse of its funds in mid-2008 will dent the confidence of foreign investors whose projects have underpinned Bulgaria's strong growth rates. This may not be altogether bad: the inflow of capital goods and raw materials required by those inward investors has helped push the current-account deficit to a staggering level. It will narrow in 2009, but only to 16.6% of GDP. The government's iron grip on the fiscal accounts will continue.

CROATIA
GDP growth:	3.5%
GDP:	$63bn (PPP: $81bn)
Inflation:	3.5%
Population:	4.5m
GDP per head:	$14,020 (PPP: $18,120)

Croatia will conclude its accession negotiations with the EU, but membership will be delayed until 2011 at the earliest. The EU feels it may have opened the door too quickly to Bulgaria and Romania, and wants to avoid a repeat. The pro-agrarian stance of the Croatian Peasants Party, on whose votes the Croatian Democratic Union-led government relies, could complicate accession talks. Rising productivity will keep economic growth above 3%.

CZECH REPUBLIC
GDP growth:	3.4%
GDP:	$223bn (PPP: $286bn)
Inflation:	3.1%
Population:	10.2m
GDP per head:	$21,860 (PPP: $28,040)

The government faces rising opposition to its fiscal-reform programme, not least from within the three-party ruling coalition. A dissident block within the dominant Civic Democratic Party is the main threat to stability. The country begins its six-month stint in the EU presidency on January 1st, and that will bring some unity, but the coalition's internal divisions will come increasingly to the fore thereafter.

To watch: Pedal to metal. The commissioning of new automotive production facilities will boost export revenue in 2009, offsetting a lacklustre trend in world trade.

DENMARK
GDP growth:	-0.4%
GDP:	$328bn (PPP: $211bn)
Inflation:	2.4%
Population:	5.5m
GDP per head:	$59,850 (PPP: $38,500)

A shaky housing market, rising borrowing rates and declining equity prices are sapping the confidence of Danish consumers. All of this will keep the economy mostly flat in 2009. The third-term prime minister, Anders Fogh Rasmussen, and his minority Liberal-Conservative coalition survive thanks mainly to support from the Danish People's Party, but there are costs, such as keeping a tight grip on immigration despite a stretched labour market.

ESTONIA
GDP growth:	-1.0%
GDP:	$25bn (PPP: $29bn)
Inflation:	6.3%
Population:	1.3m
GDP per head:	$18,550 (PPP: $21,890)

Estonia led Europe into post-credit-crunch stagflation in 2008 as the economy contracted by 1.5% and inflation topped 10%. Things will be only slightly better in 2009: GDP will shrink again as inflation falls to 6.3%. Divisions within the ruling coalition threaten its survival, but any likely replacement would maintain the same policies.

To watch: Pipe dreams. Organists from around the world will pull out all the stops at the 22nd International Organ Festival, to be held in Tallinn's historic churches from August 1st to 10th.

FINLAND
GDP growth:	1.1%
GDP:	$268bn (PPP: $207bn)
Inflation:	2.7%
Population:	5.3m
GDP per head:	$50,540 (PPP: $38,970)

Less exposed than other Europeans to financial turmoil, Finland will use its fiscal surplus for employment-boosting tax cuts. Economic growth will slow to 1.1%—tepid, but better than the rest of western Europe. The popularity of the prime minister, Matti Vanhanen, will plumb new depths, and the four-party coalition may be reduced to three if the Greens pull out over environmental policy. Still, the government should survive until elections set for 2011.

To watch: Loggerheads. A trebling of Russian tariffs on Finland's timber exports will take effect on January 1st, barring a last-minute settlement.

FRANCE
GDP growth:	-0.1%
GDP:	$2,734bn (PPP: $2,226bn)
Inflation:	1.7%
Population:	62.3m
GDP per head:	$43,910 (PPP: $35,750)

France will again test Europe's budget rules as its deficit breaks through the official ceiling (3% of GDP). This reflects the impact of slower growth on revenue collection and the effect of tax cuts unmatched on the spending side. The French economy will struggle to grow in the face of a European banking crisis, weak consumer demand and falling house prices, weakening support for the president, Nicolas Sarkozy. This will complicate the government's pursuit of the more radical of its reform proposals, including changes to the welfare system and efforts to raise purchasing power, promote competition and streamline public administration.

GERMANY
GDP growth:	0.2%
GDP:	$3,440bn (PPP: $2,989bn)
Inflation:	2.1%
Population:	82.8m
GDP per head:	$41,550 (PPP: $36,100)

Angela Merkel, the chancellor, is probably heading for re-election in September; her Christian Democratic Union/Christian Social Union (CDU/CSU) may even get enough votes to end the need for another "grand coalition" with the Social Democratic Party. With little popular appetite for market-led reforms and Ms Merkel firm in resisting populist pressures, policymaking has been reduced to uncontroversial tinkering. But a CDU/CSU-dominated government could regain some reform momentum.

Fewer jobs, higher pay

Export sales growth to the US and Asia—Germany's capital goods are much prized—will continue to fall because of weaker demand brought on by a global recession.

GREECE
GDP growth:	1.4%
GDP:	$351bn (PPP: $358bn)
Inflation:	3.0%
Population:	11.0m
GDP per head:	$31,890 (PPP: $32,600)

The centre-right New Democracy government, with a two-seat majority, could be forced to call early elections if the courts rule against it in a bribery case. On balance, though, it is likely to see out its term. The opposition Panhellenic Socialist Movement has its own troubles, and could face a leadership battle if results in the June 2009 European Parliament election prove disappointing.

The huge current-account deficit will narrow, but only because imports will slip on flagging consumer and business demand.

HUNGARY
GDP growth:	1.5%
GDP:	$146bn (PPP: $211bn)
Inflation:	4.1%
Population:	9.9m
GDP per head:	$14,720 (PPP: $21,330)

The Hungarian Socialist Party will remain in power even though it was reduced to a minority government after losing its coalition partner, the Hungarian Liberal Party, in early 2008. By contrast, the prime minister, Ferenc Gyurcsany, may face a leadership challenge as his popularity evaporates.

The economy is in dire straits as demand for Hungary's manufactured goods crumbles and the currency swings wildly, amid market turbulence. International bail-out packages are on the way to save the economy.

To watch: Word war. A rhetorical battle with neighbouring Slovakia over second-world-war property disputes may gather momentum as nationalist sentiments stir ahead of elections in 2010.

IRELAND
GDP growth:	-2.0%
GDP:	$280bn (PPP: $193bn)
Inflation:	2.3%
Population:	4.3m
GDP per head:	$64,500 (PPP: $44,470)

The economy will struggle through the rubble of the housing bust, with output falling, unemployment rising and the budget deficit smashing through the ceiling of the EU's stability and growth pact. Strains with the EU will intensify if Ireland cannot deliver support for the Lisbon treaty—which overhauls the union's institutions and governance—in a second referendum, following its rejection in 2008. The three-party coalition government led by the Taoiseach (the prime minister), Brian Cowen, will wobble, but survive.

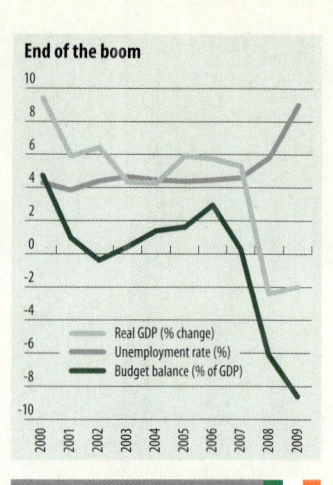

End of the boom

ITALY
GDP growth:	-0.3%
GDP:	$2,334bn (PPP: $1,872bn)
Inflation:	2.3%
Population:	58.1m
GDP per head:	$40,150 (PPP: $32,210)

Twin majorities in the two houses of parliament put the government of the prime minister, Silvio Berlusconi, on a firm footing by local standards, and disarray in the opposition after a heavy election defeat means that the government will manage to survive the year. But Mr Berlusconi's penchant for populism and strains within his coalition will prevent progress on all but the least ambitious reforms. The economy will contract and the fiscal deficit will rise, as tax revenue falls and social spending climbs.

LATVIA
GDP growth:	-1.5%
GDP:	$33bn (PPP: $42bn)
Inflation:	6.5%
Population:	2.3m
GDP per head:	$14,440 (PPP: $18,580)

The economy will contract for a second consecutive year. Sluggish demand will at least deliver lower inflation and a declining current-account deficit—though at 10% of GDP it will remain very high. The four-party coalition government, which rose from the ashes of the administration that collapsed in 2007, may succumb to the same corruption charges that finished its predecessor, but political upheaval will have little bearing on the economy.

LITHUANIA
GDP growth:	1.6%
GDP:	$49bn (PPP: $69bn)
Inflation:	6.7%
Population:	3.3m
GDP per head:	$14,510 (PPP: $20,680)

Less benighted than its Baltic neighbours, Lithuania's economy will at least grow in 2009, though by only 1.6%. This will be a sharp pullback from the country's post EU-accession burst

Baltic survivor, barely
GDP growth, %

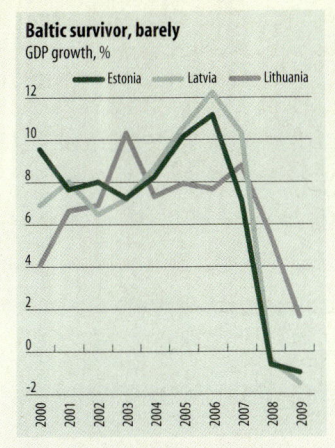

as the economy feels the effects of the global recession. Elections in late 2008 yielded a four-party centre-right coalition, but promised no respite from the instability that characterised the previous government.

NETHERLANDS
GDP growth:	0.7%
GDP:	$881bn (PPP: $702bn)
Inflation:	1.7%
Population:	16.5m
GDP per head:	$53,440 (PPP: $42,590)

The main political challenge for the prime minister, Jan Peter Balkenende, will be to hold together his three-party coalition government. The conflicting priorities of the two leading parties will limit tax and labour reforms. Slowing demand among trading partners and declining consumer confidence at home will keep growth at a pedestrian 0.7%.

To watch: Resurgent right. Rita Verdonk and her fledgling Proud of the Netherlands party will compete with the longer-standing Party for Freedom for a robust anti-immigrant voter base.

NORWAY
GDP growth:	1.5%
GDP:	$474bn (PPP: $281bn)
Inflation:	2.9%
Population:	4.9m
GDP per head:	$97,730 (PPP: $57,940)

Growing public discontent may persuade the Socialist Left Party and the Centre Party to abandon the coalition government before elections in September, leaving the Labour Party alone in a minority administration. Even if they don't, a minority Labour government is the most likely election outcome. Slower wage gains will hurt consumers and weaker export demand will limit investment, but oil revenue will keep the economy afloat.

To watch: Brussels backlash. If trade unions succeed in derailing a commitment to open services to greater EU competition, Norwegian exporters may face retaliation from Brussels.

POLAND
GDP growth:	3.8%
GDP:	$558bn (PPP: $723bn)
Inflation:	3.8%
Population:	38.1m
GDP per head:	$14,640 (PPP: $18,980)

The prime minister, Donald Tusk, and his centre-right Civic Platform (PO) will continue to head a mostly stable government. But resistance by the president, Lech Kaczynski, to key policy initiatives will limit the scope for tax and spending reform. Special pleading from the PO's partner, the Polish Peasants' Party, is another brake on policymaking; the PO could be running a minority government before 2009 is out. Economic growth will slow only moderately as trade shifts towards the EU's better-performing recent members.

PORTUGAL
GDP growth:	0%
GDP:	$242bn (PPP: $248bn)
Inflation:	2.2%
Population:	10.7m
GDP per head:	$22,680 (PPP: $23,250)

The Socialist Party (PS) government will press on with a wide-ranging reform of the public sector that has delivered notable budget savings. But the pace of change will slow as the political focus shifts to elections towards the end of 2009 and the prospect of more anti-reform protests becomes less palatable. The PS is well placed to exploit opposition weakness and win re-election. The economy will suffer amid a wider EU and global slump.

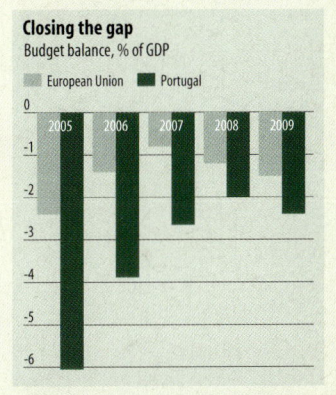

Closing the gap
Budget balance, % of GDP

ROMANIA
GDP growth:	4.8%
GDP:	$202bn (PPP: $300bn)
Inflation:	5.4%
Population:	21.5m
GDP per head:	$9,400 (PPP: $13,850)

Elections in late 2008 were likely to yield an alliance between the incumbent National Liberal Party and the opposition Social Democratic Party, but only after some noisy horsetrading. The new team, whatever its shape, will have to impose an austerity plan. An economic surge in recent years has come at the cost of loose budget control, unsustainable wage increases and a growing current-account gap. The rate of growth will ease in 2009. The slowdown is likely to be modest, but could sharpen if external conditions get much worse.

RUSSIA
GDP growth:	4.0%
GDP:	$1,680bn (PPP: $2,310bn)
Inflation:	11.5%
Population:	141.4m
GDP per head:	$11,880 (PPP: $16,330)

The campaign to recover national pride and influence has been a roaring success within Russia's borders, but has raised alarms—as the invasion of Georgia in 2008 attests—in the wider world. Russian adventurism is not over, although it will bring increasing costs as investors take fright. With the oil bonanza fading as prices fall and production flattens, the government will face a tougher economic outlook. The current-account surplus will shrink, growth will slow and inflation will remain a concern. The banks and the currency will be vulnerable to a further downturn in the financial environment.

To watch: Two's a crowd. Vladimir Putin has assumed increased powers as Russia's prime minister but its president, Dmitry Medvedev, has more, and will fight back if Mr Putin goes too far.

SLOVAKIA
GDP growth:	5.0%
GDP:	$100bn (PPP: $130bn)
Inflation:	4.2%
Population:	5.5m
GDP per head:	$18,270 (PPP: $23,720)

Slovakia adopts the euro on January 1st, though interventionist policies designed to restrain inflation and maintain competitiveness within the euro area could raise hackles in Brussels. The slowdown in the economy that began in 2008 will continue as export demand and consumer spending slacken. Political tensions could tear apart the three-party ruling coalition, though Direction-Social Democracy, the party of the popular prime minister, Robert Fico, might get a stronger mandate in subsequent elections.

SLOVENIA
GDP growth:	3.0%
GDP:	$56bn (PPP: $63bn)
Inflation:	3.5%
Population:	2.0m
GDP per head:	$27,690 (PPP: $31,430)

A coalition of centre-left parties was set to form the government after their strong showing in Slovenia's election of September 2008, and to press ahead with a consensus-led platform of social reforms, though at a slow pace. Growth will be below the high rates enjoyed in recent years, but still respectable at around 3%.

To watch: Foreign fields. Teams from 30 countries will compete in the 56th World Ploughing Contest in September.

SPAIN
GDP growth:	-0.6%
GDP:	$1,581bn (PPP: $1,470bn)
Inflation:	3.0%
Population:	45.8m
GDP per head:	$34,540 (PPP: $32,120)

Tax cuts and higher public spending may cushion the blow delivered by the collapsing property bubble in 2007-08, but the economy is still likely to shrink. The government's pump priming will show up in a sharply deteriorating

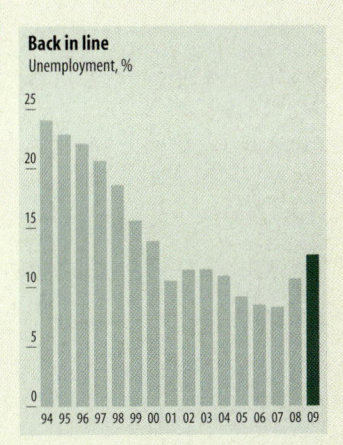

Back in line
Unemployment, %

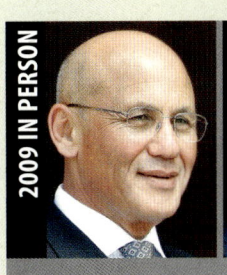

2009 IN PERSON

Demetris Christofias (right) and **Mehmet Ali Talat** (left), the leaders, respectively, of the Greek and Turkish Cypriot communities, may in 2009 resolve the dispute that has split the island since 1974. The two are ideological cousins: Mr Christofias, a Moscow-educated Communist, and Mr Talat, a former leader of the leftist Republican Turkish Party. They also share a tacit mandate from their communities and mainland sponsors to agree terms. They opened negotiations in Nicosia's no-man's-land in mid-2008; if they pull it off, expect another meeting soon—this time at the Nobel-peace-prize awards in Oslo.

budget deficit. An electoral promise to remove obstacles to faster growth, such as low productivity and over-regulation, will fade as the prime minister, José Luis Rodríguez Zapatero, concentrates on fending off union criticism and keeping sweet the regional parties whose votes he needs in congress.

To watch: Separatists. A planned vote in the Basque country in late 2008 and a Constitutional Court ruling on a new statute for Catalonia could increase political instability.

SWEDEN
GDP growth:	0.6%
GDP:	$476bn (PPP: $361bn)
Inflation:	2.6%
Population:	9.3m
GDP per head:	$51,390 (PPP: $38,940)

Tax cuts worth $2.4bn promised for the 2009 budget will provide a welcome shot in the arm to the economy, held back by weakening domestic demand and the global slump, but growth will remain far below trend. The centre-right coalition government will continue to nudge people back to work and reduce welfare dependency despite union resistance to labour-market reforms. Scandals and unpopular policy initiatives have eroded the government's popularity, but it will survive to the end of its term in 2010.

SWITZERLAND
GDP growth:	0%
GDP:	$454bn (PPP: $331bn)
Inflation:	1.5%
Population:	7.7m
GDP per head:	$58,930 (PPP: $42,940)

The move of the Swiss People's Party (SVP) into opposition—there hasn't been an opposition party since the 1950s—has upended the political system. If the SVP cannot rejoin the government on its own terms, it will continue to pursue its isolationist and anti-immigrant agenda from the sidelines. Nevertheless, an accord with the EU on the free movement of labour is likely to be renewed in a referendum.

To watch: Egg cup. Contestants will meet in Berne to fight for the trophy in the annual egg-bashing contest in March. It's like conkers, but messier.

TURKEY
GDP growth:	2.1%
GDP:	$635bn (PPP: $990bn)
Inflation:	10.8%
Population:	72.6m
GDP per head:	$8,750 (PPP: $13,630)

Turkey will continue to court political crisis as the secular establishment tries to restrain the moderately Islamist Justice and Development Party (AKP) government. The Constitutional Court fell short of banning the party in mid-2008, but upheld a charge of undermining secular principles. It may act more harshly if another case is filed. This would become more likely if the AKP tries to rewrite the constitution and, in so doing, crosses the secularists' red lines.

The global slowdown will dent growth, domestic spending and investment. Big deficits leave Turkey vulnerable to a loss of investor confidence.

UKRAINE
GDP growth:	2.3%
GDP:	$203bn (PPP: $375bn)
Inflation:	15.0%
Population:	45.8m
GDP per head:	$4,440 (PPP: $8,200)

Ukraine's politics will be dominated by manoeuvring for the 2010 presidential election. The divide between supporters and opponents of the 2004 "Orange revolution" will blur as the former battle among themselves. Relations between Orange factions soured late in 2008 (and a general election was called for December) when the prime minister, Yulia Tymoshenko, sided with the anti-Orange opposition to weaken the powers of her revolutionary ally, President Viktor Yushchenko.

With Russia jacking up the price of gas supplies, inflation rampant, the current-account gap widening and foreign debt climbing, the economy is suffering and an IMF loan may be on the cards.

To watch: Client relations. America and the EU will try to bring Ukraine more fully into the Western camp, but, given a resurgent Russia and Ukraine's own internal strife, it may find itself drifting back into Russia's "near abroad".

UNITED KINGDOM
GDP growth:	-1.0%
GDP:	$2,442bn (PPP: $2,277bn)
Inflation:	1.9%
Population:	61.9m
GDP per head:	$39,470 (PPP: $36,820)

Reeling from the credit crunch and the bursting of a homegrown property bubble—and without the fiscal wherewithal to boost demand—the economy will go backwards. The UK's highly indebted consumers will have no option but to tighten spending as they seek to rebuild their savings.

Gordon Brown's bold steps during the banking crisis have helped his image. Even so, the disgruntled Labour Party may try to oust him, and any successor will struggle to serve out the full term to 2010. If a general election is called, it will be the opposition Conservative Party's for the taking, and Labour may be cast into the wilderness from which the Tories have only recently emerged.

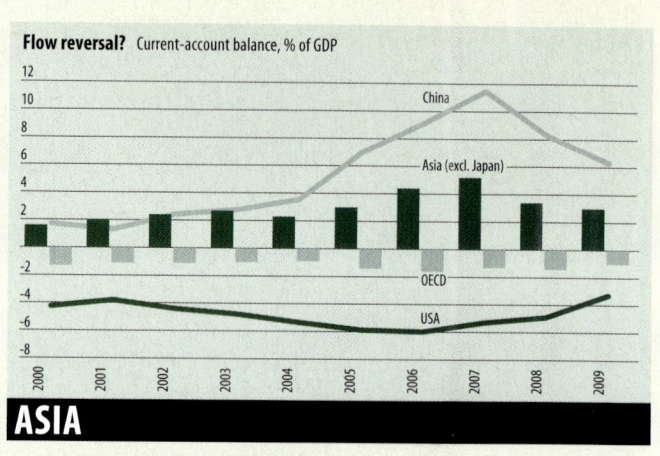

Flow reversal? Current-account balance, % of GDP

ASIA

Main event: Managing the economic slowdown in China
Asia growth (excluding Japan): 5% **ASEAN growth**: 3%

AUSTRALIA
GDP growth:	1.6%
GDP:	$755bn (PPP: $846bn)
Inflation:	3.2%
Population:	20.8m
GDP per head:	$36,250 (PPP: $40,620)

The Labor Party government will face growing criticism over a slowing economy and rising prices, but is sufficiently well-regarded by voters to weather it. The government's focus on looking different from the previous Liberal Party administration—on aboriginal rights, the Kyoto climate treaty and trade-union regulation—will persist, but on a more modest basis as the political cost of implementing related reforms rises.

CHINA
GDP growth:	8.0%
GDP:	$4,818bn (PPP: $9,128bn)
Inflation:	3.6%
Population:	1,336.7m
GDP per head:	$3,600 (PPP: $6,830)

With the lustre of Olympic gold fading, balancing the twin imperatives of sustaining growth and containing inflation will be the government's biggest challenge. A misstep in either direction could fuel the social unrest so feared by the country's rulers (though the Communist Party has won a substantial dividend from the games). A campaign against official corruption, motivated by the same fear, will continue, but broader democratic reform will not.

To watch: Strait talking. Relations with Taiwan will be smoother following the island's return to Kuomintang rule. But underlying tensions will remain.

HONG KONG
GDP growth:	1.9%
GDP:	$240bn (PPP: $330bn)
Inflation:	4.3%
Population:	7.1m
GDP per head:	$34,020 (PPP: $46,720)

The slowdown in international trade will hit exports, and inflation will gnaw at consumer demand (countered somewhat by a loose monetary stance courtesy of Hong Kong's US-dollar peg), driving growth to a very weak 1.9%. The rising cost of living, and growing discontent over increasing inequality, may renew the mid-2008 wage protests by the lower-paid.

To watch: Air today, gone tomorrow. Worsening air pollution is prompting many to leave. Without co-operation with neighbouring Guangdong province, there is little prospect of improvement.

INDIA
GDP growth:	6.5%
GDP:	$1,362bn (PPP: $3,728bn)
Inflation:	7.2%
Population:	1,140.3m
GDP per head:	$1,190 (PPP: $3,270)

The general election, to be held by May, will deliver another coalition government, but whether headed once again by Congress or by the opposition Bharatiya Janata Party is anybody's guess. Whatever the outcome, the resulting government will be beset by policy differences and personality clashes. High inflation and falling (if still

Consumer comeback % of GDP

respectable) growth will sour the new government's "honeymoon".

To watch: Caste away. Mayawati, leader of the regionally based Bahujan Samaj Party, may bid to become the country's first "untouchable" prime minister. She has an outside chance of success.

INDONESIA

GDP growth:	3.4%
GDP:	$505bn (PPP: $918bn)
Inflation:	6.6%
Population:	240.3m
GDP per head:	$2,130 (PPP: $3,870)

Voters will probably forgive and forget the painful fuel-price hikes of mid-2008 and grant President Susilo Bambang Yudhoyono a second term in the July election. But the opposition Indonesian Democratic Party-Struggle may oust his Golkar organisation as the largest party in parliament in April, complicating the task of forming a ruling coalition. A slowing economy lumbered with high interest rates and high inflation will add to the new government's many difficulties.

Inwards, upwards, downwards
$bn
- Inward direct investment (left-hand scale)
- Inward FDI stock (right-hand scale)

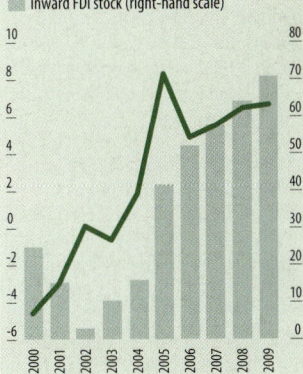

To watch: Buying in. Economic woes will not stem the surge of foreign direct investment, lured by stronger property rights, less red tape and better security.

JAPAN

GDP growth:	0%
GDP:	$5,388bn (PPP: $4,546bn)
Inflation:	1.2%
Population:	127.3m
GDP per head:	$42,310 (PPP: $35,780)

Political ructions and a snap election in late 2008 were likely to reduce the Liberal Democratic Party government's majority, leaving the prime minister, Taro Aso, the country's third in as many years, without an outright majority in the lower chamber. This means the political paralysis that scuppered his predecessor will continue under Mr Aso. He will also be burdened with a stagnant economy and slower export growth.

2009 IN PERSON

When **Ratan Tata** took over the century-old family business in 1991 he launched a modernisation and growth spree that raised the company to pre-eminence on the Indian business scene. Since the millennium, India has proved too small for the group's ambitions; a growing appetite for foreign acquisitions has allowed it to climb the global business food chain, most recently gobbling an Anglo-Dutch steel giant, Corus, and two iconic British auto marques, Land Rover and Jaguar. A brilliant entrepreneur in his own right, Mr Tata stands for a new breed of business leader in the developing world, using war chests built up in the recent growth spurt to expand into new markets. With increasing frequency in 2009, his campaign will involve the acquisition of distressed assets in the developed world.

To watch: China chill. Under Mr Aso, a foreign-policy hawk, relations with rivals China and South Korea might return to the freezer after recent thawing.

KAZAKHSTAN

GDP growth:	4.6%
GDP:	$161bn (PPP: $195bn)
Inflation:	10.4%
Population:	15.9m
GDP per head:	$10,100 (PPP: $12,290)

The current account will slip back into deficit as oil-export revenue moderates in line with prices. The rate of economic growth, though below the blistering pace set earlier in the decade, will still exceed 4%. The president, Nursultan Nazarbayev, will face no significant threat to his rule, though local business interests are showing signs of discontent.

To watch. Have a seat. Mr Nazarbayev, keen to appear democratic, may allow parliamentary elections before year-end to curb the government party's dominance (it now holds all of the seats).

MALAYSIA

GDP growth:	3.2%
GDP:	$227bn (PPP: $416bn)
Inflation:	2.5%
Population:	28.3m
GDP per head:	$8,020 (PPP: $14,720)

A comfortable majority and a growing economy will allow the Barisan Nasional (BN) coalition government to implement its legislative programme unmolested. The opposition Parti Keadilan Rakyat, led by Anwar Ibrahim, will continue a poaching campaign among the BN ranks. The economy will slow amid worsening global conditions and lower commodity prices.

NEW ZEALAND

GDP growth:	1.5%
GDP:	$115bn (PPP: $121bn)
Inflation:	3.3%
Population:	4.3m
GDP per head:	$26,630 (PPP: $27,900)

The National Party was poised to replace the Labour Party in government at the end of 2008, and pledged to continue recent tax cuts to make local jobs more attractive and cut emigration. A National government will also increase borrowing to fund a big infrastructure drive. But the economic woes that dogged Labour will persist, with the economy idling under heavy household debt, high interest rates and a gaping current-account deficit.

To watch: Trade deals. A free-trade agreement with China, the Asian giant's first with an advanced nation, will kick in gradually during 2009 and coming years. New Zealand hopes deals with America and ASEAN will follow.

PAKISTAN

GDP growth:	2.9%
GDP:	$152bn (PPP: $470bn)
Inflation:	16.4%
Population:	169.2m
GDP per head:	$900 (PPP: $2,780)

Asif Ali Zardari, the controversial widower of slain former prime minister Benazir Bhutto, easily won the presidency in 2008, but he faces a sea of troubles and a strong headwind from his erstwhile ally, Nawaz Sharif. The army, briefly out of the spotlight following the resignation from the presidency of its former strongman, General Pervez Musharraf, will remain de facto kingmaker. Pakistan may need an IMF loan to avoid a crisis.

To watch: One-day cricket. If it's safe, Pakistan will host in October the world championship in that paragon of sporting brevity, the cricket match that lasts no more than a single day.

PHILIPPINES

GDP growth:	2.0%
GDP:	$159bn (PPP: $339bn)
Inflation:	5.9%
Population:	94.3m
GDP per head:	$1,690 (PPP: $3,600)

Weakened by corruption allegations against her government and facing a deteriorating economy, the president, Gloria Macapagal Arroyo, will survive to the end of her term in 2010 provided she retains the support of the generals.

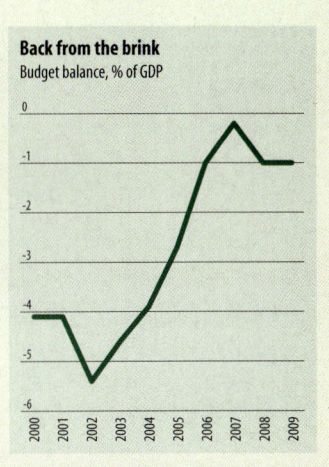

Back from the brink
Budget balance, % of GDP

She will press on with a reform programme that includes a switch from a presidential to a parliamentary system, but lack of a majority in the upper chamber of the legislature will hamper progress. Weaker export growth will hold back the economy.

To watch: Deal or no deal? After a peace deal with Islamist separatists was put on ice in late 2008, there could instead be a return to all-out fighting on the island of Mindanao.

SINGAPORE

GDP growth:	-0.1%
GDP:	$209bn (PPP: $204bn)
Inflation:	1.5%
Population:	4.6m
GDP per head:	$45,430 (PPP: $44,200)

Slumping economies in Europe and the Americas will slash demand for Singapore's exports—particularly electronics and pharmaceuticals—causing the economy to stagnate. The current account, though, will maintain a healthy surplus. The ruling People's Action Party will keep its grip on power.

To watch: Pregnant pause. The government has unveiled incentives encouraging Singaporeans to have more children; they are not expected to deliver.

SOUTH KOREA

GDP growth:	2.0%
GDP:	$893bn (PPP: $1,361bn)
Inflation:	1.8%
Population:	49.4m
GDP per head:	$18,070 (PPP: $27,550)

With a parliamentary majority for his Grand National Party and no major elections until 2012, Lee Myung-bak's position as president looks secure. His ability to govern effectively is a different story, after mass protests against the resumption of US beef imports shattered public confidence. Despite political woes and gathering economic storm clouds, the president will continue to advance business-friendly policies designed to attract foreign investment.

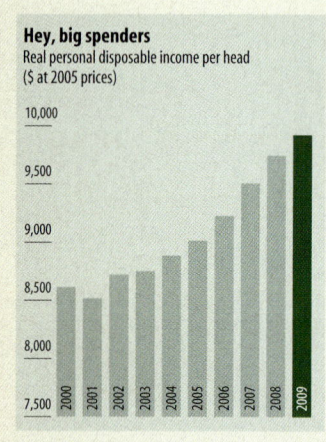

Hey, big spenders
Real personal disposable income per head ($ at 2005 prices)

To watch: Kerpoww! The International Cartoon & Animation Festival in Seoul in May will be a big draw.

SRI LANKA
GDP growth:	3.2%
GDP:	$46bn (PPP: $98bn)
Inflation:	10.5%
Population:	19.5m
GDP per head:	$2,340 (PPP: $5,040)

Despite divisions in his United People's Freedom Alliance government, the president, Mahinda Rajapakse, and his inner circle (most prominently, his brothers) will retain their grip on power. Conflict with Tamil separatists will continue until the armed forces can catch or kill the Tamil leader, Velupillai Prabhakaran. Continuing global economic weakness will hold back the economy, though growth should still exceed 3%.

TAIWAN
GDP growth:	1.5%
GDP:	$435bn (PPP: $881bn)
Inflation:	2.0%
Population:	22.8m
GDP per head:	$19,080 (PPP: $38,630)

The president, Ma Ying-jeou, will boost government spending to ease the effects of the global slowdown on the export-driven economy; growth will still be nearly three percentage points lower than in 2008. The drive by the Kuomintang government for improved ties with mainland China will continue, though progress will be mainly symbolic, apart from narrow business aims.

THAILAND
GDP growth:	3.2%
GDP:	$289bn (PPP: $596bn)
Inflation:	3.8%
Population:	67.5m
GDP per head:	$4,280 (PPP: $8,830)

The social divisions that emerged under the Thaksin Shinawatra government (2001-06)—between rural poor and urban middle class—will dominate politics. Violent protests against the pro-Thaksin People Power Party government in late 2008, and the army's ambivalent response to the government's declaration of emergency rule, make the outlook cloudy. Somchai Wongsawat, the new prime minister, does not have broad enough support to end the political crisis. Unless moderates emerge, further violence and a temporary return to military rule are on the cards. Political instability and high prices will curb domestic spending.

UZBEKISTAN
GDP growth:	8.0%
GDP:	$31bn (PPP: $80bn)
Inflation:	13.0%
Population:	27.5m
GDP per head:	$1,120 (PPP: $2,910)

Despite spiky relations with the West, a murky business climate and a harshly repressive regime, the economy will be supported by high prices for gold, cotton and gas, three key exports (though inflation will remain stubbornly high). The president, Islam Karimov, will face more questions over the constitutional legality of his election to a third term in 2007, but will deflect them with practised ease.

To watch: Divine veto. Far from the ballot box, the main threat to Mr Karimov's position is his physical survival. In ailing health, the president could be "recalled" at any time, leaving a power vacuum.

VIETNAM
GDP growth:	5.2%
GDP:	$94bn (PPP: $263bn)
Inflation:	14.0%
Population:	88.1m
GDP per head:	$1,080 (PPP: $3,020)

Cheaper
Average real wage index (local currency, 2005=100)

The Communist Party government will face rising pressure as the rate of economic growth moderates and people struggle to make ends meet. An anti-corruption drive will yield results, but is as likely to fuel public anger as to assuage it until corruption actually abates. Inflation will ease from an average of 25% in 2008 but will remain in double digits.

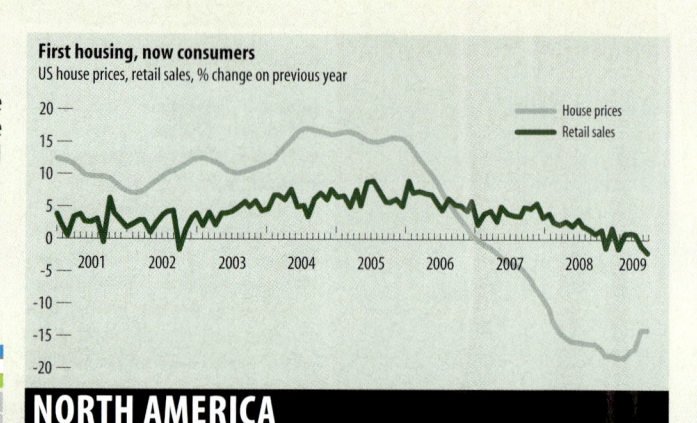

First housing, now consumers
US house prices, retail sales, % change on previous year

NORTH AMERICA
Main event: A new broom sweeps America's White House
North American (NAFTA) growth: -0.1%

CANADA
GDP growth:	0.5%
GDP:	$1,468bn (PPP: $1,357bn)
Inflation:	2.3%
Population:	33.5m
GDP per head:	$43,860 (PPP: $40,540)

An election in late 2008 produced another Conservative government under the prime minister, Stephen Harper, but one that will again rely on smaller parties for a parliamentary majority. The government's capacity to push environmental, financial and labour-market reforms will as a result be weaker than it hoped. The main focus will be the feeble economy, smothered by the slowdown in the United States, weak business investment and tighter credit. Shrinking demand at home and abroad will keep growth below 1%; the current account will post its first deficit in a decade.

MEXICO
GDP growth:	0.9%
GDP:	$959bn (PPP: $1,624bn)
Inflation:	6.2%
Population:	111.2m
GDP per head:	$8,620 (PPP: $14,610)

A truce between the ruling Partido Acción Nacional and the opposition Partido Revolucionario Institucional

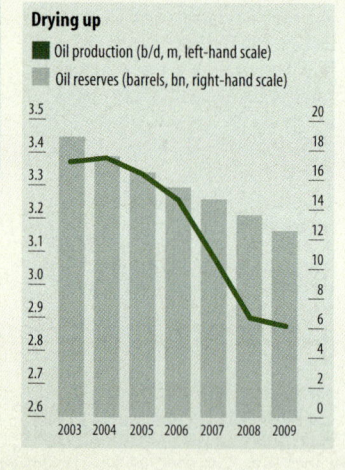

Drying up
Oil production (b/d, m, left-hand scale)
Oil reserves (barrels, bn, right-hand scale)

will come to an end as the July mid-term elections approach. The results delivered by a period of co-operation, including legislation to boost investment in the energy sector, should pay dividends over time. But the price of compromise was a watered-down bill that will not do enough to address falling oil output.

The policy bind caused by a weak economy and high imported inflation will persist. Growth will decline for a third year running.

To watch: Truncheons and tear-gas. Civil disorder may increase as opposition groups use unpopular reforms, a flagging economy and persistent drugs violence to mobilise support.

UNITED STATES
GDP growth:	-0.2%
GDP:	$14,839bn (PPP: $14,839bn)
Inflation:	2.0%
Population:	306.6m
GDP per head:	$48,400 (PPP: $48,400)

The promise of a new president with fresh ideas will be overshadowed by more sober developments: a shrinking economy, soaring unemployment and a shattered financial system. Stiff new financial regulation and economic stimulus plans will be the order of the day, but confidence will not be easily restored.

After George Bush's last, lethargic years, a new political agenda will take shape. Greater international co-operation on global issues such as climate change will feature prominently. The American military presence in Iraq will also begin to wind down. Despite the warmer outreach, trade policy will become more protectionist and commercial tensions with China will intensify.

To watch: Home repair. The worst property crisis since the 1930s will bottom out as house prices begin to stabilise. But with a huge backlog of homes on the market, a sustained recovery will have to wait until 2010.

The world in figures Countries

The return of risk
Government bond spreads over US Treasuries, basis points
(Argentina, Brazil, Venezuela, Colombia, Panama, Peru, Ecuador)
Source: JPMorgan

LATIN AMERICA

Main event: Argentina on the turn **Latin American growth**: 2.2%

ARGENTINA
GDP growth:	2.5%
GDP:	$319bn (PPP: $606bn)
Inflation:	9.9%
Population:	40.1m
GDP per head:	$7,950 (PPP: $15,100)

President Cristina Fernández de Kirchner will struggle with growing economic imbalances, the result of supercharged pump-priming introduced during the recovery from the 2001 slump. She will lose friends both outside and within the ruling Peronist party, with big losses likely in October elections. Further economic missteps risk a harder landing.

BOLIVIA
GDP growth:	3.4%
GDP:	$20bn (PPP: $46bn)
Inflation:	10.9%
Population:	9.9m
GDP per head:	$2,040 (PPP: $4,710)

Bolivia will open the year under a new constitution that emphasises the indigenous majority; this will further anger the country's wealthier eastern areas. As the east's campaign for autonomy gathers momentum and President Evo Morales's redistributive policies bite, violence will increase. Weaker demand for commodities will slow the economy.

To watch: No preference. A US law that gives Bolivia preferential market access to the US will expire in January. Doubts over renewal will mar export prospects.

BRAZIL
GDP growth:	2.7%
GDP:	$1,308bn (PPP: $2,114bn)
Inflation:	6.3%
Population:	194.4m
GDP per head:	$6,730 (PPP: $10,880)

Conservative management by Luis Inácio Lula da Silva's government should allow the economy to weather the slowdown in demand and financial market strains. But inflationary pressures will require tighter fiscal and monetary policy, squashing consumer spending and curbing growth. The race to succeed Lula in 2010 will dominate politics.

CHILE
GDP growth:	2.8%
GDP:	$184bn (PPP: $262bn)
Inflation:	6.4%
Population:	16.9m
GDP per head:	$10,850 (PPP: $15,470)

Slow growth and high prices are eroding confidence in President Michelle Bachelet and her government. Elections in December will provide the test, with the centre-right Alianza coalition poised to take over. Export growth will weaken, but the outlook for the important mining sector will be helped by the inauguration of Codelco's Gaby copper mine.

COLOMBIA
GDP growth:	2.5%
GDP:	$176bn (PPP: $363bn)
Inflation:	5.7%
Population:	48.3m
GDP per head:	$3,640 (PPP: $7,510)

Colombia's president, Álvaro Uribe, will enter the final years of his second term more popular than when he began his first, thanks mainly to a successful anti-rebel strategy and the spectacular rescue of 15 hostages from their FARC guerrilla captors in mid-2008. Friends will spend the year trying to remove a constitutional ban on a third term ahead of 2010 elections.

CUBA
GDP growth:	4.5%
GDP:	$60bn (PPP: $118bn)
Inflation:	6.4%
Population:	11.2m
GDP per head:	$5,330 (PPP: $10,540)

The journey to a more permissive post-Castro era will continue, but at a crawl rather than a rush. Government-controlled prices will be allowed to rise a little closer to market levels, measures will be introduced to improve labour productivity and raise incomes, and some powers will be devolved to regional government. A new US president may allow for some warming of relations.

To watch: Youth programme. A new generation of leaders (in their 50s rather than their 70s) may be anointed at Cuba's Communist Party congress late in the year.

ECUADOR
GDP growth:	2.0%
GDP:	$50bn (PPP: $111bn)
Inflation:	7.3%
Population:	14.0m
GDP per head:	$3,560 (PPP: $7,900)

President Rafael Correa will go to the polls early in the year, boosted by approval for his new constitution in a late-2008 referendum. His popularity is waning, but is much stronger than that of the divided opposition, so if he seeks a new mandate he will get it. The economy will deteriorate as oil prices fall and production declines. Growth of 2% will be in line with recent years—a poor showing for an oil exporter during a commodities boom.

PARAGUAY
GDP growth:	2.7%
GDP:	$16bn (PPP: $31bn)
Inflation:	9.0%
Population:	6.4m
GDP per head:	$2,500 (PPP: $4,920)

Former cleric Fernando Lugo's first full year as president will provide a stiff test for his faith in the power of secular politics. Surrounded by unreliable allies and remnants of the corrupt single-party state he overthrew at the ballot box, he will find the going hard. A platform combining conservative economic policies with redistributive initiatives such as land reform will threaten powerful interests.

To watch: Holy communion. The Mennonite World Conference will be held in Asunción in July. Paraguay has 32,000 Mennonites, including the former first lady.

PERU
GDP growth:	6.4%
GDP:	$138bn (PPP: $271bn)
Inflation:	5.0%
Population:	29.4m
GDP per head:	$4,680 (PPP: $9,210)

President Alan García, who during a previous stint (1985-90) enjoyed soaring popularity even as he enacted policies that wrecked the economy, is suffering a ratings slump just as he seems to be getting things right. This time, he is likely to serve out his term, but public protest and labour militancy will rise. Economic growth will slow to 6.4%, but that will be the best in the Americas.

URUGUAY
GDP growth:	3.5%
GDP:	$31bn (PPP: $45bn)
Inflation:	7.4%
Population:	3.3m
GDP per head:	$9,260 (PPP: $13,580)

Politics will be dominated by campaigning for the October congressional and presidential elections, which the ruling centre-left Frente Amplio (FA) coalition is a narrow favourite to win. Danilo Astori, a former finance minister, will probably be the FA's candidate; primaries will be held in June.

A weak world economy will weigh on exports, but the damage to growth will be limited by strong business spending.

VENEZUELA
GDP growth:	1.8%
GDP:	$417bn (PPP: $381bn)
Inflation:	40.0%
Population:	28.1m
GDP per head:	$14,860 (PPP: $13,590)

President Hugo Chávez will celebrate ten years in power in 2009, but things have got a lot tougher of late. He faces a public backlash against the more radical elements of his socialist programme, rising dissent in the government ranks and stirrings of unity in the fractious opposition. Still, there is little question Mr Chávez will survive at least to the end of his term in 2013. Even given a decline in the oil revenues that have funded his revolution, there is fuel in the tank for a few more years.

Sebastián Piñera, a billionaire Chilean businessman and leading light in the opposition Alianza coalition, was narrowly defeated in the 2005 presidential election by the present incumbent, Michelle Bachelet. It seemed that Chilean voters, though put off by infighting in the centre-left Concertación coalition, were not yet ready to elect rightist forces associated with the dictatorship of Augusto Pinochet. In December Mr Piñera, himself a public critic of the Pinochet regime, will contest the presidency again, and the voters may well be ready this time. Mrs Bachelet hasn't lived up to expectations and her government looks tired. Above all, Mr Piñera's election would show that the Pinochet era had been put to rest.

2009 IN PERSON

Countries The world in figures

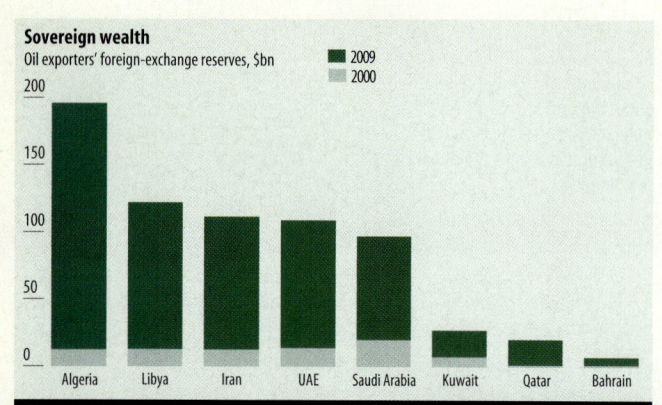

Sovereign wealth
Oil exporters' foreign-exchange reserves, $bn
- 2009
- 2000

Algeria, Libya, Iran, UAE, Saudi Arabia, Kuwait, Qatar, Bahrain

MIDDLE EAST AND AFRICA

Main event: Jacob Zuma takes over as South Africa's new president
Middle East & North Africa growth: 4.8%
Sub-Saharan Africa growth: 4.8%

ALGERIA
GDP growth:	4.6%
GDP:	$172bn (PPP: $302bn)
Inflation:	3.9%
Population:	34.9m
GDP per head:	$4,940 (PPP: $8,670)

The president, Abdelaziz Bouteflika, will celebrate a decade in power by seeking a third term in the April election—and will probably win. This will heighten interest in the ongoing shift in power from the old military-led ruling class to the presidency, and the lack of a clear path of succession. Islamist terrorists will kill and maim, but will pose little real threat.

Economic growth will accelerate (a rarity in 2009), as new hydrocarbon projects are brought on stream.

ANGOLA
GDP growth:	9.8%
GDP:	$76bn (PPP: $100bn)
Inflation:	11.8%
Population:	18.0m
GDP per head:	$4,200 (PPP: $5,550)

A crushing win in the September 2008 legislative election gives the ruling Movimento Popular de Libertação de Angola the majority it needs to reform the constitution. This it will do with an eye mainly on securing its own

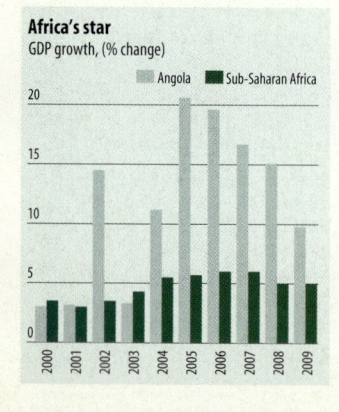

Africa's star
GDP growth, (% change)
- Angola
- Sub-Saharan Africa

hegemony. President José Eduardo dos Santos, celebrating 30 years in power in 2009, will probably win another term in September. Rising oil production will keep growth among the world's highest.

CAMEROON
GDP growth:	3.5%
GDP:	$22bn (PPP: $41bn)
Inflation:	3.5%
Population:	19.3m
GDP per head:	$1,130 (PPP: $2,120)

The government, led by 75-year-old President Paul Biya, will face no meaningful political opposition (the last time the president's position was threatened was in a failed coup in 1984). Cameroon will court foreign investment in the country's natural resources, and the commissioning of new projects will keep economic growth steady despite lower global commodity prices.

To watch: Reluctant reunion. Violence is likely on the Bakassi peninsula as Cameroon seeks to exert its authority over the region, ceded by Nigeria in 2008 after international arbitration.

EGYPT
GDP growth:	5.7%
GDP:	$184bn (PPP: $486bn)
Inflation:	9.1%
Population:	78.6m
GDP per head:	$2,350 (PPP: $6,190)

Tensions will remain high as rising prices, static wages and uncompromising political repression fuel discontent. The regime's main focus will be to ensure continued dominance beyond the 2010 presidential election. The government will press on with an ambitious economic-liberalisation programme, but a harsh global environment means the pace will be slower than intended.

To watch: Middle way. The belly-dancing world cup will be held at the Sinai resort of Taba Heights at the start of the year.

ETHIOPIA
GDP growth:	7.0%
GDP:	$31bn (PPP: $71bn)
Inflation:	15.0%
Population:	87.0m
GDP per head:	$350 (PPP: $810)

The Ethiopian People's Revolutionary Democratic Front is firmly in power, but political tensions will rise as all parties plan for the next general election, due in 2010. Events in the Horn of Africa will dominate foreign policy. A border dispute with Eritrea will stay hot, and their proxy war in Somalia shows little sign of subsiding. Strong growth in services and agriculture will yield a healthy economic expansion of 7%. Donor financing is likely to be scaled up after post-election violence in 2005 led to a temporary downturn in flows.

IRAN
GDP growth:	3.8%
GDP:	$387bn (PPP: $902bn)
Inflation:	25.0%
Population:	72.9m
GDP per head:	$5,310 (PPP: $12,370)

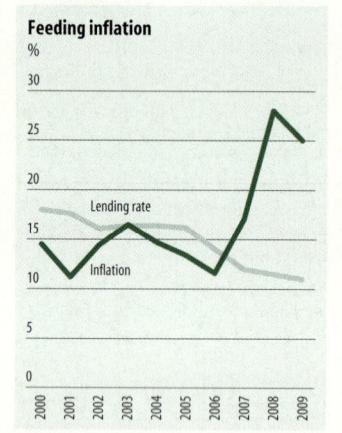

Feeding inflation
%
- Lending rate
- Inflation

Mahmoud Ahmadinejad's populism will serve him well when (health permitting) he seeks re-election as president in June. So will the backing of the supreme religious leader, Ayatollah Ali Khamenei. Mr Ahmadinejad's sometimes bizarre economic policies and their perverse impact on prices will work against him, and government spending will continue to rise. The threat of international oil sanctions will scare off many foreign oil companies. Economic growth will slip to 3.8% as global oil prices fall.

To watch. Mighty atom. The nuclear programme will make relentless progress despite intense diplomatic pressure, creating more tension in the region.

IRAQ
GDP growth:	6.7%
GDP:	$92bn (PPP: $125bn)
Inflation:	5.4%
Population:	29.9m
GDP per head:	$3,090 (PPP: $4,200)

The year promises a virtuous cycle in which improving security allows greater economic stability, boosting the government to the detriment of the militias. Iraq's armed forces will assume a greater combat role, leaving a diminishing but still substantial American troop presence to keep the peace. The prime minister, Nuri al-Maliki, has gained support by facing down the belligerent Shia militias, but Sunni groups remain aloof. Inflation will fall to 5.4% from over 30% in 2007; fiscal spending will rise sharply, but the budget will stay in surplus.

To watch: Breaking away. Fears of outright civil war are fading, but tribal, ethnic and sectarian interests will clash and a bid for secession by the Kurdistan regional government should not be ruled out.

ISRAEL
GDP growth:	2.7%
GDP:	$209bn (PPP: $215bn)
Inflation:	3.2%
Population:	7.4m
GDP per head:	$28,120 (PPP: $28,940)

Tzipi Livni's victory in the ruling Kadima party's leadership election will not heal divisions in the government, and elections are likely early in the year. The right-wing Likud party under a former prime minister, Binyamin Netanyahu, is best placed to lead a new coalition government, but it will be little stronger than its predecessor. A weak government and the lack of unity in the Palestinian Territories will stymie progress in the Israeli-Palestinian conflict. The face-off with Iran over the Islamic state's nuclear programme will smoulder, but may not ignite.

Economic liberalisation will advance, but at a slower pace. Export diversification will help the economy weather the global downturn, but growth will nonetheless slow to 2.7%.

JORDAN
GDP growth:	4.0%
GDP:	$21bn (PPP: $32bn)
Inflation:	3.6%
Population:	6.3m
GDP per head:	$3,320 (PPP: $5,070)

Inflation, which soared to nearly 15% in 2008, causing much discontent, will decline to around 4%, easing pressure on the king, Abdullah II, and his government. The Islamic Action Front, the main opposition force in parliament, suffers from internal divisions and will pose no political threat, though sporadic violence by Islamist interests outside politics will rumble on. A weaker global economy will limit the scope for market-based reforms, but growth should be helped by an ongoing stream of infrastructure projects.

WE LOVE THE NEW KNOWLEDGE.

**LEADING REGION IN EUROPE
NORTH RHINE-WESTPHALIA**

▶ Even robots are being taught in North Rhine-Westphalia. Maha Salem and Stefan Krüger are working at the Bielefeld University with scientists from all around the world on the interaction between people and robots. For further information about North Rhine-Westphalia as a location visit www.welovethenew.com

NRW INVEST GERMANY

All this space and nowhere to hide.

Set in over 150 acres of English parkland – just a half hour journey from London – Ashridge has all the space you'll need to prepare for future leadership.

Yet, for a world-class business school, we offer a surprisingly intimate learning experience.
In a class of just 30 people, you can expect high levels of personal participation and individual attention from your tutors. There's nowhere to hide.

RECRUITING NOW for our next intake:
The One-year Full Time MBA – starts January
The Two-year Executive MBA – starts September.

Contact us to experience the 'MBA in a Day' at Ashridge or meet us in venues internationally.

ASHRIDGE

**The Ashridge MBA.
It's personal.**

call: +44 (0)1442 841483 | visit: www.ashridge.org.uk/mba-economist | email: mba@ashridge.org.uk

Registered as Ashridge (Bonar Law) Memorial Trust. Charity number 311096.

KENYA

GDP growth:	3.5%
GDP:	$35bn (PPP: $67bn)
Inflation:	7.0%
Population:	39.6m
GDP per head:	$880 (PPP: $1,700)

By keeping his friends close but his enemies closer, the president, Mwai Kibaki of the Party of National Unity, has drawn the sting of his main rival, the prime minister, Raila Odinga of the Orange Democratic Movement. This has pulled Kenya back from the brink of renewed violence after the disputed election. Still, hostilities could yet resume. Improved political stability should allow for respectable economic growth, and inflation will be tamed as commodities come off the boil.

LEBANON

GDP growth:	3.1%
GDP:	$28bn (PPP: $46bn)
Inflation:	6.0%
Population:	4.2m
GDP per head:	$6,570 (PPP: $10,980)

The national-unity government will focus on keeping a lid on tensions between pro-Western and pro-Syrian factions until parliamentary elections scheduled for mid-year. The election result is uncertain, and the losing side may in any case refuse to abide by it. Sectarian grievances will smoulder and communities will rearm. The potential for political stalemate and renewed violent flare-ups will be high. Economic reform will be put on the back burner.

LIBYA

GDP growth:	6.9%
GDP:	$62bn (PPP: $112bn)
Inflation:	9.6%
Population:	6.4m
GDP per head:	$9,720 (PPP: $17,500)

Frustrated by the country's failure to reap a dividend from restored ties with the West, the national leader, Colonel Muammar Qaddafi, may go through with plans to abolish most government agencies at the start of the year and

Volatile prices
Inflation, %

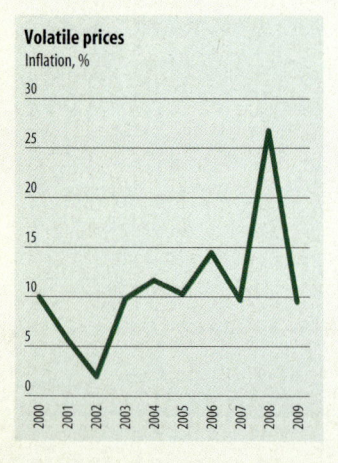

distribute oil revenue directly to the people. The justice, defence, foreign and interior ministries will survive, but everything else would be handed over to local structures. Rising oil output and inflows of foreign investment will support growth, sustaining the current-account surplus at a heady 44% of GDP.

MOROCCO

GDP growth:	4.5%
GDP:	$94bn (PPP: $150bn)
Inflation:	3.2%
Population:	31.9m
GDP per head:	$2,930 (PPP: $4,710)

The stability of the political system, in which King Mohammed VI enjoys loyal support from many political parties, is also a source of potential discontent, with outlets for alternative views sharply limited. As global economic conditions weigh on local living standards, disaffection will rise. In this atmosphere, Islamist groups outside the formal political system will find it easier to win recruits, and the sporadic campaign of amateurish armed militancy may become more threatening. Government spending to reduce poverty, partly intended to address this threat, will be constrained by the cost of an onerous price-subsidies system.

NIGERIA

GDP growth:	5.6%
GDP:	$184bn (PPP: $303bn)
Inflation:	10.0%
Population:	152.2m
GDP per head:	$1,260 (PPP: $2,060)

Rising production from offshore oil reserves will offset the effects of violence on output from the Niger delta. With non-oil sectors also showing some growth, the economy will expand by 5.6%. President Umaru Yar'Adua will face rising criticism from an opposition emboldened by its success in forcing re-runs of some of the 2007 legislative contests, by the slow pace of government reform, and by the government's difficulties in quelling violence in the delta. But his position looks secure.

To watch: Bank tellers. Monitors from the central bank will be posted at each of the country's leading banks to watch for excessive risk-taking during an aggressive drive for market share.

SAUDI ARABIA

GDP growth:	3.3%
GDP:	$393bn (PPP: $648bn)
Inflation:	10.3%
Population:	25.8m
GDP per head:	$15,230 (PPP: $25,130)

Economic and social liberalisation will creep forward in 2009, but at a pace defined by the overriding priority of King Abdullah and the Al Saud family:

Black economy
Oil and oil products exports, % of total

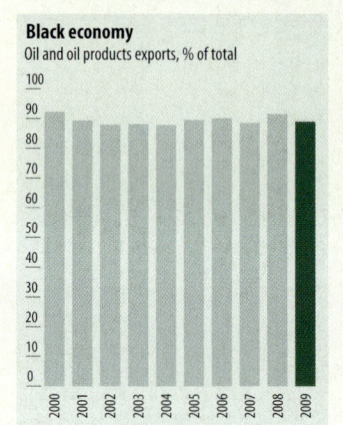

staying in control. The massive budget surplus will shrink as global prices fall, as revenue is hit by the rising investment needs of the state oil company, Saudi Aramco, and as spending climbs for social projects and public-sector wage increases.

To watch. Off the peg. There is an outside chance that the central bank will revalue the riyal, pegged at SR3.745:$1 since 1986. Gulf Co-operation Council plans for monetary union will require a revaluation at some point, and it would help ease inflationary pressures. But the central bank will not take lightly a measure that could undermine its hard-won credibility.

SOUTH AFRICA

GDP growth:	2.7%
GDP:	$282bn (PPP: $529bn)
Inflation:	7.3%
Population:	48.0m
GDP per head:	$5,870 (PPP: $11,010)

Kgalema Motlanthe, the deputy leader of the African National Congress, replaced Thabo Mbeki as president in September, but this is an interim move; Jacob Zuma, current head of the ANC, will take over the reins at the April general election. The economic focus will remain firmly on boosting growth and investment to create jobs and reduce inequality, with infrastructure projects, especially

2009 IN PERSON

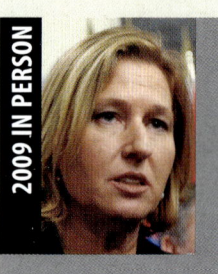

On succeeding Ehud Olmert as leader of the Kadima party in September 2008, the first task for *Tzipi Livni* was to try to form a stable government out of the disparate interests that make up the ruling coalition. When that failed, snap elections were on the cards for early 2009, after which she will hope to get a second go. There's no guarantee she can find a way to power, but if she does become the country's first female prime minister since Golda Meir she could be the person to give a shot of adrenalin to the moribund peace process. A former Mossad agent and brought up by militant Zionist parents, she has conservative credentials that give her credibility as a negotiator. She is also a pragmatist, and has worked hard in recent years in favour of a two-state solution to the Israeli-Palestinian conflict. But before tackling the Palestinians she must make peace within Israel's own tribal politics, and right now that looks just as tough a challenge.

for electricity, an important element. Economic growth will slow to 2.7%, reflecting power-supply shortages, high interest rates and a weak global economy.

TANZANIA

GDP growth:	6.9%
GDP:	$19bn (PPP: $51bn)
Inflation:	7.7%
Population:	41.1m
GDP per head:	$460 (PPP: $1,240)

President Jakaya Kikwete's government will press on with market-oriented economic reforms designed to boost private-sector growth, largely by building new infrastructure and addressing some of the weaknesses of the legal system. This drive, like a high-profile campaign against corruption, will deliver only gradual and limited results. Nevertheless, the economy will steam ahead, with growth just short of the 2008 figure of 7.1%. Construction, tourism and mining are expected to perform well. The current-account deficit will decline, but only to 11.6% of GDP and only thanks to donor funding.

ZIMBABWE

GDP growth:	-4.4%
GDP:	$1.5bn (PPP: $2.1bn)
Inflation:	NA
Population:	13.3m
GDP per head:	$110 (PPP: $160)

A power-sharing deal in late 2008 between the president, Robert Mugabe, and the opposition leader and now prime minister, Morgan Tsvangirai, holds out a wobbly promise of some improvement in political stability. If the unity government survives, it will allow the resumption of international aid flows and may begin to address the egregious problems facing the shattered economy, including hyperinflation, which exceeded 11m% in mid-2008 (and is now almost beyond forecasting). But real improvement in the daily lives of the long-suffering population will be hard to spot.

The world in figures: Industries

Automotive 123
Consumer goods 123
Defence 123
E-commerce 124
Energy 124
Entertainment 124
Financial services 124
Food and farming 125
Health care 125
Information technology 125
Media 125
Property and construction 126
Raw materials 126
Telecoms 126
Travel and tourism 126

For an interactive version of these pages, go to:
www.economist.com/theworldin

BUSINESS ENVIRONMENT

The Economist Intelligence Unit expects most of the developed world to be in recession in 2009. The global economy will grow by 2.6% (on a purchasing-power parity, or PPP, basis), the slowest pace since 2002. The big industrialised countries will expand by a mere 0.3% in 2009, while developing-world growth will slip to 5.9%, a full percentage point lower than in 2008.

World trade will increase by 3% in 2009, a third of the rate in 2006. Trade growth in emerging markets will be healthier, at 8-9%, but this is not entirely good news: emerging Asia's openness to trade will leave it exposed to the downturn in the wealthier countries. Central and eastern Europe will be hurt by a lacklustre euro zone and Latin America will feel some of the pain from the downturn in the United States.

Weaker global demand will push commodity prices lower, including oil. As China and India slow infrastructure spending, sub-Saharan Africa's miners will feel the pain.

The US and European central banks will cut interest rates as economies slide and inflation recedes. With more than half a trillion dollars of assets already written off by global banks, a return to normal credit conditions remains far away.

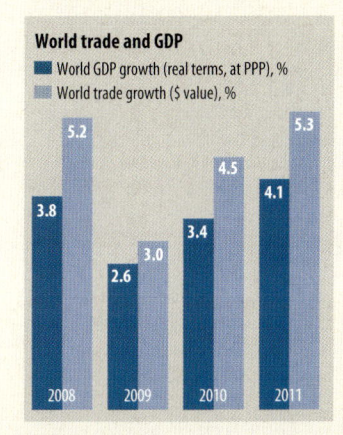

World trade and GDP
- World GDP growth (real terms, at PPP), %
- World trade growth ($ value), %

Year	GDP	Trade
2008	3.8	5.2
2009	2.6	3.0
2010	3.4	4.5
2011	4.1	5.3

2009 forecasts unless otherwise indicated. World totals based on 51 countries accounting for over 95% of world GDP.

Source: **Economist Intelligence Unit**
london@eiu.com

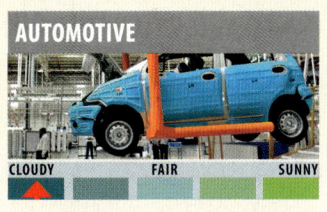

AUTOMOTIVE
CLOUDY – FAIR – SUNNY

The outlook for cars in 2009 depends on which part of the world you examine. Sales in the US, Europe and Japan will stagnate or shrink, but demand in emerging markets will still advance. China, which recently overtook Japan as the world's second-largest car market, will record 8-9% growth in car sales, markedly lower than in recent years. India and Russia, two other emerging car giants, will expand at nearly the same rate as China.

Passenger-car registrations, m

Asia and Australasia	16.4
North America	13.5
Western Europe	13.5
China	6.7
Eastern Europe and Russia	6.0
Latin America	4.7
Japan	4.2
Middle East and north Africa	1.6

The US car market will remain in meltdown, a reflection of the poor state of the economy. Ford, General Motors and Chrysler will find things tough, having failed to meet demand for fuel-efficient cars in the face of high oil prices. Despite its travails, the US will remain the world's largest passenger-car market, accounting for around one-quarter of total sales in 2009.

Chinese and Indian manufacturers will increase production rapidly, adding to global oversupply and denting profit margins all round. This will lead to more reorganisation as companies seek to share costs and increase critical mass. America's Chrysler, for example, may strike a deal with Fiat, with the aim of leasing manufacturing capacity to the Italian company. Nissan, Japan's second-largest carmaker, may join its partner, France's Renault, in the tie-up Renault agreed with Russia's AvtoVAZ.

Going the other way, General Motors may shed both Saab (Sweden) and its iconic gas guzzler, the Hummer. Ford may dispose of Volvo. Wherever they are, manufacturers will develop more energy-efficient cars, particularly the diesel variety, thanks partly to the advent of cleaner diesel fuel.

To watch: Air cars. New York-based Zero Pollution Motors and India's Tata Motors are close to marketing the first Air Car. The engine mimics old locomotives, except that compressed air, not steam, moves the engine's pistons. The car will be glued, not welded, and can cover 800 miles between charges.

CONSUMER GOODS
CLOUDY – FAIR – SUNNY

With America's economy in the doldrums and emerging-market growth less buoyant, bargain hunting will hit new heights in 2009. Global consumer spending will increase by only 2%, lifted by demand in developing countries. In the rich world, retailers will suffer as consumers—though prepared to pay a premium for the occasional high-quality brand—flock to cheaper own-make and cut-price products. Discount stores will remain hot properties in mature markets.

As the high price of fuel makes online shopping in the United States more appealing than a trip to the mall, the shopping-centre format will find new life in emerging markets. France's Carrefour and American giant Wal-Mart will continue to increase the number of big stores in China in 2009, increasing their focus on smaller cities. In India, Wal-Mart, which has joined hands with Bharti Group, will open the first of a line of stores in March. The world's third-largest retailer, UK-based Tesco, will open its first cash-and-carry in India, part of an ambitious five-year investment plan.

In Russia, OAO Magnit, the country's second-largest supermarket chain, plans to continue opening a store a day in its home market. Given strong wage growth in recent years, sales of food, drink and tobacco in Russia will jump by nearly 18% in 2009.

In the developed world, consumer spending on electrical gadgets, which has grown well over the past few years, may ebb in 2009 as jobs disappear and wages grow at less than the rate of inflation.

Not all will be doom and gloom, however. Manufacturers of pricier Blu-ray Discs (BDs) and BD players, which can create cinema-quality entertainment at home, will see sales take off. As demand gradually eases, the price of BDs will slide. Sales of the longer-playing format will overtake conventional DVDs by 2011.

To watch: Edible optics. Scientists at Tufts University in the US have come up with a way to stamp a colour-changing hologram pattern on an edible membrane of pure silk. Uses will range from environmentally friendly sensors for contaminants in packaged food to edible silk underwear.

DEFENCE
CLOUDY – FAIR – SUNNY

Despite Russia's continued military build-up and growing adventurism, it is unlikely ever to match the might of the United States, which still accounts for 48% of global defence spending, according to the International Institute for Strategic Studies. The US Congress has been asked to spend at least $607bn on defence in the 2009 fiscal year. That includes the Defence Department's baseline budget of $515.4bn—an increase of nearly 74% since President George Bush took office—as well as $21bn for the Energy Department's nuclear-weapons programmes and at least $70bn for Iraq and Afghanistan.

Bucking the general trend, Taiwan will scale back its military spending by just over 3% in 2009, as relations with China improve. At NT$315.2bn ($10bn), defence will still account for a massive 17.2% of the government's budget. But opposition parliamentarians fear the island is sending the wrong message to allies like the United States and Japan about its determination to defend itself.

China's true spending on defence will

Industries The world in figures

THE WORLD IN 2009 — Economist Intelligence Unit

2009 IN FOCUS

Russia's military budget is expected to rise to Rb1.3trn ($53bn) in 2009, a jump of some 23%. In addition to procuring more advanced weapons, such as T-90 battle tanks and Iskander missiles, and boosting its S-400 air-defence system, there are plans to raise troop wages. Overall, Russia plans to cut its defence payroll from 1.13m troops to 1m by 2013, mainly by increasing its reliance on hardware and reducing the overall number of non-combat positions. Paying soldiers more will be key to honing the country's conscript army into a more professional force.

remain a closely guarded secret—but will probably be about one-sixth that of the United States.

Despite a narrow vote by Israel's cabinet to postpone earlier budget allocations for increased spending on defence, the armed forces will nevertheless receive an additional NIS900m ($251m) in 2009 and NIS1.03bn in 2010. Some of the funds will be used for internal security and welfare programmes.

To watch: Iran. Although Iran's economy is the same size as that of the US state of Connecticut, and its military budget is comparable to Sweden's, its nuclear programme will remain a political flashpoint. US intelligence fears Russia will supply its advanced S-300 anti-aircraft-missile system to Iran if America pushes NATO membership for Georgia and Ukraine. The system can reportedly track up to 100 targets while engaging 12 at the same time.

E-COMMERCE

CLOUDY | FAIR | SUNNY

Almost a quarter of the world's population—1.5bn people—will use the internet regularly in 2009. Half of them will make online purchases. A further 400m people will join the online world by 2012. By then, over 1 billion people will buy things over the web, contributing to a global business-to-consumer (B2C) market worth $1.2trn.

Broadband subscriber lines
per 100 people

Western Europe 29.5
North America 27.9
Japan 26.7
Eastern Europe and Russia 9.2
Latin America 6.7
Asia and Australasia 5.7
Middle East and north Africa 2.2
World 9.2

Business-to-business (B2B) e-commerce by then will be just as mainstream and worth ten times as much.

While the number of devices with internet connections will double to 3bn over the next few years, the real shift will be in the way users access the web—by smartphone and other portable devices, rather than by personal computers, according to IDC, a consultancy. In 2009, 600m people will have mobile internet access, twice as many as in 2006.

Online retailing will continue to grow, but not as quickly as offline purchases based on web research. eMarketer reckons web-influenced store sales in the US will grow by 19% to $667bn in 2009, while retail e-commerce will expand by 12% to $170.6bn. Combined, the two will account for 28% of all retail sales by 2012.

To watch: Mind games. San Francisco-based Emotiv Systems, developer of a headset that allows gamers to control play with their thoughts, has linked up with IBM to explore web-based business applications, such as training, design or sophisticated simulations.

ENERGY

CLOUDY | FAIR | SUNNY

Demand for oil in the rich world will fall in 2009 by around 1% because of elevated prices and slowing economic growth. Oil prices will average around $75 a barrel for Brent crude. The growth of oil demand in emerging markets will slow to 3.1%, with total global consumption edging up by only 0.7%. For suppliers, the picture will be far from bleak. OPEC's capacity cushion will double to as much as 3.6m barrels a day and, outside OPEC, oil production will improve as Brazil, Azerbaijan and the US all boost capacity.

Coal's share in global energy will continue to climb because of its relative cheapness and abundance, especially in the two largest coal-producing/consuming countries, the US and China.

In the US, more coal-fired than gas-fired power plants will come on stream in the next two years. Globally, demand for coal will rise by 4.6% in 2009 to 6.8bn tonnes; this trend will gather speed as countries with large reserves aim to reduce their dependence on oil imports.

Demand for natural gas will accelerate, led by India, the rest of Asia and the Middle East. Natural-gas substitution in electric power generation and heating is gathering pace. Among alternative energy sources, solar panels suffered in 2008 because the price of pure silicon, the main component of most solar cells, hit record levels. But UK-based New Energy Finance expects the output of silicon for the solar industry to double in 2009, leading to a 40% price drop.

To watch: Waste-based biofuels. British oil major BP has formed a partnership with a US biofuels start-up, Verenium, to speed the development of ethanol made from non-food sources, such as corn crop waste and the woody bits of sugarcane.

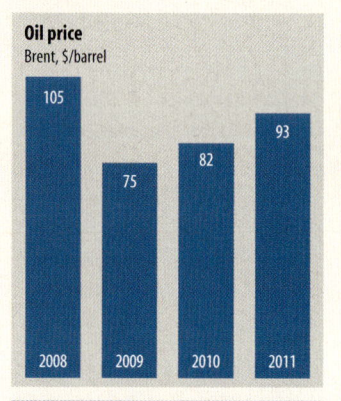

Oil price
Brent, $/barrel

2008: 105
2009: 75
2010: 82
2011: 93

ENTERTAINMENT

CLOUDY | FAIR | SUNNY

New multiplexes and digital cinemas will help Asia's box-office revenue grow at an average annual rate of 8.5% through 2012, reaching $10.4bn, according to PricewaterhouseCoopers. In the US, download-to-own movies streamed over the internet will rise 51.4% a year, to $900m in 2012. Casinos and gaming will be the fastest-growing entertainment segment in the Middle East and Africa, with revenue rising 12% annually over the next few years. But major resort developments in places like Macau will make Asia the biggest gaming and casino destination in the world.

Wireless-network upgrades and specialised handsets will propel mobile music spending, which will be worth $2.1bn in the Europe-Middle East-Africa market in 2012, says PwC. Rising broadband penetration in Asia will drive online gaming, particularly MMOGs (massively multimedia online gaming, which can support hundreds of thousands of players simultaneously). Across the region, online game revenue will increase at an annual rate of 13.3%, reaching $5.6bn in 2012.

Established Hollywood players such as Pixar Studios will face competition from new players. The first 3D animation design film made in Russia is set to be released in early 2009.

To watch: MOD DVDs. According to *Screen Digest*, by 2012 consumers in the US and Europe will spend $1.1bn buying DVDs "manufactured on demand". About two-thirds of this will be new spending by consumers downloading TV shows or events at home onto a disc; the rest will replace traditional DVD purchasing. Currently, most of the $33m custom DVD market is conducted through Amazon.com's CreateSpace unit, but in-store kiosks are set to proliferate.

FINANCIAL SERVICES

CLOUDY | FAIR | SUNNY

The global credit crunch will mark its second grim anniversary in August, when the worst of the crisis will be history. Still, after writing off more than half a trillion dollars in 2008, the financial sector will remain highly risk-averse and lending will be subdued. After a 7.2% increase in global lending in 2008, led by emerging markets, borrowing will be stagnant in 2009.

The entire structure of the financial-services industry is changing. Traditional investment banks proved vulnerable as Wall Street imploded in 2008. Fundamental financial techniques such as securitisation will be subject to new scrutiny. A substantial increase in government regulation is inevitable as taxpayers in the US and elsewhere are exposed to bail-outs worth hundreds of billions of dollars.

As economic growth sputters, a wider range of commercial banks in rich countries will suffer from costly credit and continuing losses, even with plans to inject cash into banks, guarantee bank debt and buy troubled assets. Banks will also confront much-reduced demand for many of their most complex, lucrative products and as a result will hold additional funds against loans they are no longer able to sell on in securitisation markets. M&A deal volumes will also be subdued, with the exception of bottom-fishing by more adventurous investors.

The world in figures Industries

2009 IN FOCUS

Rapid urbanisation and a growth in sedentary living are helping to drive **epidemics** in diabetes and cardiovascular complaints across Africa, the Middle East, Asia and Latin America. India, for example, will have more than 30m diabetes sufferers in 2009, the most of any country. That number is expected to more than double in the next 20 years. China, in a different illness, is estimated to have more than 100m hypertension sufferers, with 3m new cases expected each year.

As property markets stagnate or continue to fall in the developed world, foreclosures and home-loan defaults will persist. The US, UK, Spain and Ireland have suffered the most, and the pain is not over. Credit difficulties will spread beyond housing to car loans, commercial-property finance and general corporate credit in 2009 in those economies where growth is weakest.

To watch: Banking 2.0. Internet-based peer-to-peer lending will proliferate as consumers look for alternatives to the traditional banking model. Sites such as California-based Lending.com match lenders and borrowers directly via the internet. Sites that allow borrowers to auction their lending needs, eBay style, will also flourish.

FOOD AND FARMING

CLOUDY | FAIR | SUNNY

After surging in 2008, prices of basic foods such as rice, wheat and soybeans will slide. The Economist Intelligence Unit's food, feedstuffs and beverages index—up a colossal 30.2% in 2008—will plummet by 25% in 2009. Global consumption of wheat will inch up by 1% in 2009 to 450m tonnes. Ample crops from China, the US, Bulgaria, Romania and the former Soviet Union will offset weaker production in the Middle East, so supply will not be a problem. Subdued economic growth in eastern Europe and Russia will lead to lower growth in meat consumption and ease demand for animal feedstuffs. After years of increases, the prices of maize, wheat and soybeans will drop by about 25%.

Rice production will rise by 1.4% to 444.3m tonnes, according to the UN Food and Agriculture Organisation. After jumping an alarming 107% in 2008, rice prices will fall by 19% as export restrictions by some major suppliers—notably India and Egypt—remain.

Cocoa, tea and coffee prices will ease, although sugar prices will rise. The soaring cost of high-fructose corn syrup, a sugar substitute, has made it less competitive, sending food processors back to the traditional sweetener.

Despite widespread drought, Australian wine-grape production will increase by 6.7% in 2009 to 1.78m tonnes, according to the Australian Bureau of Agricultural and Resource Economics. As they did with twist-top bottles, exporters will shock European producers by increasingly replacing glass with plastic—lighter for picnics, and also cheaper on fuel for long-distance transport.

While millions will still go hungry in developing countries, consumers in wealthier nations will increasingly seek out foods that offer health benefits. The market for foods containing "nutraceuticals"—ingredients with human-health benefits beyond basic nutrition, ranging from herbal extracts to omega-3 sourced from fish oils—will boom. According to Cygnus, a consultancy, the global market for nutraceuticals will be worth nearly $140bn in 2009, an annual growth of 7%.

To watch: Edible packaging. To date, a polysaccharide such as starch has been the most commonly used material in edible packaging, but it has a drawback—it breaks down in water. But now a scientist at the University of Manitoba, Jung Han, claims that adding beeswax to starch from peas produces an edible material that can be spread into a water-resistant, plastic-like film. Depending on what it tastes like, the days of plastic packaging could be numbered.

HEALTH CARE

CLOUDY | FAIR | SUNNY

The average life expectancy of a woman in 2009 will be 75 years for the first time in history. Men will reach a life expectancy of 70 two years later. Recession or no, global health-care spending will expand in 2009 as longer-lived consumers place a premium on having the latest therapies or drugs.

In the developing world, the swelling ranks of the middle class will increase demand for pharmaceuticals, while rising government-provided benefits for the elderly will ensure continued growth

Pharmaceutical sales
$bn (manufacturers' sales)

- North America: 420.9
- Western Europe: 249.0
- Asia and Australasia: 145.2
- Japan: 67.5
- Latin America: 43.2
- Eastern Europe and Russia: 35.0
- World: 902.4

of the sector. Health-care spending per head will rise by 4.3% in 2009 and pharmaceutical spending by 7.2%. Total drug sales will be worth $1.2trn in 2012.

The explosion in the amount of chronic disease in the developing world will push down the cost per treatment. Annual spending for a single diabetes patient is around $10,000 in the US. Even if India spends one-tenth of that per patient, it will be faced with a staggering bill, for a single disease.

Although governments around the world have launched anti-obesity campaigns, they may have come too late. The World Health Organisation says 10% of children and 20% of adults in Europe and Central Asia will be obese by 2010 unless drastic action is taken.

To watch: Sniffing out cancer. Researchers from the University of Oklahoma are developing a device that aims to detect cancer at an early stage by analysing a patient's breath. The key will be a sensor with lasers that can detect specific marker gases.

INFORMATION TECHNOLOGY

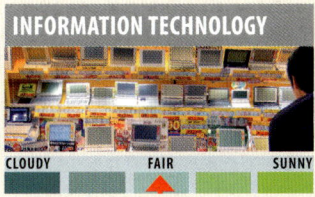

CLOUDY | FAIR | SUNNY

With the lessons of the dotcom crash still fresh, the IT industry is better placed to navigate tougher times. Given technology's role in productivity, cost

Personal computers
Stock per '000 people

- North America: 896
- Japan: 757
- Western Europe: 666
- Eastern Europe and Russia: 307
- Latin America: 240
- Asia and Australasia: 144
- Middle East and north Africa: 99
- World: 250

control and competitiveness, IT spending will outpace GDP growth in rich countries as well as developing ones.

According to the Economist Intelligence Unit, spending on hardware, software and services will edge up by around 3% in 2009. Although most of that growth will be in emerging markets, IT spending in western Europe will still continue to run ahead of GDP growth. The need for network security, sophisticated data-storage tools and mobile computing will spur growth as companies globally shift processes and transactions online, a process known as cloud computing.

Growth in the sales of personal computers will continue to slow in 2009, although demand will remain relatively strong in emerging markets. The falling cost of laptops and the growing availability of cheaper internet-enabled devices will help to fuel demand worldwide. As a result, laptops will outsell desktop computers for the first time in 2009.

With factories running at close to 90% of capacity, the global semiconductor industry will see stable prices in 2009, helped by demand for chip-heavy laptops, high-end TVs and satellite navigation systems.

Not to watch: Mobile-internet devices. Despite strong support from companies like Intel, tablet-sized computers will remain a non-starter as consumers upgrade to smartphones instead.

MEDIA

CLOUDY | FAIR | SUNNY

Much of the advertising world will have a hard 2009. Carat, part of the Aegis marketing empire and Europe's biggest media buyer, has lowered its forecasts for global advertising because of the slowdown in key markets, especially the US and western Europe. In the UK, Carat now expects advertising growth of 2.2%, half its original estimate. Worldwide, growth of 4.8% is expected.

Developing markets will pick up some of the slack, contributing 63% of ad-spending growth between 2007 and 2010; their overall global market share will rise to 33% from 27%, according to ZenithOptimedia. Asia Pacific will overtake western Europe in 2010 to become the second-largest advertising domain, while the BRIC countries will march up the international rankings. Between 2007 and 2010, China will rise to fourth from fifth, Russia to sixth from 11th, and Brazil to seventh from ninth.

Industries The world in figures

2009 IN FOCUS

On-demand digital programming systems—"personal TV"—will be up and running in 2010, ahead of an industry-wide shift between 2012 and 2018 when high-definition TV will also at last go mainstream with free-to-air channels. In 2009, film giants Viacom, Paramount, MGM and Lionsgate will join forces to launch a premium TV and video-on-demand service in the autumn. And, following its acquisition of Naviq, which works with big cable companies like Time Warner to provide targeted TV advertising, Microsoft aims to challenge Google's TV ads business.

Having broken through the 10% share barrier in 2008, global internet ad spend will be worth $64bn in 2009 and attract 13.6% of all advertising by 2010.

To watch: Multiple messages. Digital billboards, which show sequential ads that change every eight or so seconds, will proliferate in the US, from 500 to more than 500,000 over the next few years. It's easy to see why: digital displays can generate up to 20 times the revenue of a poster displaying a single ad.

PROPERTY AND CONSTRUCTION

The world's tallest skyscraper, the Burj Dubai, is due to open in September, soaring to more than 818 metres (2,684 feet). Work will also continue in Dubai on the 618 metres, 120-floor Pentonium, which will become the highest all-residential complex in the world when it opens in 2011. Projects such as the Russia Tower in Moscow, the Incheon Tower in South Korea and the Chicago Spire will set new standards in their regions by 2012.

Back on the ground, the situation will be rather more gloomy, as the credit crunch weighs on homeowners on both sides of the Atlantic—and increasingly in other rich countries. With companies finding it harder to secure debt-finance, commercial-property markets will suffer too, except in a few places such as the UAE, where the number of deals should hold steady.

In the US, home prices should stabilise in 2009 but will not rise much for another year. In a vicious circle, demand will be further constrained by a softening job market and tighter lending criteria.

Persimmon, Britain's largest homebuilder by market value, will run a leaner operation in 2009 after cutting more than a fifth of its 5,000-strong workforce, saving some £65m ($119m). Jeremy Helsby, chief executive of Savills, an upmarket estate agent listed on the London Stock Exchange, expects house prices to fall 25% from their peak by the end of 2009. Even the luxury end of the market—properties worth £5m or more—is not likely to remain immune.

The emerging markets will provide a few bright spots, though. In Brazil, for example, despite slower economic growth, demand for housing should hold up, either for first homes or for holiday homes in popular resorts.

To watch: Aquaculture. Architect-designed floating homes are already popular in the water-savvy Netherlands, but Frits Schoute, a former Delft University professor, is developing a stabilising platform-and-barrier system to allow communities to live in the middle of oceans, unaffected by waves. He expects people to start living on such platforms by 2020.

RAW MATERIALS

Base-metal prices will fall in 2009 as the economic downturn in the richer countries slows the construction and transport sectors that are so important to miners. Metals producers will be doubly vulnerable as resource-hungry Asian and Middle Eastern economies slow. Only gold producers will have a reason to smile in 2009, as prices will remain at near-record levels.

With less call for steel, the price of iron ore is expected to drop in 2009 by more than 50% to $0.65 per dry tonne unit.

EIU's industrial raw-materials index
% change in $ prices
— Rubber — Fibres — Metals — Industrial raw materials
2008 2009 2010 2011 2012

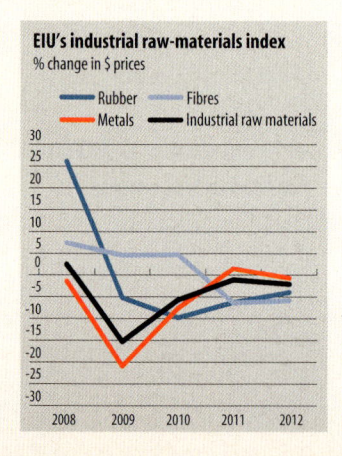

Disruptions to supply, such as power outages in African and Chilean mines, will not prevent aluminium and copper prices from falling. Prices will still contract by 25% and 19% respectively.

The fall in oil prices will once again make synthetic rubber more attractive than the natural product for manufacturers of items like shoe soles.

Reduced cotton plantings in the US, Latin America and Australia—as farmers switch to grains—and sustained demand from Chinese textile-makers will make cotton one of the few commodities to see a solid price increase in 2009.

To watch: Mars. Its red hue is due to a high iron oxide content in the soil, and there is speculation that asteroid-impact sites could yield rich deposits of copper, nickel and other metals. Florida-based 4Frontiers is working on a prototype of what it believes a colony on Mars would look like, but it will be 2025 before Martian mining could take off.

TELECOMS

From the world's poorest countries to the very richest, the demand for mobile phones will not be derailed by tougher economic times. Globally, subscriptions will swell by 8%, bringing the total to some 4bn worldwide. In the developed world growth will be spurred by the need to upgrade to ever more powerful, internet-enabled phones, while in emerging economies heavy investment in network infrastructure will mean that virtually anyone, just about anywhere, will be able to get reception.

In recession-hit economies, however, customers will delay their upgrades and cut back on pricier usage plans. Falling revenue will hit the big telecoms companies in slower-growth economies. But cash-rich telecoms groups in emerging markets will be increasingly well-placed to expand into Europe or the US.

In Kuwait, for example, Zain has made no secret of its wish to join the top ten telecoms companies worldwide by 2011. Other ambitious players include STC of Saudi Arabia, Egypt's Orascom and Qatar Telecom. Flush with cash from years of monopoly status, these companies are facing domestic competition for the first time and are eager to expand internationally.

To watch: Self-powered phones. An Idaho-based start-up, M2E Power, is developing a device based on a lithium ion battery and a series of coils and magnets that can generate small amounts of electricity for devices such as mobile phones when they are in motion.

Mobile-phone subscriptions
per 100 people
- Eastern Europe and Russia 132
- Western Europe 129
- North America 92
- Japan 91
- Latin America 79
- Middle East and north Africa 67
- Asia and Australasia 48
- World 66

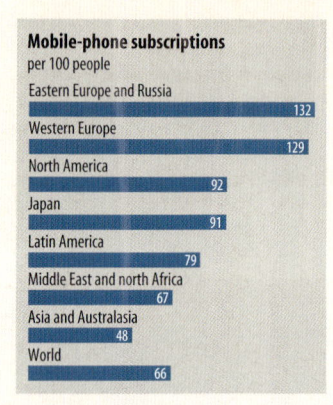

TRAVEL AND TOURISM

The global travel and tourism business will post its sixth consecutive year of growth in 2009, but only just. High energy prices, climbing air fares and a slowdown in consumer spending in the US and Europe will take their toll. Global tourist arrivals will rise by only 2.7% and spending on hotels and restaurants will grow by 3.8%.

Old-world charm will ensure that France remains the world's most popular destination for tourists in 2009, with around 83m visitors. For the first time, China will rank as the world's second-favourite destination, with 65m visitors, pushing Spain into third place with 62m. The United States will hold on to fourth place with around 57m. In spending terms, America will easily outstrip its rivals, collecting nearly $110bn in international tourism receipts in 2009, compared with Spain's $71.2bn and China's $68bn. Germany will continue to export the most globe-trotters, followed by the US and the UK.

Airlines will struggle in 2009. The International Air Transport Association predicts $4.1bn in losses, most of this from US airlines. Asian-based carriers and budget hotels will thrive.

To watch: Air taxis. The US National Aeronautics and Space Administration is designing a four- to eight-seater passenger jet that can be operated without a pilot's licence and will be affordable for small businesses or rich individuals. Computer-display technology will enable landings in low visibility on badly lit landing strips at small airports.

How can we meet consumer demands as fast as they arise?

The Siemens answer: Digital engineering for more flexibility and lower costs.

What businesses need today is the ability to react to market needs – quickly and flexibly. We are the only company worldwide providing products and solutions that cover the whole product lifecycle: from virtual product design and development right through to manufacturing. This saves valuable time and makes products more affordable. www.siemens.com/answers

Answers for industry.

SIEMENS

"I could see we had won the account before he even started speaking…"

POLYCOM®
Telepresense

Find out how to hone your business perceptions, visit:
www.polycom.com/go/telepresence/UK

Business

Also in this section:
India's middle-class consumers 130
Prosperous brands 132
Lakshmi Mittal:
A new economic order 134
Retailers sniff out business 135
Barbie turns 50 135
China's globetrotting tourists 136
Managing a career change 137
All change in health care 138
The year of the CFO 140
Farming after a food crisis 142
Jeff Immelt: Time to
re-embrace globalisation 144

No more business as usual

Matthew Bishop NEW YORK

Now for the corporate crunch

Hopes were high at the start of 2008 that the effects of the credit crunch would largely be contained within the global financial system, and that non-financial firms would be able to carry on regardless, expanding sales and piling up record profits. Nobody is expecting business as usual in 2009: for many firms, the top priority will be survival, while for others a tougher economic environment will provide unexpected opportunities.

In uncertain times, cash is king, and those (mostly mature) firms that have fat margins and strong cash flow will have a definite edge over firms that are in critical phases of their investment cycle, especially start-ups that are burning rather than breeding cash. Many firms will slash discretionary spending, and scale back growth plans to conserve cash until they get a clearer sense of the economic outlook. Before the market panic of October 2008, the OECD predicted that business investment in the leading economies would slump through the first half of 2009, rebounding a bit in the second half, but to a much lower growth rate than had been the norm until recently (see chart). And that rebound scenario assumes a relatively mild recession—a forecast that now looks optimistic. There will be a surge in cost-cutting outsourcing, especially to low-cost providers in emerging markets.

Among firms that are not generating much cash, some will fare much better than others because they took advantage of the loose credit markets before they abruptly froze in summer 2007 to lock in credit lines on favourable terms. Many companies will find themselves close to death; having debt that is "covenant lite" or has a "toggle" that allows them automatically to add interest to the loan amount outstanding rather than pay it may be what keeps some alive. Bankruptcies have already started to rise, not only in America, and market prices in the autumn of 2008 suggested investors were expecting default rates on high-yield American corporate bonds that were last seen in the recessions of 1991 and 2002—around 12% of all bond issues, up from an actual rate of 3.4% in the 12 months to September 2008.

Many of those bankruptcies will be in industries exposed to rich-world consumers, who will splash cash less freely—if only because creditors won't let them. Yet even within those consumer-oriented sectors, some firms will do better than others, especially if they provide value for money. Restaurants, bars and cinemas may suffer as people opt to stay at home with a DVD and a six-pack. That will be good news for Chinese takeaways.

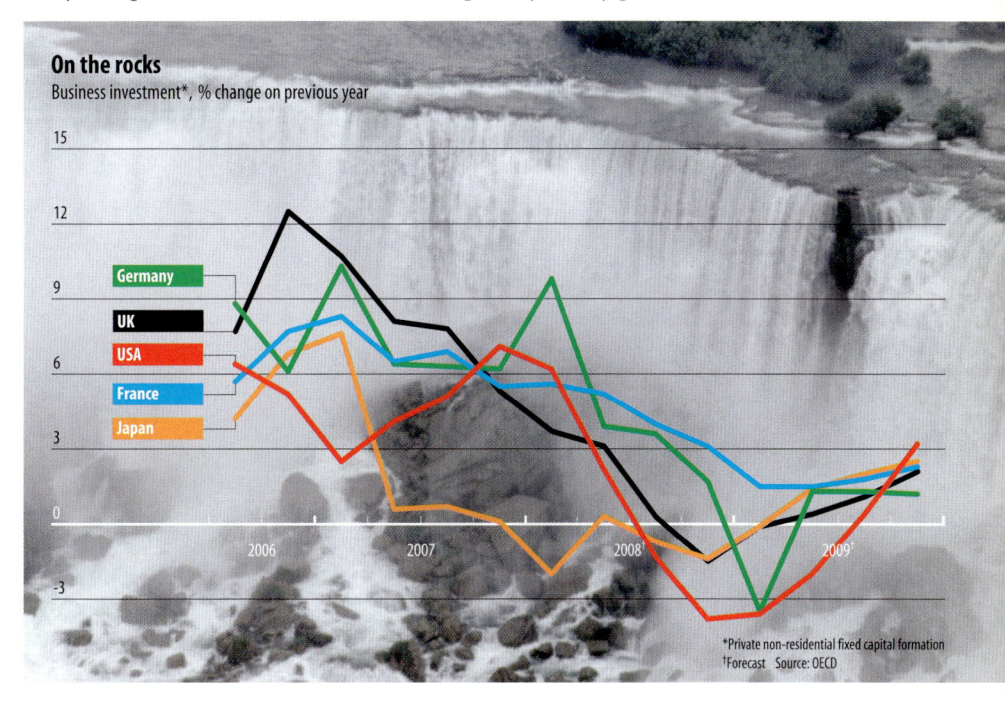

When the credit crunch first started to slow growth in the developed economies, leading firms said they would simply accelerate their growth plans in emerging markets, where demand was still growing fast, as the "next billion" consumers started to earn incomes with which they could afford higher-value branded goods. Now, the idea that emerging economies had "decoupled", and would continue to boom even as the economies of America and other rich countries grapple with recession, has been exposed as fanciful.

So multinationals will have some tough decisions to make about these growth plans. Those, such as General Electric and Cisco, betting on an infrastructure boom in the emerging markets are likely to have more reason to stick to their guns, given the relatively strong fiscal positions of many emerging-country governments, than

In uncertain times, cash is king

On the rocks
Business investment*, % change on previous year

Germany, UK, USA, France, Japan

*Private non-residential fixed capital formation
†Forecast Source: OECD

2009 IN BRIEF
Saudi Aramco brings **new oil fields** onstream, boosting Saudi Arabia's production capacity to 12.5m barrels a day.

Matthew Bishop: American business editor, *The Economist*; co-author of "Philanthrocapitalism: How the Rich Can Save the World" (Bloomsbury)

To have and to hold

Simon Cox DELHI

India's middle-class aspirations will give way to anxiety in 2009

In the recent Bollywood film, "Saas Bahu aur Sensex", a divorcee, recently arrived in Mumbai, raises eyebrows when she steals away from the parties and television soap operas that occupy middle-class wives to consort with an unknown gentleman. The man, it turns out, is her new stockbroker, who initiates her into the mysteries of the Bombay Stock Exchange.

The film closes with couples paired off and the Sensex (India's best-known share-price index) crossing 30,000. The real stockmarket, alas, did not stick to this script. The Sensex peaked at 21,206 in January 2008 and lost a third of its value by the time the film opened in September.

In those nine months, India's triumphant middle class lost a bit of its swagger. In June, the price of liquefied petroleum gas, which fires middle-class stoves, was raised by 16%. In August, car sales fell for the second month in a row. Banks have become warier of prospective borrowers, and depositors have become warier of their banks.

In decades past, India's middle class craved security. Their most coveted station in life was a government job, which epitomised their "status quoist mindset", as Rama Bijapurkar puts it in her book, "We Are Like That Only". Cocooned in a shady bungalow and a closed economy, the middle class was shielded from the glare and dazzle of unbridled capitalism.

In the past 15 years, however, a new middle class has superseded the old. These people are driven by aspiration, not anxiety. They are, says Ms Bijapurkar, "in a hurry", busy acquiring the accoutrements of prosperity. Economists and marketers struggle to define them. But they define themselves by what they own: from watches to air conditioners.

The new middle class are more willing to borrow than their cautious predecessors. Debt no longer carries a stigma. It is a statement of confidence in one's ability to repay, not a sign of intemperance. In India's cities, housing and consumer debt grew by over 40% a year on average from 2001 to 2006.

In July 2007 A.C. Nielsen, a market-research firm, carried out a survey of consumers in 46 countries. India's were the most confident of the lot. A year later, their spirits had flagged a little. But they were still more optimistic than anyone bar the Norwegians.

Common Sensex

And yet their position is precarious. Unlike the Norwegians, they cannot count on the dole if they lose their job or a state pension when they retire. Only 12% of India's workers have any formal provision for retirement. For many Indians, family is the closest thing to social security.

As a consequence, Indian households save a lot. In the year to March 2007, they set aside almost 24% of GDP. Without that thrift, India could not have mustered the astonishing rates of investment that underpinned its remarkable rate of economic growth in the past five years.

Indeed, in 2009 the economy will become more reliant than ever on household thrift. In a slowing economy, companies will not be able to count on retained earnings to finance their investment plans. The government will also need bankrolling as it adds to its growing pool of red ink, including a salary hike for civil servants, fuel and fertiliser subsidies, as well as a loan write-off for farmers.

India's households save a lot, but they do not necessarily save well. They put more than half of their saving in physical assets, such as property or gold, rather than in the financial system, which in normal times could make it work harder. India's financial industry needs to compete harder for funds against the stuffed mattress and the gold necklace. Insurers are enjoying some success. In the year to March 2008, life insurers issued almost 51m policies, annuities and pensions. They underwrote premiums of $38.40 per head in 2006, compared with only $9.90 in 2000. Even so, this pales in comparison with China, where the 2006 figure was $53.50.

If the Indian economy is to thrive, it needs to harness middle-class saving as well as consumption. That may mean flogging fewer microwaves and air conditioners in 2009 and beyond, and more pension plans and mutual funds. It will be a long film. But that is the only hope of the Sensex surpassing 30,000 by the end. ■

Simon Cox: South Asia business correspondent, *The Economist*

---

those betting on the emergence of middle-class consumers (see box). Equally, in the rich world, infrastructure firms may find themselves better-placed than they expected, if governments try to revive their economies by investing in rebuilding their crumbling roads and sewers—assuming governments have any money left after bailing out the banking system.

Another tough question will be what to do about those costly corporate-citizenship commitments that big firms have made in recent years. These commitments—such as Coca-Cola's investments in water projects in developing countries—have lately been justified as a core part of long-term profit-maximising strategy. The coming year will test whether they really believe that.

One final opportunity will be for companies with cash to acquire weaker rivals. Helpfully, there is unlikely to be any quick return of the debt-fuelled private-equity buyers that drove prices too high for ordinary companies to make strategic acquisitions. Indeed, private-equity firms may be willing sellers as they struggle to deal with a growing number of troubled firms in their portfolio that they have burdened with far too much debt.

The mood in many boardrooms will be defensive, but 2009 will offer opportunity for some firms that take bold contrarian bets. It is often in tough times that the greatest fortunes are made. To the brave, the spoils. ■

2009 IN BRIEF
Google's **search revenues** overtake Microsoft's revenues from Windows.

www.qfc.com.qa

Issued by Qatar Financial Centre Authority

The world's largest

With its wealth of proven natural gas reserves and the investment of $15bn in new carriers, the pulse of Qatar's growth is quickening.

liquid natural gas exports

Qatar Financial Centre is at the heart of this development program. For opportunities in project finance, insurance, reinsurance,

are fuelling Qatar's

corporate and private banking, asset management and Islamic finance, QFC provides access,

rapid growth

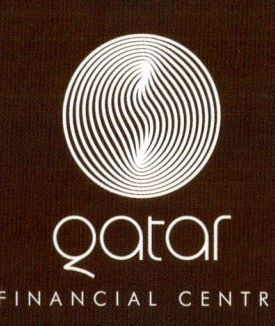

qatar
FINANCIAL CENTRE

facilities and an independent regulatory authority operating to internationally recognised standards. Contact: stuartpearce@qfc.com.qa

Business

Flight to value

Tamzin Booth PARIS

No-nonsense brands will prosper in 2009

2009 IN BRIEF
Transparency International, namer and shamer of corrupt governments, issues a report on **corruption and the private sector**.

On September 29th, when the United States Congress rejected the first bail-out plan for Wall Street, the Standard & Poor's 500 index plunged and all of its constituents fell in value, except one: the Campbell Soup Company. Investors flocked to the iconic brand, which makes some of America's favourite broths, such as chicken noodle and cream of mushroom, and its shares went up by 0.3%. That is a very good clue to the type of brands that will prosper in 2009: those that represent good quality, no-nonsense and excellent value for money.

To safeguard their own profits, advertising firms always insist that any brand can do well during hard times if owners continue to lavish money on marketing. But the reality is that consumers are likely to change their habits dramatically during a downturn. Fast-moving consumer goods have little to fear, but products priced for status are likely to suffer.

One victim will be organic products. Any brand built around do-gooding notions of organic, corporate social responsibility or caring for the environment may need to rethink, according to Interbrand, a marketing consultancy, as value for money rises up the consumers' agenda. Two early beneficiaries of consumers' changing mood, on the other hand, have been Aldi and Lidl, big German hard-discount supermarket chains which are expanding across Europe and eating into the market share of established giants such as Tesco and Carrefour. It used to be shameful for middle-class families to shop at hard-discounters, but now their brands suggest intelligent buying. Aldi and Lidl and their imitators will gain more ground in 2009.

Luxury brands are in for trouble. The industry has argued that it can resist a downturn: the seriously rich, after all, will still have plenty of cash to throw around. But that underestimates its achievement in selling luxe to the aspiring middle classes as well as to the wealthy. Louis Vuitton bags, after all, are sported by middle-class women as well as by the private-jet class. In Japan, where office workers typically save up for years to buy from Louis Vuitton and other luxury-goods firms, demand is falling. Their best hope will be to find ways to offer cheaper goods without compromising their image. Luxury car brands such as Porsche and Audi, for instance, are revamping their certified "pre-owned"—ie, second-hand—product ranges. Top fashion labels are hoping that fashionistas will buy the season's hot new sunglasses even if they can no longer afford a $3,000 handbag.

In Interbrand's 2008 ranking of the world's top 100 brands, the combined brand value of four financial institutions—Merrill Lynch, AIG, Morgan Stanley and Goldman Sachs—was estimated at some $37 billion. Since then, Merrill has ceased to exist as an independent entity, AIG was bailed out at the taxpayers' expense and Goldman Sachs and Morgan Stanley have thrown themselves under the protection of federal regulation as deposit-taking institutions. Banks will have a hard time in 2009 rebuilding any kind of confidence, let alone strong brands. On the other hand, they desperately need to compete with each other on this front in order to shore up their balance sheets with new deposits.

> Luxury brands are in for trouble

Brand new

On the brighter side, 2009 will see the arrival of big emerging-market brands into the developed world. Companies in China, India, Brazil and Russia have built strong brands at home, but they have mostly stayed there. Mahindra, an Indian conglomerate with a strong brand, which sells everything from tractors to insurance, will launch a small, fuel-efficient sport-utility vehicle in America. Strawberry Frog, the advertising agency working on the launch, says that emerging-market brands such as Mahindra can leapfrog rich-world marques by using guerrilla-marketing techniques and new media. If the Indian firm succeeds, more will surely follow. ■

Tamzin Booth:
European business editor, *The Economist*

Stock up

aim: zero emissions

We are committed to preserving the delicate balance between man and nature.

We've come a long way since we launched our first hybrid car 10 years ago. But our goal goes beyond reducing exhaust emissions. We apply innovative environmental solutions to every aspect of the vehicle's life cycle: from design, manufacture and use, right through to recycling. It's the only way to reach our ultimate aim: zero emissions.

www.aimzeroemissions.eu

TOYOTA

A new economic order

Even before the most extreme events affecting financial institutions in 2008, forecasters agreed that global economic growth would slow in 2009. Some developed economies may enter the new year in recession; and even the fastest-growing emerging markets are likely to see slower growth than in the recent, astonishing, past.

In time, we will understand much better the link between sophisticated financial markets and the physical world of goods manufactured and sold. We should bear in mind that, looked at from inside a G8 economy, a gloomy outlook seems prudent, if not inescapable. But the world is not just the G8, and developments outside the most advanced group may come to the rescue of us all.

At root, the subprime crisis originated in the United States from excess credit extended against insufficient security to those least capable of servicing, let alone repaying, the loans. Yet many families in the developing economies aspire just to have a roof over their heads; ownership is a distant dream. This is something to bear in mind when we ponder the human cost of the credit crunch.

It may also explain why so far the slowdown in the G8 has not had an equal effect in pulling down the faster-growing economies. The near double-digit growth rates from the BRICs (Brazil, Russia, India and China) and other developing economies have been one of the most transformational economic trends of the past few years. From the perspective of my own industry—steel—the demand from these countries, and in particular from China, has been one of the main factors behind the industry's resurgence.

Catching up with the leaders

Today there is a substantial difference in the rate of growth between the developed world and the emerging markets and this is set to continue. This "growth-rate gap" will see the BRICs and their smaller counterparts begin to catch up with the G8 countries, even if the wealth gaps within and between nations are huge and likely to remain so.

We are witnessing the establishment of a new economic order, one in which the great economic powers such as the United States will continue to wield considerable influence but where new economies such as China will have an ever-growing weight. For example, the UN predicts that in ten years half the population of China will live in cities—a momentous change.

The process of economic globalisation has been under way for some time. It has brought great benefits to many millions of people in the developing world, with the potential to influence positively a billion more. Improvements in infrastructure, agriculture and industrial efficiency have led in turn to advances in health care and education. The increasing wealth of developing countries has yet to bring them close to the standard of living of advanced economies, but even so the world's average wealth, defined as GDP per head, is being spread more evenly with each successive year. Indeed, the economic power of the developing economies is now such that to some extent they can grow independently of the developed world and have found their own momentum, beginning a process of industrialisation that encompasses more than 1.5 billion people.

The developed world should be thankful for this trend. As consumers in the advanced economies retrench from unsustainable levels—American consumer spending alone accounts for 21% of global GDP—shoppers in the BRICs will take up the slack.

But there are also concerns, the critical one being to what extent this economic power will manifest itself as political power—a process that history suggests is inevitable.

So perhaps the more pertinent question is: how will these countries exercise this power? Will they want better terms in deals over climate change, for instance? Or want to keep an increasing portion of the world's natural resources for themselves?

I am an optimist and I believe that as the world's economy becomes more interdependent, we will see better collaboration. We must hope that the developed economies will become more generous with their intellectual property and financial resources; and, in return, that the emerging economies will supply not just their raw materials and cheaper workers, but more importantly their sheer human vitality and inventiveness. You don't have to travel far to see that this is already happening.

In 2009 we may not know the absolute answer to the fundamental question of how the new map of economic power will be drawn. But the question is the most important of this relatively new century. We are living through a pivotal time in establishing a new economic order. What matters is that globalisation has started and in my view it cannot—and indeed should not—be stopped. ■

Lakshmi Mittal, CEO of ArcelorMittal, argues that the shift in power towards emerging economies is at a critical point

The developed world should be thankful for this trend

Led by the nose

Jonathan Rosenthal

Retailers will try out a baffling array of smells, sounds and sights on hapless shoppers

A scent of chocolate wafted through the women's shoe section. That of cut grass floated through the outdoor-furniture department, accompanied by the far-off sounds of children laughing, jumping into pools and of sausages sizzling on an open fire. Lime and basil infused the till receipts. Never a store to do things by half-measures, London's Harrods, the world's best-known purveyor of luxury, went for maximum impact when it played with scent for a few weeks in 2008. No fewer than 12 different fragrances permeated its sumptuous departments, in the boldest experiment yet in the use of aroma in retailing.

In 2009 several other stores will follow the Harrods lead, in Britain and beyond. They will include at least one large supermarket, the owner of several shopping malls and a fast-food chain. All will try out an array of new smells, sights and sounds on their customers, hoping not just to entice people in but to make them stay longer, spend more and come back again.

If history does indeed rhyme, rather than simply repeat itself, it does so with remarkable symmetry in retailing. For the Darwinian world of shopkeeping has long thrown up all manner of innovation. Harrods, for instance, installed the world's first escalator in 1898, drawing huge crowds of gawpers. Those brave enough to ride it were offered a stiff brandy at the top.

For all its magic, however, the past century of retailing has been dominated by attempts to appeal to the eye. In Britain, for instance, two Americans threw out the rulebook for running shops and introduced a radical new form of retailing when, in 1909, they opened Woolworths, a cheap general dealer, and Selfridges, a de-

2009 IN BRIEF
The number of **mobile-phone** subscriptions passes 4 billion, according to Finland's Nokia.

Jonathan Rosenthal: European business and finance correspondent, *The Economist*

Happy birthday, Barbie

Suzi Parker LITTLE ROCK

What will a superdoll do at 50?

No doll outshines Barbie's celebrity. If all the Barbies and her family members—Skipper, Francie and the rest—sold since 1959 were placed head to toe, they would circle the Earth more than seven times. And sales are sure to boom in 2009, when the fashion doll celebrates her 50th birthday on March 9th.

Barbie will star at an array of global events honouring her milestone, possibly including a glitzy affair at New York's Fashion Week in February (most of the world's top fashion designers, from Givenchy to Alexander McQueen, have designed haute couture for her). On her birthday, Mattel, the company that makes her, will launch a souvenir doll honouring the original Barbie in her black-and-white striped swimsuit and perfect ponytail. It will be available for purchase only that one day. Another Golden Anniversary doll targets collectors. Barbie fans have planned hundreds of events, including the National Barbie Doll Collectors Convention in Washington, DC, which is already sold out.

When Ruth Handler created Barbie in 1959, a post-war culture and economy thrived but girls still played with baby dolls. These toys limited the imagination; so Handler introduced Barbie the Teen-Age Fashion Model, named after her daughter, Barbara. Jackie Kennedy soon sashayed onto the world stage and Barbie already had a wardrobe fit for a first lady. Barbie bestowed on girls the opportunity to dream beyond suburbia, even if Ken at times tagged along.

Barbie entranced Europe in 1961 and now sells in 150 countries. Every second three Barbies are sold around the world. Her careers are myriad—model, astronaut, Olympic swimmer, palaeontologist and rock star, along with 100 others, including president. Like any political candidate, controversy hit Barbie in 1992 when Teen Talk Barbie said "Math class is tough" and girls' education became a national issue. She has been banned (in Saudi Arabia), tortured (by pre-teen girls, according to researchers at the University of Bath's School of Management) and fattened (in 1997).

Feminists continue to bash Barbie, claiming that her beauty and curves treat women as objects. But others see her as a pioneer trendsetter, crashing the glass ceiling long before Hillary Clinton cracked it.

High-tech entertainment now attracts girls and Barbie also faces fierce competition from various copycats including the edgier, but less glam, Bratz dolls. The Bratz suffered a setback in 2008. Mattel sued MGA Entertainment, Bratz's producer, for copyright infringement. A judge awarded Mattel $100m in damages.

Mattel has smartly ensured that Barbie products reflect current trends. Through two Barbie websites, girls can design clothes, network and play games. The pink Barbie brand is licensed for products from DVDs and MP3 players to bicycles and even 24-carat gold and crystal jewellery. Barbie collectors fuel an entire global industry on eBay and at conventions. To entice collectors, Mattel regularly releases pricey limited-edition dolls based on characters in films and popular culture.

Industry analysts believe Barbie will remain a bestselling and lasting icon regardless of competition. "Barbie's been out in the world and had fun, and she's ready for her second career," says Rachel Weingarten, a pop-culture expert. "I don't see her adopting five children from five different countries, but I could see Barbie with a conscience, activist Barbie." At 50 Barbie will also be a marvel of plastic surgery and eternal youth. And she still knows how to party. ■

Suzi Parker: author and journalist

The Chinese are coming
Steve King

Prepare for an influx of tourists

It is difficult to picture the Eiffel Tower, the Trevi fountain or the gates to Buckingham Palace without also picturing throngs of camera-toting Japanese tourists. But the Japanese will face growing competition in 2009 as they jostle for prime photo position. The World Tourism Organisation predicts that by 2020 some 100m Chinese will be travelling overseas.

Wolfgang Arlt, director of the China Outbound Tourism Research Institute, notes that most Chinese travellers get no farther than Hong Kong or Macau. Fewer than 4m a year venture beyond Asia. "In 2007, 27 out of 1,000 Chinese visited Asian destinations, while only three out of 1,000 visited destinations outside Asia."

But hoteliers expect Chinese travellers—especially rich ones—to have a significant influence on their industry. Like the Japanese, Arabs and Russians before them, the Chinese will subtly transform the services offered by high-end hotels. "It is a gradual process," says Christopher Norton, general manager of the George V in Paris, part of the Four Seasons portfolio. "A new class of upscale Chinese traveller is just starting to emerge."

Mandarin will become mandatory among front-of-house staff at top hotels. Signs and menus will become more characterful. And private dining rooms will proliferate. "Privacy is hugely important to the Chinese," says Daniel Ford, director of public relations in Asia for Ritz-Carlton. "In any of our hotels in China, you might find as many as a dozen private dining rooms." Those wooing Chinese travellers abroad will have to adopt the principles that apply back home.

So where will you find all these Chinese tourists, Mandarin-speaking hotel staff and private dining rooms in 2009? Mainly in Hong Kong, which remains their favourite "foreign" destination, but also in Europe, South-East Asia and Australia. More Chinese will discover America too. "What they are really interested in is seeing how the West measures up," says Mr Arlt. "They want to see it in all its brilliant modernity to understand to what degree China has been able to catch up—and whether the struggle is worth it." ■

Steve King: works for *Vanity Fair*

2009 IN BRIEF
Colour television, now boasting the glories of **high-definition**, turns 60 and analogue TV ends in America.

partment store offering luxury to the middle classes. Although aimed at very different parts of the market, they transformed shopping in a similar way. Both brought goods out from behind their Victorian counters and put them where customers could see and touch them. "Display was everything," says Kathryn Morrison, an architectural historian.

A whiff of innovation

Now smell is the new frontier. One reason for this is that mainstream shops have suffered a steady haemorrhaging of spending to cheaper internet sites and "big-box" warehouses on the outskirts of towns. In response, they are trying to make shopping more entertaining and to offer customers experiences that they cannot get online, says Ira Kalish, a retailing expert at Deloitte. With sight and sound easily delivered in bits of data to the home, retailers are now experimenting with the two senses that don't transmit: touch and smell.

This is not entirely new. Canny supermarkets already ensure shoppers are hit with the smell of freshly baked bread as they enter. But now retailers and marketers are playing with a whole bouquet of smells in new and radical ways that often seem unconnected with the products on sale, be they chocolate or women's shoes.

Indeed, a second reason for a smellier future is the innovation that will flow from advances both in our understanding of how different smells affect the mind and in new techniques to deliver them. Brain scans, for instance, can show how different smells fire up the brain's pleasure centres. Some aromas have shown a remarkable ability to get customers to browse longer, spend more and come back to the store more often, says Eric Spangenberg of Washington State University, who has published several papers on the subject.

> Get the smell right and you can bypass rational thought

Simon Harrop, chief executive of BRAND sense agency, reckons the power of scents comes from their close association with emotion and memory. Get the smell right and you can bypass rational thought. Field trials in stores have shown that aroma can achieve the holy grail of marketing. It can prompt customers to try new brands, and to stay loyal to them, he says.

But retailers and their marketers are treading a path full of pitfalls. What are the ethics, for instance, of enticing obese people to buy snacks by wafting the smell of popcorn at them? And how much damage will be done to a company's brand if its customers realise that it has, quite literally, been leading them about by the nose? ■

Basic instinct

The upside of a downturn

Martin Giles SAN FRANCISCO

Fired with enthusiasm

"You're fired!" has become a catchphrase for Donald Trump and other hosts of "The Apprentice", a well-known TV show about aspiring business stars that has made its way around the world. Those same chilling words will be heard in many workplaces in 2009, as companies faced with a sluggish economy continue to cut one of their biggest costs: people. Although losing a job will be a very traumatic experience for many employees, such lay-offs will also be accompanied by opportunities.

A few leavers will be lucky enough to get some job-hunting assistance from their former employers. The outplacement industry, which provides such advice to jobseekers, is already gearing up for a bumper year. Online networking and job sites, such as LinkedIn and France's lesjeudis.com, will also see a rise in traffic as the newly displaced use such sites' electronic tentacles to reach out in search of new positions.

Some of those ousted from their jobs will find it easier to get a new one than others. A recent study by Right Management, which is part of Manpower, an employment-services giant, shows that many people laid off in the pharmaceutical industry in north-eastern America in 2007 and early 2008 went on to find new positions—often at an equivalent or a higher salary—elsewhere in the same industry or in the fast-growing biotech sector. The fledgling green-energy industry will be another big recruiter in 2009, given that it faces a dire shortage of talented engineers and other experienced staff.

Not all those who find themselves unemployed will want to head straight back into the same line of business, though. Many job-hunters will explore several possible careers before charting a new course for themselves. One way to do this will be to seek out people who are already working in new areas and ask them what life is like there. But second-hand anecdotes are a poor substitute for first-hand experience. So there will be a demand for services provided by companies such as VocationVacations, an American firm which lets its customers try out a new career by working for a period with a "mentor" who is already active in the business of their dreams. Popular targets for "vacationers" will include catering (restaurants, bakeries), as well as the sports, entertainment and environmental industries.

Some of the newly unemployed will seek inspiration in education. Places on business-school courses will be popular with ousted employees who can afford to pay the hefty fees. The coming year will be a record one for applications to full-time MBA programmes, partly stimulated by demand from job-hunters who hope to use the schools' career advisers to help them identify suitable potential jobs while they are busy polishing their skills in the classroom. Vocational courses that develop industry-specific skills will also see a surge in applications.

I used to be a senior manager

Hire yourself

Rather than studying business, what about starting a company from scratch? If history is any guide, a significant number of people who are laid off over the coming year will do just that. Carl Schramm, the head of the Kauffman Foundation, a non-profit organisation that promotes entrepreneurial activity, points out that start-ups tend to flourish in the year that follows a sharp downturn. Rather than head back to another corporate bureaucracy, some of those made redundant will take a shot at being their own boss.

And these new entrepreneurs will not just be young whippersnappers. In America, in particular, older workers are increasingly likely to start a second—or third or fourth—act after a lay-off, in part because they fret that they do not have enough money saved up for their retirement. According to statistics from Challenger, Gray & Christmas, an outplacement consultancy, the number of self-employed workers over 55 in America has risen by 10% since 2005. That figure will grow again in 2009.

Those victims of downsizing who do end up launching their own businesses will have no shortage of role models. Michael Bloomberg, Steve Jobs and Michael Dell are just a few of today's business behemoths who were thrown out of a job at some point in their careers. Like them, some of 2009's crop of corporate outcasts will go on to prove that triumph—and millions of newly minted jobs—can be born out of adversity. ■

> Start-ups tend to flourish in the year that follows a sharp downturn

2009 IN BRIEF

The Eastern Africa Submarine Cable System (EASSy), using **fibre-optic cable**, will connect 21 African countries, from South Africa to Mozambique, to each other and the rest of the world with high-speed internet.

Martin Giles: senior business correspondent, *The Economist*

Intensive scare

Vijay Vaitheeswaran NEW YORK

Several disruptive innovations will soon make life harder for health care's established giants

Health care has long been a cosy industry dominated by monopolies in the provision of service and lumbering giants in the provision of pills. Profit margins have historically been fat, growth prospects rosy and disruptive innovations rare indeed. But all this looks set to change in 2009. Thanks to a swirl of new technologies, business models and, possibly, a push from the American government, the established dinosaurs of health care may well be forced to dance.

Big Pharma will feel the force of generic competition in earnest in 2009. Billions of dollars of branded blockbuster drugs are due to go off-patent in 2009 and 2010. Aggressive pricing by generic-drugs manufacturers is sure to drive the prices of those drugs down by 80% or more, battering the profitability of branded firms. The ongoing consolidation of the generics sector will reach full strength in 2009, producing several giant firms with the global reach, marketing savvy and research capability to threaten established global drugs firms such as America's Pfizer and Britain's GlaxoSmithKline.

Meanwhile, two different sorts of disruptive innovations promise to upend America's health-care system, a $2.4 trillion colossus that is ripe for change. One is the spread of cheap-and-cheerful retail health clinics located next to the pharmacist at drug stores, in shopping malls and even inside Wal-Mart outlets. The second is the coming boom in American medical travel to faraway places such as Thailand and India.

A retail revolution

In 2006 there were hardly 200 retail clinics in America, but in 2009 the number will easily top 1,000. This innovative business model has attracted powerful players, from CVS (a big pharmacy chain) and Wal-Mart to Revolution Health (set up by Steve Case, a co-founder of AOL). By offering cheap and convenient care they expose the costly incumbents of health-care delivery.

Those thus challenged must also brace themselves for the coming boom in medical tourism. Traditionally, that meant only the elites in poor countries who travelled to Paris, for example, or to America's Mayo Clinic for medical care they could not get at home. In recent years some Europeans have been travelling to developing countries to get round lengthy queues in their state-funded health systems. But Americans have never been a big part of this globalisation of health.

This is about to change. Some 46m Americans lack health insurance, and tens of millions more are woefully under-insured. As they face huge out-of-pocket expenses, deductibles and "co-payments" for operations, they are increasingly heading overseas to cheaper facilities. Many common operations can be done in world-class hospitals abroad for a fifth or less of the price charged by American hospitals.

As more employers and health-insurance firms add the "global option" to their plans, the number of American health tourists will soar to over 2m in 2009—rising to 10m by 2012, according to forecasts by Deloitte, a consultancy. This exodus will have a direct impact on the established firms of American health care (and, in time, on their European counterparts too), as the millions of operations conducted overseas will mean tens of billions of dollars in lost revenue back at home. And by, in effect, importing competition, medical tourism will increase price transparency and bring much-needed reform.

Yet another great disruption in 2009 will be the arrival, at long last, of the internet age into this most arcane of industries. Most doctors' offices in America still rely on paper-pushing to maintain medical records. Doctors and hospital administrators have been quick to adopt information technology for financial operations such as billing and claims processing, but not for dealing with actual medical matters. Google and Microsoft have both recently launched efforts to tackle online medical records, but have got off to a slow start.

Watch for outsiders to break into this space in 2009. The two giant firms have not made headway because their online efforts have not gone far enough to address doctors' concerns about ease of use, and patients' concerns about privacy and security. But venture capitalists in Silicon Valley are betting heavily on firms with better technology and smarter business models for tackling this problem. Several are expected to emerge from stealth mode in 2009.

In sum, 2009 will be a crucial year for health reform. Not only will the politics of health care be taken up by the new American president, which is sure to disrupt business as usual, but emerging technologies and business models also promise to turn up the heat. Happily, all of these changes—cheaper pills, more convenient clinics and online records, and the option to save money by travelling abroad for care—promise to benefit the long-suffering patients even as they punish the dinosaurs. ■

> **Billions of dollars of branded blockbuster drugs are due to go off-patent in 2009 and 2010**

Out patients
Forecast number of US patients travelling abroad for medical care, m
Source: Deloitte Centre for Health Solutions

2009 IN BRIEF
As the world's airlines endure a second year of net losses, **passenger traffic falls** in North America, the industry's biggest market.

Vijay Vaitheeswaran: health-care correspondent, *The Economist*

When policies change every five minutes, make sure your ducks are in a row.

(Duck labels: Legal Hold, Active Policy, Regulatory Requests, Information Governance, Archiving)

9 of 10 top banks use Autonomy to automate **regulatory compliance**.

As the rules are redrawn, you must comply with changing regulations. Corporate-wide systems including archives and legal hold must be in place to ensure that no relevant data is deleted.

Autonomy manages billions of emails, Bloomberg, IM and voice messages each day across 6,000 servers and 5 secure data centers. We'll help you get your ducks in a row.

Find out how at autonomy.com/governance.

Autonomy®

World's Largest Online Archives

The year of the CFO

Lucy Kellaway

Corporate life won't be funny

Prepare for the year of the finance director. In 2009 the world will find out just how bad corporate balance sheets really are, and companies—most of which escaped the early effects of the credit crunch—will start to find it trickier to raise money. Add to that the upward push in costs and downward slide in demand, and the chief financial officer (CFO) will be called upon to shore up the P&L too.

The implications of his ascendancy will be felt far beyond the figures and will last much longer than it takes to make them look healthy again. There will be a shift in the balance of power in the boardroom, which will affect how companies are managed, what it feels like to work in them, the culture of business and even its language.

For the past decade the prevailing wind in boardrooms has been gentle. Emotional intelligence and innovation have been what counted, and what leaders professed to value. But those ideas are all but finished. No one will talk of EQ ("emotional intelligence quotient") any more. It will be EVA ("economic value added") instead. Thinking outside the box (an over-rated activity at the best of times) will not be celebrated. Ticking boxes will be.

As financial skills are valued more highly, CFOs will make it to the corner office in greater numbers than before.

Recession, credit crunch and the increasingly complex nature of global companies will all play directly into the bean counter's hands. Nominations committees will throw their trust behind the guy who has protected the creditworthiness of a company in hard times and won the trust of the market; they will pick him for the top slot rather than poaching an expensive star CEO from outside. This will be bad news for headhunters (who will vainly try to make good the shortfall by meddling in internal succession instead), but also bad news for CEOs' bank balances as top salaries will halt their ever-upward march.

Leadership style at the top will change. Big personalities have been out of fashion at the top for some years; in 2009 they will be more out than ever. However, egalitarianism and empowerment will also be on the way out; management by fiat is going to make a stealthy return.

In the boardrooms, the firm slap of leadership will be felt. "Execution" will no longer be a management fad, it will be a part of daily life. We will hear less of "vision" and much more of "value".

Goodbye "talent", hello "staff"

The biggest loser in the struggle for power will be the human resources director. In the past five years HR has been enjoying the greatest power it has ever had. The "war for talent", which companies have fought tooth and nail, will be over in 2008, neither lost nor won: there will be a ceasefire brought on by lack of funds and exhaustion of the troops. An old truth will be whispered by the brave: most workers are not terribly talented and most of them don't need to be, as most jobs don't require it. In 2009 a more elitist shift will occur: companies will worry about the performance of those at the top of the pyramid, while everyone else will be managed like a commodity. "Talent" will be a word we wave goodbye to. In 2009 the word "staff" will make a comeback, as will "headcount".

In this new world the HR director might just cling on to his title, but his job

> Thinking outside the box (an over-rated activity at the best of times) will not be celebrated. Ticking boxes will be

will be downgraded to personnel and in particular to payroll.

The marketing director will also lose out. He has already been kicked once by the decline of advertising and kicked again as the power of the internet has made his traditional tools useless. In 2009 his budgets will fall further, as will his status. As for the corporate-social-responsibility supremo, he will be told to take a gap year indefinitely.

The firm financial leadership will be welcome in that it will help companies survive, yet being a corporate foot-soldier in 2009 is not going to be enjoyable. Moaning will be on the rise as inexorably as expenses will be on the decline.

There will be less foreign travel, which will make work more efficient but duller. And there will be no more free champagne in first class—it will be steerage only. Expense-account lunches and subsidised health clubs will be slashed, and stationery cupboards will be thinly stocked.

One blessed thing will be cut: weekend offsite meetings in luxury hotels. Instead, if managers feel the need to bond at all it will be done more quickly over a cup of tea from the vending machine. There will be no more laughter workshops led by an outsourced facilitator—but then in the new world of 2009 there is not going to be a lot to laugh about. ■

Lucy Kellaway: columnist at the *Financial Times* and author of "The Answers: All the Office Questions You Never Dared to Ask" (Profile)

KONICA MINOLTA

The essentials of imaging

Do you still believe that one skill is enough to win?

Is speed the decisive factor when it comes to success?
Speed is important, no doubt about that.
But it only makes sense if it comes with outstanding quality.
Of course, you want your business documents as fast as possible.
But you also want them to be as professional as possible.

Does cost efficiency mean going for the cheapest solution?
Sometimes, one player makes all the difference between two teams.
He's probably not the cheapest one.
Konica Minolta helps you save money by offering you printing solutions with
an attractive Total Cost of Ownership and a wide variety of applications to
support your cost management / control.

Last but not least, what about networking?
Every football player knows that he would be nothing without the rest of the team
behind him.
If you strive for the best results you need to get the best out of your network.
Konica Minolta supplies you with equipment and applications to do exactly this.

But which skill is the one that makes you a winner?
You don't have to choose if you can actually have all of them.
Your office needs a colour output system that is a printer, copier,
scanner and fax.
And it needs software applications to help you maximise
flexibility and performance.

Your office needs a Konica Minolta solution.

SPEED
QUALITY
SECURITY
NETWORK
COST MANAGEMENT

bizhub

In our team, we only accept the best members.

Konica Minolta. The skills to win.

konicaminolta.co.uk/skills

Old Macdonald gets some cash

John Parker

After the year of food crisis, the year of the farmer

2009 IN BRIEF
Abu Dhabi hosts its first Formula One **grand prix**. Other venues may fall by the wayside for lack of money.

In 2008, food-price rises sent tens of millions tumbling into direst poverty. Those same higher prices mean that, in 2009, farmers will grow bumper crops. Bigger harvests will, in turn, moderate the price rises, giving belated relief to hard-pressed consumers. But although prices will fall back somewhat, the upshot will be that, in many countries (not all), farmers will produce good crops at prices higher than they have been used to for 20 years. In the year ahead, markets in world farming will begin to move back towards equilibrium.

The process is under way. According to the United Nations Food and Agriculture Organisation, the world wheat harvest in 2008 may have been some 9% above the 2007 level; total grains (rice, maize and the like) were about 4% up. These increases were achieved even though farmers are risk-averse: it usually takes them a season or two to respond fully to higher prices. The supply response will speed up in 2009. The International Grains Council, a trade body, reckons the 2008-09 season will see rises of between 4% (for total grains) and 11% (for wheat). Barring unforeseeable droughts or floods, both the wheat and cereals harvests in 2009 will set records.

There are three reasons for these improvements. One is that countries are at last getting rid of the self-defeating anti-farmer policies that they imposed at the height of panic over rising food prices in early 2008. Thirty countries implemented measures like export restrictions (to increase domestic supplies) and food-price controls. These policies caused the worst of all worlds: they did little to reduce prices at home; they increased world prices (by 40%, in the case of rice); and local farmers were cut off from international markets. As supplies rise, countries will feel confident enough to get rid of these state-sponsored perversities. Kazakhstan (one of the top ten wheat exporters) has allowed its wheat export ban to expire. Russia lifted taxes on wheat. More countries will follow.

Second, markets will do what they always do: encourage investment into areas where the returns are good. Farming is no exception. The share prices of farm-machinery makers outperformed the stockmarket's (admittedly miserable) averages in 2007 and 2008. Agricultural land prices in Britain rose by their fastest recorded amount in 2008. It is true that this is not always a sign of good health: soaring land prices in America in the early 1980s bankrupted many farmers who borrowed too heavily to buy land. But this time, in combination with other indicators, they suggest rising confidence in the future of agriculture.

Most important, higher prices seem to have changed the attitudes of governments in developing countries. This matters because public investment in farming underpins rural productivity there. Public investment has been declining for years but the decline has been reversed in the biggest countries. China's government increased central budget spending on agriculture by a stunning 30% in 2008, and has promised to boost it further. In his 2008 budget, India's finance minister said capital formation in agriculture needed to rise to 16% of national income by 2012 (from 12.5% in 2007). Of course, it is one thing for governments to make promises, another to deliver on them. Still, after many years of suffering from neglected irrigation, bad rural roads, intermittent or non-existent electricity and so on, farmers in emerging markets can hardly fail to benefit from the renewed attention.

Over the past dozen years, world farm output has barely kept pace with increased demand. In the past three years, output actually fell short: the world was eating more food than it grew. In 2009 output will surge ahead again, relieving some of the pressure on developing countries that, in 2008, caused the first global outbreak of food riots for more than 30 years. But it will not provide much relief. The forces behind the increase in demand—a growing appetite for meat in fast-growing countries such as China and India; policies encouraging the production of fuel from crops, especially in America—have not abated. They will keep prices from falling back to anywhere near the levels of the early 2000s.

> **Both the wheat and cereals harvests in 2009 will set records**

In 2008, the World Bank reckoned that higher food prices drove 100m people into poverty. That may have been a bit of an exaggeration because many rural parts of developing countries also benefited from dearer food. But the urban poor suffered a great deal and the majority of developing countries were hit by higher inflation and lower living standards. The good news is that 2009 will be a year of recovery for farmers. But it will take more than a year for the world as a whole to recover from the food crisis of 2008. ∎

A higher priority for agriculture

John Parker: globalisation correspondent, *The Economist*

There's 💧 energy 🔥 security 🌬 in ☀ energy 🌱 diversity.

There's strength in numbers, and security in having a number of energy sources. That's why, as the largest single producer of oil and gas in the UK North Sea, BP is using the latest technology to find new reserves and to increase recovery from existing fields. We are also investing in a major biofuels facility in Hull and expanding our global wind power generation and production of solar panels. It all adds up to a more dependable energy future. Learn more at bp.com

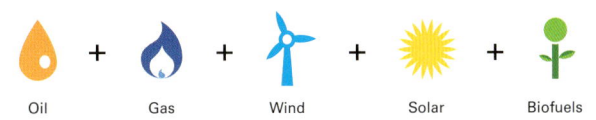

Oil + Gas + Wind + Solar + Biofuels

bp

beyond petroleum

Time to re-embrace globalisation

In turbulent economic times, globalisation has become regarded as a dirty word, tainted by a toxic mix of misinformation, misconception and misanthropy. It is time, in 2009, for leaders in business and government to reset the debate, informing their constituents that free and fair trade is good for the health and wealth of their operations and their nations, especially as governments and businesses navigate through the extraordinary financial turmoil.

It seems as if globalisation has been around for ever, but the concept probably didn't crystallise into its current form until the early 1980s. And at that time there was one enormous example of it, one that was then thought threatening: Japan, which was going to globalise the rest of us right out of business. When I joined General Electric in 1982, Japan was the ultimate global threat. Its awesome arsenal of technology innovation, financial acumen and process expertise was going to annihilate American business and we were all going to end up working for a Japanese company—if we even had a job.

The best Japanese companies that learnt to become global just happened to be based in Japan. It was Toyota, it was Canon, and they had evolved to become remarkable global enterprises. So we had to get global—and at significant scale—fast. We had to evolve into a truly global company that happened to be based in America. It sounds simple today, but it was revolutionary and signalled the initial tectonic rumblings of a flattening earth.

In the intervening 25 years, international trade, and the global economic integration resulting from it, have raised standards of living in both developed and developing economies, facilitated the flow of ideas and people, spurred innovation, strengthened the rule of law and lifted hundreds of millions of people out of poverty. Is integration always perfect? No, but China and eastern Europe are examples of adept change.

Points of principle

There's a dangerous tendency to resort to protectionism when things get tough. In 1929, American tariffs turned a domestic financial crisis into a global economic crisis that inflicted damage for years to come. And although we've learnt a lot from that mistake over 80 years, you wouldn't know it today. If you put globalisation to a vote in America, Europe—pretty much anywhere—the general public would probably vote it down.

Business and government leaders must reset the debate, re-establishing why interdependent economies and healthy competition are good for the world. At GE, we believe six principles should underpin this debate:

1. A strong international trade system is fundamental. Such a system, overseen by the World Trade Organisation (WTO), is vital to the global economy and to the employees of all companies operating globally.

2. Continued economic liberalisation enhances growth. Particularly at a time of global economic duress, market liberalisation can play a role in stimulating growth, saving jobs and enhancing living standards. Comprehensive multilateral, regional and bilateral trade agreements have been critical to spurring such liberalisation in the past and should continue to be pursued actively.

3. Protectionism must be resisted. Trade and investment barriers deter foreign participation in domestic markets, add cost to what consumers buy, hamper innovation, limit growth, and ultimately reduce living standards at home and abroad.

4. Global trade must be fair. All participants in the global economy must live by international trade rules: property rights (including intellectual property) should be protected; markets should be transparent; baseline international labour and environmental standards should be honoured; technical standards should not be used to bar access; governments should refrain from trade-distorting subsidies; and WTO dispute-resolution decisions should be respected.

5. Governments must pursue domestic policies that allow their citizens to thrive in the global economy. The solution to global competition is improved competitiveness, not isolation. Governments should strengthen the health and education of their citizens and build necessary trade-related infrastructure.

6. Each of us must contribute. Developed and developing countries, governments and industry, shareholders and employees—we all share a responsibility to make meaningful contributions to protect and strengthen the international trading system.

Thomas Edison, GE's founder, used to say that people don't recognise opportunity because it "usually goes around wearing overalls looking like hard work". To succeed in our swarming global economy, leaders must not resist the challenge but relish the opportunity, especially in these harder economic times. True leaders must re-embrace globalisation. ■

Jeff Immelt, chairman and chief executive of General Electric, urges business and political leaders to embrace competition, not protectionism, as the way through economic turmoil

There's a dangerous tendency to resort to protectionism when things get tough

CIMA
Chartered Institute of Management Accountants

'CIMA has enabled me to create value by providing rigorous financial analysis. For example, as finance leader I supported the set up of a distribution hub in Singapore that changed the dynamics of our Asian supply chain.'

Stephen Howe, ACMA
Head of Decision Support,
DIAGEO Global Supply Scotland

CIMA *m*AKES BUSINESS SENSE

CIMA is the most relevant international accountancy qualification for business. Chartered Management Accountants are financially qualified business leaders operating in all areas of the organisation. They create value by applying leading edge techniques with a commercial and forward looking focus, adapting to the changing needs of the business.

Download the CIMA global employer pack today
www.choosecima.com/diageo

FINANCIAL MANAGEMENT   BUSINESS MANAGEMENT   FORECASTING   STRATEGIC INSIGHT   ACCOUNTING   PERFORMANCE MANAGEMENT   REPORTING   DECISION MAKING   TRANSACTION PROCESSING   PROJECT APPRAISAL AND MANAGEMENT   PLANNING   CHANGE MANAGEMENT   BUDGETING   ENTERPRISE GOVERNANCE   RISK MANAGEMENT   PARTNERSHIP MANAGEMENT   STRATEGY   SYSTEMS AND PROCEDURES   CORPORATE FINANCE

General Insurance
Life Insurance
Risk Management

Zurich HelpPoint™

One global insurance program for your expanding business. Even for places you've never been.

Zurich HelpPoint™ is here when you need more than just insurance. So we offer the Zurich Multinational Insurance Proposition (MIP)*. It helps you keep global insurance programs compliant when you expand your business to a new market and expose yourself to new risks. The strength of Zurich MIP lies in a transparent and thorough set of solutions for writing and maintaining global insurance programs in over 170 countries. Our game-changing solution can help you sleep better at night, no matter the time zone. For more details about *Zurich HelpPoint*™, visit www.zurich.com

Here to help your world.

ZURICH®

Because change happenz

Zurich Insurance Ireland Limited, UK Branch: Registered in England and Wales No. BR7985. Authorised and regulated by the Irish Financial Regulator and regulated by the Financial Services Authority for the conduct of UK business. Zurich Insurance Ireland Limited, a limited liability company registered in Ireland under registration no.13460. Registered Office: Eagle Star House, Ballsbridge Park, Dublin 4. * patent pending.

Finance

Also in this section:
Microcredit's moment 148
Defaults, distressed debt and deleveraging 150
The downside of banking 152
And its emerging winners 153
Where are the bulls? 154
A mightier dollar 155
Josef Ackermann: Lessons from a crisis 156

Whatever next

Zanny Minton Beddoes WASHINGTON, DC

The balance between governments and markets in finance will shift—a bit

In the autumn of 2008, Western finance almost collapsed. That catastrophe was staved off by the biggest state interventions since the 1930s. To restore confidence and unblock credit, governments across the rich world flooded banks with liquidity and offered guarantees on deposits and bank debt. They injected hundreds of billions of dollars of public capital, leaving the state as part-owner of many of the rich world's biggest banks. In America, champion of free markets, and Britain, the birthplace of modern privatisation, many titans of finance enter 2009 as semi-nationalised creatures of the state.

The coming year will determine the consequences for the balance between markets and government, and for the Anglo-Saxon model of capitalism. Already many have declared the death of the Thatcher-Reagan revolution and the end of an era of "free-market fundamentalism". "Laissez-faire is finished," argues Nicolas Sarkozy, France's president.

In fact, the balance between the state and markets will swing less than many now imagine. And it will be determined more by economies' performances than by grand intellectual redesigns. The rich world faces a nasty recession but that recession need not be calamitous. The shallower the downturn, the more muted will be the appetite for wholesale economic change. That is why comparisons to the 1930s are overstated. The Depression was a catastrophe: in America output fell by a third and unemployment hit 25%. That protracted collapse led to the redrawing of boundaries between governments and markets well beyond finance—from farming to interstate trucking.

A better parallel lies in other modern banking collapses. Dozens of countries, from Sweden to Japan, have suffered systemic banking crises in recent decades. The vast majority used public funds to recapitalise their banks. In the best cases, governments quickly got out of cleaned-up banks. In the worst cases policymakers dithered and botched their rescues.

Western governments have not dithered. And 2009 will be the test of whether they use their cash infusions to good effect. The temptation will be to get too closely involved in banks' decisions. Britain's government, for instance, has demanded that banks which receive public capital must pledge to keep lending to consumers and small businesses at the pace of 2007. In America, if the sad tale of the state-sponsored mortgage giants, Fannie Mae and Freddie Mac, is a guide, the pressure for political

> The temptation will be to get too closely involved in banks' decisions

2009 IN BRIEF
Short-sellers of financial stocks return in January to the London Stock Exchange, and to Iceland's, too.

Zanny Minton Beddoes: economics editor, *The Economist*

2009 IN BRIEF
America's new administration fills vacant, politically sensitive spots on the **Federal Reserve** Board.

meddling will grow too—even if the recession is mild.

Expect, then, endless congressional and parliamentary hearings on whether taxpayers' investments are being appropriately used and whether there should be special help for struggling industries and homeowners. With luck, the public spotlight will bring benefits—for instance, by jump-starting new pay packages that better align bankers' incentives so that they don't take excess risks—without inducing politically motivated lending.

The politics will set the stage for the more lasting decisions of 2009: how far should finance be re-regulated? Much depends on what becomes the dominant narrative of the financial crisis. Was it the result of deregulation, speculative excess and greed? Or was it a perfect storm in which policy failures (such as excessively low interest rates, poor supervision and, in America, government meddling in mortgage markets) played just as big a role?

Much of the to-do list is already clear. Transparency and oversight must be improved in the newer, more exotic reaches of finance, such as credit-default swaps. Regulators will grapple with whether oversight should be extended to hedge funds and other frontiers of the new finance; how capital rules should be rewritten to ensure that they are less "procyclical", or prone to amplify booms and busts; and how to keep track of risks across the industry and not just within individual firms.

America will begin a modest overhaul of its labyrinthine structure of financial supervisors—though because of entrenched bureaucracies it will still have too many disparate regulators. Internationally, regulators will update the Basel II rules on banks' capital and central bankers will debate whether monetary policy or regulatory rules ought to be used to combat asset-price bubbles. The ugly new, ill-defined buzzword will be "macro-prudential" supervision.

There will be plenty of grand global conferences, but the result will be an update of regulation, not a wholesale overhaul. And even a modest overhaul will be superseded by changes within finance itself. The crisis of 2008 transformed the financial landscape far beyond the governments' rescues. The "shadow" banking system—the money-market funds, securities dealers, hedge-funds and other non-bank financial institutions—is shrinking fast. Western finance will be increasingly dominated by a few huge universal banks, with a new aversion to risk. Politicians will grandstand about remaking finance. They will find that finance has remade itself. ■

Small is beautiful
Leo Abruzzese

Want a safe bet for 2009? Try microcredit

Wall Street's titans minted money in good times but now find it hard to repay their debts, if they are in business at all. Ironic, then, that many of the world's poor are better credit risks than the once-high-flyers at Lehman Brothers. This is one of the attractions of microcredit, the lending of tiny sums—as little as $50—to people at the bottom of the economic pyramid. It is an increasingly bright light in the gloom of the financial world.

Micro-borrowers range from farmers in rural areas to shopkeepers, artisans and street vendors in cities. In places where banks do not reach the poor, micro-lenders (often NGOs and non-profit organisations) provide capital to people who can put it to good use. If you think this looks like another subprime scheme—lending money to people who should not be borrowing—cheer up. Micro-borrowers have a stellar repayment record: Muhammad Yunus, founder of Bangladesh's Grameen Bank and recipient of the 2006 Nobel peace prize for his work in microfinance, says repayment rates are 95-98%. American credit-card holders are not that dependable.

Microcredit is not a solution to poverty: the very poorest often do not have the wherewithal to start businesses or the income stream to make regular loan re-

The loan's come through

payments. Processing so many small loans is also expensive for the lender, so interest rates can be high. But they are usually much lower than the local loan shark's, and poor people seem generally happy to have a reliable source of finance.

Increasingly, mainstream financial firms see money to be made. A study by the *MicroBanking Bulletin* puts the inflation-adjusted returns for lenders at around 2.5% of assets, on a par with commercial banking. Advocates of the poor worry that too much commercialism will ruin microfinance, but a decent return will attract more capital, broaden its reach and make the whole enterprise more sustainable.

Microcredit's marriage with technology is opening new opportunities. Mobile phones and a local shopowner willing to handle the cash can extend microlending to a wider audience. XacBank, in Mongolia, is planning a mobile-banking programme that could cover as many as 300,000 people—no small feat in a nomadic country where livestock outnumber people 13 to one. Another bad year on Wall Street and goat-herding may look attractive there as well. ■

Leo Abruzzese: editorial director, North America, Economist Intelligence Unit

The world's favourite Turkish bank.

❀ Garanti

garantibank.com

Dirty words

Henry Tricks

Derivatives, defaults, disaster...

The ugliest letter in finance is D, and 2009 will be full of them. Whether or not talk of depression is borne out, defaults, distressed debt and deleveraging will be on the rise. Ordinary companies will collapse in droves. In the process, the massive market for credit derivatives will be put to an even bigger test than it has been in 2008. It will end up thoroughly discredited—and quite possibly dead.

Creative destruction, by which unprofitable companies go bust and profitable ones rise in their stead, is capitalism's way of reinventing itself. But unless banks are able to lend again to good companies, there will be little that is creative in 2009.

One reason is the amount of borrowing that needs to be repaid. Another is the deteriorating business climate as the world staggers towards recession and unemployment rises. A third is the plethora of hedge funds and other "new-age" creditors, who will yank the plug on struggling firms at the first whiff of trouble—something banks in the past would have tried to avoid doing.

Debts where default is a possibility are rated speculative grade (better, and more aptly at this point, known as "junk") by the rating agencies. By some estimates, the amount of junk bonds that need to be repaid jumps to almost $30 billion in 2009, from less than $15 billion in 2008. Edward Altman, a professor of finance at New York University, reckons more than $100 billion of leverage loans are also maturing, many of which were used in buy-outs. Credit spreads on junk bonds, which are an indication of future default rates, rose from 260 basis points over Treasury notes in early 2007 to 1,200 basis points in late 2008 (see chart). All this promises soaring default rates in 2009.

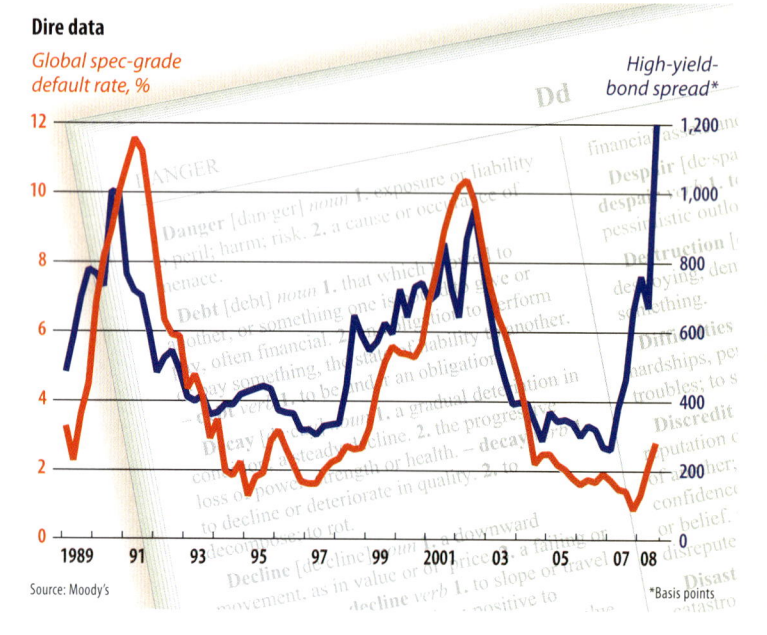

During the past few years, borrowers took advantage of low interest rates and eager creditors to refinance their borrowings, and assumed this blissful state would last. Unfortunately, they engaged in the corporate equivalent of subprime borrowing and went in way over their heads. According to Standard & Poor's, a rating agency, two-thirds of all borrowing in 2007 (the year the credit bubble peaked) was junk, almost double the level during the previous housing boom in 1990. Defaults on such debts generally pick up sharply from two years after issuance—which means from 2009.

Who will be hit? If any group is in the direct line of fire, it is those private-equity firms that paid fortunes for leveraged buy-outs in 2006-07, and whose debts come due in 2009. At the time, the buy-out barons argued that diversity would protect them. But they did not reckon on a credit squeeze affecting good companies as well as bad ones, nor on an economic downturn that threatens to inflict pain indiscriminately. There are sectors that appear particularly vulnerable, because they borrow a lot but have cyclical sales, such as leisure, media, restaurants, retail, consumer products and travel.

> The only people sure to come out smiling are the lawyers

Such failures can become self-reinforcing. The default rate closely tracks the unemployment rate; bankruptcy throws people out of work, which means people spend less, which makes retailers and other consumer businesses even more exposed to ruin, and so on.

Just as troubling is what will happen to failing firms. During the borrowing binge, creditors were so eager to throw money at companies that they doled out far more loans than bonds—even though loans are much less exposed to public scrutiny. On top of that, they relaxed many of the conditions usually put on borrowers, known (formerly with biblical reverence) as covenants, giving away their right to monitor the loans.

The $55 trillion question

What is more, as the numbers of creditors have multiplied to include hedge funds and other unregulated firms, so have the difficulties of dealing with bankrupt companies. They cannot sit around one table and bully each other into submission, as bankers used to do. They might have hedged their positions using newfangled credit derivatives, which would make them less willing to reach a settlement, or even used those same derivatives to bet on a company going bankrupt, in which case they would set out to block a settlement. The only people sure to come out smiling are the lawyers.

All of which leaves a $55 trillion question. If companies fail en masse, what will happen to the derivatives that insure against default, known as credit-default swaps (CDSs)? The collapse of Lehman Brothers, an investment bank, and other financial disasters, raise fears that the sellers of these products, namely banks and insurance firms, will not honour their commitments. Somewhere out there are $55 trillion of them. A cascade of defaults could be multiplied many times through derivatives, blowing yet another hole in the financial system. Once considered a marvellous tool of risk management, CDSs now look as though they will magnify, not mitigate, risk. ■

Dire data

Global spec-grade default rate, %
High-yield bond spread* (Basis points)

Source: Moody's

2009 IN BRIEF
The **World Social Forum**, challenger to Davos, meets in Brazil to take an anti-capitalist view of the banking crisis.

Henry Tricks: finance editor, The Economist

Together.
Free your energies

We are one of the world's foremost providers of consulting, technology and outsourcing services. Together, we can help you to unleash your company's full potential, and transform it into tangible results and new levels of performance. We endeavour to ensure that this transformation gives you greater room for manoeuvre. And because your problem is unique, the solution will be too: we work together to find the best answer for you. At Capgemini, we call this the Collaborative Business Experience®. It is our trademark. It boosts flexibility, proactivity and creativity, qualities that can help drive your performance.

Visit us at www.uk.capgemini.com

Capgemini
CONSULTING.TECHNOLOGY.OUTSOURCING

No end of trouble

Andrew Palmer

The first of two articles on banking focuses on the downside of 2009. More misery lies ahead

2009 IN BRIEF
Damascus at last manages to open its **stock exchange**, threatening to use chalk on a blackboard if necessary.

The credit crunch has had more false bottoms than a trafficker's suitcase. Since money markets first froze in the middle of 2007, bankers have pointed to one event after another, from the collapse of Bear Stearns, an investment bank, to the nationalisation of Fannie Mae and Freddie Mac, two American mortgage giants, as a signal that the worst is over. As the crisis has spiralled and government intervention in the sector has grown ever more dramatic, the optimists have become quieter. The authorities have shown they are prepared to do whatever they have to in order to keep the financial system alive. But 2009 will, at best, be a year of painful convalescence for the banks.

Two forces will weigh them down. The first is the grisly state of the real economy. The credit crisis has long since moved beyond the woes of investment banks forced to slash the market value of exotic securities. As actual defaults (as opposed to mark-to-market writedowns) rise, banks are racking up ever higher credit losses. To make matters even worse, new accounting rules mean that commercial banks have lower levels of loan-loss reserves than in previous downturns, so provisions have to be plumped up at just the wrong time.

That sinking feeling

Smaller, regional banks look most vulnerable to rising losses. Compared with larger peers, their earnings are less diversified and their arguments for more capital, private or public, less persuasive. A lot of American regional banks will go under in 2009, straining the resources of the Federal Deposit Insurance Corporation (FDIC), a government agency which guarantees retail deposits up to a certain limit. There are similar worries about the health of European banks that are too small to save, from Spanish *cajas* to German *Sparkassen* and British building societies.

Housing will remain a major drag on banks' earnings. Most in the industry reckon that only when house prices in America reach their floor will the cycle really turn, but few are confident that this inflection-point will come in 2009. As prices fall further, more households will enter negative equity, in Europe as well as America. There are still plenty of mortgages with burning fuses. Perhaps the most widespread are America's interest-only mortgages, which give homeowners a temporary holiday from principal repayments. Many of these borrowers will face a nasty payment shock in 2009.

Housing is not the only area under strain, of course. The squeeze on consumers is already visible in areas such as car loans and credit-card debts. But many bankers will be watching two other asset classes in 2009. One is commercial property, where lending surveys suggest that banks are now being especially cautious. Exposures to this asset class tend to be big and concentrated, so the failure of even a handful of property developers can cause significant damage to banks' balance-sheets.

> A lot of American regional banks will go under in 2009

The other is longer-term corporate borrowing (see previous story). Companies have so far been able to take advantage of vast undrawn credit lines in order to keep financing themselves, but those facilities will not last for ever and banks are disinclined to extend cheap credit. The coming year will tell us just how bad things are going to get in banks' corporate portfolios (and also test the vast derivatives market in corporate debt).

Given how awful the past year has been for the banks, a grinding recession would almost come as welcome relief. But the banks will still have to cope with continued uncertainty about their future. Governments and central banks have been forced to step in to replace private capital throughout the banking industry, acting as necessary sources of short-term liquidity, longer-term funding and equity. They will not quickly depart from the scene. The nerves of private creditors and investors are frazzled, and the banks must refinance great slugs of maturing debt in 2009.

Although once it seemed likely that the banks would escape wholesale regulatory change, that is now impossible. The banks are already paying a price for their dependence on the public purse, in ways both substantial (higher capital ratios) and symbolic (lower pay packages). Even more dramatic ▸

Andrew Palmer: banking correspondent, *The Economist*

The return of the gentleman banker

Lionel Barber

Introducing the winners of 2009

Over the past decade Americans, Britons, even the staid Swiss embraced the model of the all-singing, cross-selling investment bank. But the Great Credit Drought claimed many high-profile victims. In 2009 a familiar if somewhat forgotten figure will head the winners' queue. Capital will remain scarce and trust in short supply. In these hard times, no commodity will be more valuable than high-calibre, impartial advice. The gentleman banker will make a comeback.

Those most likely to thrive will include boutique investment banks such as Evercore, Greenhill, Gleacher Shacklock, Perella Weinberg and the advisory arm of Blackstone, a private-equity colossus. Many of these firms' partners are defectors from the big investment banks: Joseph Perella (Morgan Stanley), Peter Weinberg (Goldman Sachs) and John Studzinski (HSBC, Morgan Stanley). The boutiques were hiring in 2008 and most expect to continue in 2009.

Do not expect a merger-and-acquisitions glut in 2009. With credit still tight, deals will take time to move through the pipeline. But the boutiques will muscle in, exploiting personal relationships and the trend towards consortia advisers. Large cross-border deals such as Mittal-Arcelor (in the steel industry) and BHP Billiton-Rio Tinto (a massive mining merger whose outcome will be settled in 2009) have often included as many as five or six different investment banks on each side.

The proliferation of advisers will continue, says one investment-banking CEO, "because corporate boards want to hedge against risk and to hell with the fees."

The gentleman banker's renaissance reflects a broader shift in the balance of power on Wall Street and in the City of London, principally at the expense of the traders. True, Lloyd Blankfein (Goldman Sachs) and John Mack (Morgan Stanley) remain on top. But the elevations of John Thain (Bank of America-Merrill Lynch) and, above all, Sir Win Bischoff, chairman of Citigroup and a City grandee par excellence, epitomise the prevailing mood of prudence at the expense of risk. This will endure over the next year as bankers brace themselves against a regulatory backlash after the excesses of the credit boom.

The other big winners in financial services in 2009 will be those best able to mobilise capital and spot undervalued assets. The latter sport claimed plenty of victims in the first year of the credit crunch. Sovereign-wealth funds from Asia and the Gulf provided rescue finance for Barclays, Citigroup, Lehman and Merrill Lynch, assuming they were buying into blue-chip stocks; in fact, they were catching falling knives.

In 2009 they will be more circumspect, but will still be eager to put their excess capital to work. Increasingly, they will team up with private equity. This will mark a big shift on both sides, but it reflects a convergence of mutual interest.

Until recently, private-equity bosses regarded sovereign-wealth funds as competitors in the hunt for assets, but beggars for capital cannot be choosers. Similarly, funds from places such as Abu Dhabi, Dubai and Qatar will be keen to allay concerns in the West about their investment strategy; and they need top talent to make sound returns (excluding their investments in English football clubs).

Deep pockets will count more than ever in 2009. Not only will well-capitalised banks be able to withstand further squalls in the credit markets. They will also be able to exploit their balance sheets to scout for deals in real estate and distressed debt, both virtual no-go areas in 2008. In 2009 there will be opportunities for brave bottom-fishers among hedge funds and private equity.

Capital gains

Three banks stand out as likely winners in 2009: Banco Santander of Spain, Goldman Sachs and JPMorgan Chase. In 2008 a capital-strong Santander targeted distressed Alliance & Leicester and Bradford & Bingley, building on its successful integration of Abbey National. JPMorgan Chase rescued Bear Stearns and Washington Mutual for a song. In 2009 both these predators will look to consolidate their position in a still struggling banking sector.

Few would bet against Goldman Sachs (though enough did in 2008 to persuade the investment bank to change its status to a regulated, deposit-taking bank). Its traders made the right bets, early on. It managed the inherent conflict of interest between proprietary trading and relationship banking. At the same time, many of its bankers set up shop elsewhere in boutiques and hedge funds.

The Goldman diaspora will grow in 2009 as bankers (not all of them gentlemen) succumb to the lure of bigger returns at smaller institutions.

In financial services, small will be beautiful—if not nearly so profitable. ■

Lionel Barber: editor-in-chief, *Financial Times*

---

redrawing of the regulatory landscape will not happen quickly but discussions on how to overhaul the rules and infrastructure of global finance will intensify throughout 2009.

Amid the gloom, some will do better than others (see article above). The gaps between strong and weak institutions will widen further. Stronger banks will attract more deposits and will have the pick of the strongest borrowers at favourable terms. At the opposite end of the spectrum, weaker banks will face a double whammy of higher costs and a deteriorating credit pool as their best customers migrate to competitors. Governments will help to accelerate this polarisation by making it clear which institutions they will stand behind and which they are prepared to see disappear. Bankers used to complain bitterly about state intervention. In 2009, the thing they fear most will be state abandonment. ■

Who's a bull?

Philip Coggan

The markets may start to think the worst will be over

The notion that the markets are always right, that prices are set at an "efficient" level, has taken a severe beating. The world saw in 1999 and early 2000 what a bubble looked like, when dotcom stocks with no profits and barely a business plan were valued in billions of dollars; it saw in 2008 what a panic looked like with some of Wall Street's biggest names disappearing in the course of a weekend.

Getting ready to charge

Surely the pace of events in 2009 cannot be as turbulent as during 2008, when big investment banks variously failed, were taken over or reclassified themselves as deposit-taking banks, and when governments nationalised, or took stakes in, some of their leading banks. All that was due to a freezing of the money markets, which saw a run on the banks led, not by nervous retail depositors, but by institutional investors and the banks themselves. America's Federal Reserve was compelled to unveil a plan to lend to companies directly, bypassing the banks.

In the face of all that, 2009 will be a triumph simply if markets function normally, with money flowing freely between banks, companies and consumers. Recession is certain in many countries; indeed, investors will be relieved if a deeper depression is avoided.

More regulation is inevitable as payback for the public money put into the financial sector. Governments will insist that banks have more capital (or, put another way, use less leverage) and this will reduce their willingness to take big trading positions. They may also keep hedge funds on a tight leash. That will make markets less liquid, which could, of course, lead to their being even more volatile.

As to the prospects for a rally, the good news is that markets are a discounting mechanism. They will hope that American house prices reach their nadir some time during the year and that lower oil prices and lower interest rates will fuel an economic rebound in late 2009 and early 2010. Indeed, it seems likely that interest rates will fall in many countries to historically low levels and stay there. Eventually, that will lead to the kind of speculative risk-taking that marked the late 1990s as well as the binge of 2004-06.

In the meantime the rebound will help investors cope with awful news from the corporate world. In 2008, the pain was in finance. In 2009, the bad news will shift to industry, and particularly the consumer-linked sectors, as unemployment rises and people struggle to repay their debt. The hope is that sentiment will improve at the prospect of an upturn in 2010.

If so, investors may be able to take some comfort from valuations. In the middle of October investment-grade bonds reached their cheapest levels since 1925; in Britain, the price-earnings ratio was in single digits while the dividend yield on the FTSE All-Share was above the yield on ten-year gilts. Investors were betting that dividends were not going to rise over the medium term. That has happened only once before since the late 1950s—in March 2003, before a four-year bull run.

Clues from the past

History is on the bulls' side. Since 1926, the United States stockmarket has fallen only one year out of every three—but it has suffered four such years already this decade. If the American stockmarket falls in any given year, there has been a 60% chance of a rebound in the following year.

However, an important note of caution is that there have been some alarming sequences of down years: the crash of 1929-32, the stagflation of 1973-74, the end of the dotcom bubble from 2000 to 2002. Turn bullish too early and you will make an expensive mistake.

For emerging markets, 2008 was a timely corrective to the view that they were "safe havens", thanks to their current-account surpluses and rapid growth rates. The collapse of the Chinese stockmarket boom and the need for Russia to suspend trading on the Moscow market on several occasions illustrated that these markets are still vulnerable to the whims of hot money or falls in commodity prices.

The danger is of a repeat of Japan's travails of the 1990s or, even worse, a global depression like the 1930s. The hope is that central banks and politicians have learnt from the mistakes of the past. Any revival of protectionism would be the worst possible sign for markets.

Nevertheless, a lot of debt has been accumulated in developed economies. There are only two ways to get rid of high debt: default on it or inflate it away. Defaults threaten a depression, which governments are determined to avoid; hence their desire to assume or "socialise" private-sector debt. In the long run, they can repay that debt through higher taxes or inflation.

That dilemma may become clear to government bond investors, for whom 2009 could be a turning-point. Such bonds were a safe haven during the credit crunch. But lending money to profligate governments at 4-5% for 30 years may start to look like a bad deal. Instead of an equity-market crash, we could have a bond-market rout by the end of 2009. ■

Philip Coggan: capital markets editor, *The Economist*

Currency comeback

Patrick Lane

Why the financial crisis helps the dollar

Even in quiet times, predicting the paths of exchange rates is a fool's errand. Economists can come up with the most reasonable of arguments for why this currency will rise and that will fall, only to have their forecasts overturned by small shifts in the financial weather. In 2008, working out where foreign-exchange markets might be in a week's time, never mind a year's, has been about as easy (and as sensible) as holding a finger to the wind in a tornado.

To make matters trickier still, past financial crises have been national or regional—meaning that analysts have had only a few currencies to focus on. This time the turmoil is much broader, and America and western Europe are in the thick of it. And whereas economies as a whole can suffer or stockmarkets around the globe can fall, in foreign-exchange markets it is relative prices that count: whether the world economy is doing badly or well, some currencies must go up and others down.

Even so, some trends are discernible. And those trends do not look at all bad for—of all currencies—the dollar, even though the financial crisis began in the United States and America's economy is in hard times. Indeed, as the crisis intensified during 2008, the dollar's six-year decline against the euro and some other leading currencies went into reverse. There are good reasons to think that the dollar will hold up in 2009.

Everything is relative

The demand for a currency depends on the return that investors expect from holding it. That in turn depends largely on the interest rates on offer and on underlying rates of economic growth. At first sight, little of this favours the dollar. American official short-term interest rates are far more likely to go down than up. The rates on Treasury notes have at times fallen to almost zero: at almost any price, the safety of government paper trumps risky-looking banks. And America's growth prospects for 2009 are poor. Some economists have even argued that the financial crisis could spell the end of the dollar's long reign as the world's premier reserve currency—doing for the greenback what the Depression did for the gold standard.

Look around the world and there are, to be sure, better bets on offer than the dollar: the yen is one, even though Japan's economy is faltering. For Japanese investors, prospects are no better abroad than at home; and the carry trade—borrowing cheap yen and buying assets denominated in high-yielding currencies—has become a much harder game to play. The Chinese yuan is not about to reverse its climb either, even if exports and the economy slow down. But European currencies are a different story.

In both Frankfurt and London, central banks have more room to cut rates than in America, and are likely to use it. That would narrow transatlantic differentials. The outlook for growth in Europe is no better—and is perhaps even worse—than in America. Housing markets in Britain, Ireland and Spain were every bit as bubbly as in America.

Moreover, the backing of Uncle Sam still counts for something. That will help the dollar if a slowing world economy gives investors in emerging markets a lasting bout of the collywobbles. (It seems a fair bet that it will.) Treasury notes are still regarded as a safe haven—and they will continue to be trusted, even if America has to issue many more billions of dollars' worth to finance the bail-out of its banks. Stephen Jen, an economist at Morgan Stanley, points out that in past years there have been huge flows out of dollars and yen into European and emerging-market currencies, which will have to return. He has a long list of currencies that could come under severe pressure, which includes the Indian rupee, the South Korean won and the Brazilian real, as well as "most" east European currencies.

A faltering world economy will also weigh down commodity producers' currencies: the Australian and New Zealand dollars, which lost ground in 2008, may lose more in 2009. The most vulnerable currencies when financial storms break, however, belong to countries whose banks, companies and households owe large amounts of short-term debt denominated in foreign money. In the Asian crisis of 1997-98, that meant a collapse of the Thai baht, the Indonesian rupiah and others. This time the most conspicuous victim has been the Icelandic krona. Even if they are not in for such a rough ride, other countries may be exposed too.

All in all, if 2009 brings a currency crash, the dollar is unlikely to be the victim. ■

> The backing of Uncle Sam still counts for something

Buck up
Dollar against the euro, inverted scale
Source: Thomson Datastream
*Economist Intelligence Unit forecast from October 2008

2009 IN BRIEF
The five-nation **East African Community** hopes to launch a common market by the end of the year, with a common East African shilling to follow—eventually.

Patrick Lane: deputy business affairs editor, *The Economist*

Lessons from a crisis

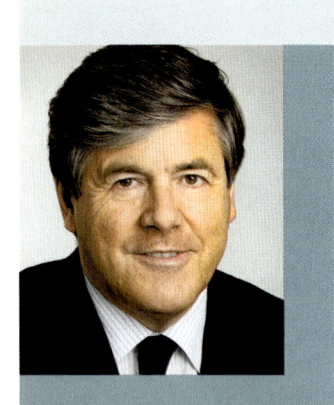

How to restore the financial markets to health? **Josef Ackermann**, chief executive of Deutsche Bank, gives his answer

The crisis that engulfed first the financial industry and then entire economies is a watershed event. Broad segments of global financial markets stopped working. Structures and institutions that had been the bedrock of the system for decades disappeared literally overnight. And in response central banks and governments deployed counter-measures on an unprecedented scale.

History will record 2009 as the year that reshaped the global financial system. Banks will need to restore not only their capital base, but their clients' trust. They will have to reconsider their business models and products. The authorities, for their part, will need to continue doing what is necessary to maintain the functioning of the financial system while designing the building-blocks of a regulatory and supervisory system that is commensurate with global, interdependent financial markets.

The financial industry is vigorously addressing all areas in which deficiencies have been revealed. The Institute of International Finance and the Counterparty Risk Management Policy Group have presented a wide range of recommendations and these are being implemented by banks worldwide.

Three issues stand out. First, liquidity. This is at the heart of the stability of any financial system. Yet the crisis revealed that the assumption of continuously available liquidity can no longer be upheld, and our understanding of market dynamics in times of illiquidity is poor. The repercussions for the valuation of illiquid assets in a mark-to-market accounting regime need to be addressed with urgency.

Second, transparency. It would be wrong if the focus of this issue were limited to greater transparency about banks' exposures. Rather, it must extend to better disclosure of a bank's institutional arrangements for risk management, risk models and techniques. Moreover, greater transparency must be achieved for financial products, especially the complex structured credit products at the heart of this crisis. Investors will return to these markets only if originators disclose sufficient data in the underlying assets so as to enable investors to make their own due diligence rather than rely passively on the judgment of originators and rating agencies. Even this will not save these markets from shrinking dramatically as investors' preferences shift to simpler products.

Third, we need to strengthen the infrastructure of financial markets, the "plumbing". In order to increase price transparency, transaction data should be pooled and made available. To reduce settlement risk and enable netting in over-the-counter markets, central counterparties will be established. Greater automation in these markets will also reduce settlement risk, but will obviously require a higher degree of standardisation.

Not by banks alone

Although banks' own efforts will be sufficient and successful in many areas, intervention by standard-setting bodies and authorities will be needed in others. On valuation issues, for example, reforms must recognise that this is more than merely an accounting issue. Mark-to-market accounting imposes stricter discipline on banks' risk management and increases market discipline, because it acts as an early-warning system, where losses show up in banks P&L accounts before they materialise in the real economy. Any changes must respect these benefits of fair-value accounting, but must at the same time address the issues of illiquid markets, pro-cyclicality and consistency between accounting standards.

International co-ordination is essential for these efforts and for any state action aimed at stabilising financial markets and banks. For sure, state action needs to be attuned to individual circumstances. But unco-ordinated action using a plethora of diverging instruments will only create yet more uncertainty, spread the virus and distort competition.

This holds particularly true for the European Union, where member states will be faced with a stark choice. They can either act jointly and at last create a supervisory system that is commensurate with a truly integrated financial market, or relapse into a system of essentially separate national markets.

More calls for tighter regulation will be heard in 2009. This is understandable. The financial crisis will cost us dearly and the financial industry bears as much responsibility for this as past mistakes in both macroeconomic and regulatory policies. But it must not result in the dissolution of financial-market integration and the stifling of financial innovation.

Though it seems hard to believe these days, the market-based financial system has made a big contribution to global growth. Reverting to fragmented, nation-based and over-regulated banking markets is not the answer. What we need is greater resilience via sophisticated market participants, as well as stronger market infrastructure and supra-national structures for the regulation and supervision of the global financial system. ■

History will record 2009 as the year that reshaped the global financial system

THE WORLD IN 2009   157

Also in this section: | Gene therapy gets to work 159 | The latest in biomimetics 160
Human microbes and how | Shedding light on dark | Paul Allen:
they can help 158 | matter 160 | Piece of mind 161

Science

A year of astronomy

Alun Anderson

The search for life beyond Earth

No discovery in science could be more dramatic than finding life elsewhere in the universe. If it were intelligent life that would be even better but evidence of even the simplest forms of life on a planet circling a distant sun would be the find of the century. That discovery can't be promised for 2009 but we will see a giant leap in our capability to find Earth-like planets that could provide good homes for life. In April NASA will launch Kepler, a powerful space telescope that can monitor simultaneously 100,000 stars and look for the faint signal that reveals an orbiting planet.

The choice of the name Kepler is timely, for 2009 is the 400th anniversary of two of the most momentous events in astronomy. Both are to be celebrated in the International Year of Astronomy, a global festival designed to "help the citizens of the world rediscover their place in the Universe". The first of those events was the publication by Johannes Kepler, a mathematician living in Prague, of *Astronomia Nova*, a tract which laid out the fundamental laws governing the movement of the planets. The second was the first use of an astronomical telescope by Galileo Galilei. With it, as he wrote in "Starry Messenger", "all the disputes which have tormented philosophers through so many ages are exploded at once by the irrefragable evidence of our eyes." He could see that the moon was not a perfect celestial body but was covered with spots (craters), that Jupiter had a set of moons of its own and that there were vast numbers of previously unknown stars. With Galileo's discoveries, the religious dogma that all the heavens revolved around the Earth became increasingly difficult to believe. Now, four centuries later, we know that the Earth is a small planet circling a minor sun on the edge of just one of an estimated 125 billion galaxies. Out in space are a thousand billion billion suns that may have planets supporting life.

The Kepler telescope will be launched amid a flurry of discoveries of planets circling distant stars. Since the first "exoplanet" was found in 1995 by Michel Mayor at the Geneva Observatory, more than 300 have been charted. Europe's COROT space telescope has been particularly successful and will find many more planets in 2009. These discoveries have been of large fast-orbiting planets which are so close to their suns that they are far too hot to support life of any kind. Among them are gigantic gas planets called "hot Jupiters" and "hot super-

2009 IN BRIEF
China piggy-backs on a Russian launch vehicle to send up its first **Mars probe**. The probe will circle Mars for a year.

Alun Anderson: former editor, *New Scientist,* and writing a book on the future of the Arctic

Life on Man

Alun Anderson

Why you should be happy to be hybrid

If you have gone through life blithely thinking of yourself as a "human being", then 2009 will bring the shocking news that it is time to think again. You are a "human-microbe hybrid" or "super-organism", dependent on a vast number of microbes that live in your body, do vital jobs for you, and both influence and provide unique indicators of your health.

These bugs live in your mouth, eyes and reproductive parts; they love your gut. Their numbers are staggering: 100 trillion microbes live in the average human. Given that the body contains only 10 trillion cells, some scientists joke that the human-microbe hybrid is 10% human and 90% microbe. Their total weight is only slightly less than that of your own liver.

In 2009 we will learn a lot more about them. By the end of the year, the Human Oral Microbiome Project will succeed in giving names to the 600 or so different microbes that live in the mouth. In the gut, over 1,000 species have been labelled already. More important, the DNA of these bugs has been found to contain 60,000 genes, twice the number found in your own DNA. Those extra genes carry the code for many enzymes that humans don't have and do things that humans can't do. Gaining access to them is why you should be proud to be a human-microbe hybrid rather than a mere human.

In the colon, microbes synthesise vitamins for us and provide 10% of our calories by breaking down dietary fibre we cannot process. Many intimate new connections are just beginning to emerge. Gut bacteria can affect how fats are processed, change the likelihood of obesity, alter cholesterol levels and affect chances of developing diabetes. New data suggest that they might affect brain development and influence the early immune system and allergies. And they certainly alter individual reactions to medicines.

Scientists are wondering how to improve health by meddling with your microbes. A start is being made by collecting signatures of all the chemicals that microbial interactions create in the body. Computers can hack through these vast lists of data and look for "metabolic profiles" that correlate with health and disease. Then scientists can search for ways to alter them. That might include drugs, diet, probiotics that contain helpful bacteria and functional foods that encourage the right bacteria to grow. "The implications if it can be done properly are astronomical," explains Jeremy Nicholson of Imperial College, London, a pioneer of metabolic profiling. "You could change the face of 21st-century medicine." In the future, loving the 90% of you that is microbe may just seem common sense. ■

Check out those microbes

---

earths" that are just a few times larger than our Earth. Kepler is the first telescope to be designed to find Earth-sized planets that orbit in the "habitable zone" where temperatures are neither too hot nor too cold for water to remain in its liquid state.

The Kepler telescope will hang in orbit and stare continuously at a field of 100,000 stars in the Cygnus-Lyra region of the Milky Way. Kepler will watch them all for three-and-a-half years and wait for the light from any of them to dim ever so slightly. That could be the sign of a planet passing in front of its sun. If this miniature eclipse is repeated at regular intervals, for the same length of time, then the odds are that an orbiting planet has been detected. Our Earth orbits our sun once a year. To find similar planets, Kepler will have to spot a transit and then wait another whole year to see if it is repeated and then another year to check that it saw a genuine repeat and not just a second planet sailing by.

Staring into space

"If Kepler is successful it will be NASA's most boring operation," says David Koch, an astronomer at NASA Ames Research Centre, which runs the Kepler project. "But the results will be sensational."

Kepler's scientists estimate that the telescope should find at least 50 Earth-sized planets in one-year orbits, plus many bigger planets. They even expect to find quite a few planets orbiting pairs of stars. "A pirouette of two stars and a planet can be stable," explains Dr Koch. "The planet may orbit one of the pair of suns if it is in close enough, or both suns." Living on such a planet might be a little strange, with multiple sunrises and sunsets.

If all goes well Kepler will leave us with a catalogue of planets that could support life. That will help plan future missions. The next logical step would be a space telescope capable of picking up the chemical signatures of life, including the presence of oxygen, water vapour and carbon dioxide. Whether such a project will attract funding is, as Dr Koch says, "politics".

> The telescope should find at least 50 Earth-sized planets

Until we have those signs, we will be haunted by the Fermi paradox. The physicist Enrico Fermi famously asked why no extra-terrestrials have shown up on Earth when there are likely to be so many solar systems where life could have evolved. Where are the visitors from civilisations far more advanced than our own?

One answer is that our Earth really is unique in this vast universe and we are alone. Another is that aliens visited Earth and found our planet so dull that we didn't even merit a rating on their interstellar travel guide. A more sobering possibility is that advanced civilisations inevitably destroy themselves; in which case intelligence is an evolutionary dead-end and extinction our fate. With luck, the Kepler launch will help us to find clues to our destiny in good time. ■

2009 IN BRIEF

The European Space Agency's **Mars Express** spacecraft ends its mission after circling Mars and collecting data for more than two Martian years, each lasting some 687 days.

Cancer killers

Jan Piotrowski

After many a false dawn, gene therapy's experimental promise will at last turn into clinical reality

Ever since scientists twigged how to manipulate genes, doctors and their patients (especially those suffering from debilitating genetic ailments) have pinned their hopes on this knowledge being transmuted into readily available medical procedures. The initial spark came in 1990, with gene therapy's striking preliminary success against a rare condition known as severe combined immuno-deficiency, or SCID. SCID sufferers lack an immune system and they usually die in childhood, as their bodies are unable to deal with even the simplest of infections.

Various other therapies (for example, bone-marrow transplant, antibiotics or isolation) have proved inadequate, but a gene-based treatment helped cure nearly two dozen children. However, this came at a high price, with five patients developing leukaemia and one dying as a result.

At the last count, over 1,400 clinical trials deploying gene therapy to fight various diseases have been pursued worldwide since 1989, with 47 having reached phase III, the final stage required before possible regulatory approval. Yet, largely because of undesirable side-effects like those in the SCID trials, none has hitherto been granted the ultimate go-ahead by health authorities in America and Europe. (In 2003 the Chinese regulators did approve the first gene therapy, for head and neck cancer, but many Western researchers have expressed doubts about its efficacy.)

Enter the Trojan horse

In 2009 this is set to change, with the commercial rollout of two products. Advexin, devised by Introgen, an American company, is aimed at combating head and neck cancer; and London-based Ark Therapeutics' Cerepro targets malignant glioma, a fatal brain tumour. Both companies have already filed applications for marketing approval, and now await regulatory decisions.

All gene therapy rests on the idea that instead of attacking a disease directly, for example by administering a drug to replenish the amount of some vital substance or sweep up a harmful one, the patient's genes can be manipulated in such a way that the organism fixes itself. This can be done in one of two ways. One is to use drugs to regulate the expression of an existing gene, in other words to hamper or boost the gene's activity. This, in turn, alters how much of the protein encoded by the gene is synthesised, which can profoundly affect the way the body behaves.

An alternative approach is to insert foreign genes, known as transgenes, to replace or repair the malfunctioning ones at the root of the illness. Transgenes are delivered into the patient's cells on the back of a carrier, called a vector. The most widespread approach is to use what Len Seymour, a researcher at Oxford University, describes as "Trojan horse" vectors. These are usually viruses, which have a natural ability to insert their own genes into host cells. Normally, this can lead to illness. But by tinkering with the viral genome, scientists have been able to eliminate the disease-causing genes and replace them with desired transgenes. All that remains is to infect the target cells with the engineered virus, and let nature work its magic.

Both Cerepro and Advexin rely on this mechanism. Cerepro harnesses an adenovirus, a type of virus which carries its DNA in double-stranded form, to transmit a gene responsible for the production of a protein called thymidine kinase. It is administered by a series of injections into the healthy brain tissue of patients who have had solid tumour masses surgically removed. Next, patients are given an antiviral drug, ganciclovir, which the thymidine kinase then converts into a substance that destroys all dividing cells. Since healthy brain cells do not divide, they remain unaffected by the treatment, but any proliferating cancerous cells are killed. In the case of Advexin, which also uses an adenovirus for transport, the beneficent payload is the p53 gene, a naturally occurring tumour-suppressor which, injected into cancer cells, kills them, again leaving healthy cells unharmed.

There will be other advances in gene therapy in 2009. For instance, one problem with using viruses as vectors is that they tend to provoke an immune response, which is useful in combating unwanted infections but can suppress the type sought by gene therapists. Dr Seymour has been developing a "stealthing" polymer coating which protects viral vectors from being neutralised in this way. Hybrid Systems, a company he co-founded, has a broad portfolio of patents in this area and will begin clinical trials in 2009. Given the pace of progress on these and other fronts, gene therapy is at last ready to mature from a soundbite into sound clinical practice. ■

> Over 1,400 clinical trials deploying gene therapy have been pursued worldwide since 1989. Yet none has hitherto been granted the ultimate go-ahead

2009 IN BRIEF
Saudi Arabia opens the King Abdullah University of Science and Technology, the country's first science-focused graduate-level research centre.

Jan Piotrowski: winner of 2008 Richard Casement science internship, *The Economist*

Science

Dark secrets

Geoffrey Carr

The physics discovery of 2009 may come from Yorkshire

It was supposed to be the year that saw the discovery of the long-sought Higgs boson, which physicists need to explain why matter has mass. The Higgs, as many readers will be aware, is the principal quarry of a $10 billion particle accelerator known as the Large Hadron Collider that is located on the outskirts of Geneva. However the LHC, which was commissioned to great acclaim in September 2008, closed down in a rather embarrassing puff of helium gas from its cooling system nine days later. The repairs will take so long that the likelihood of its finding anything dramatic before the end of 2009 is now remote.

That gives a rather less flashy project the chance of making the physics discovery of the year. The Boulby Underground Laboratory is stuck at the bottom of a potash mine in northern England. The aim of its three experiments, known as Zeplin-II, Zeplin-III and Drift-II, is to detect dark matter—for another of the things that physicists don't know is why the visible sort of matter that stars, planets and people are made of seems to be only a sixth of the total.

The best guess is that dark matter is made of different types of particle from "ordinary" matter. The LHC has a good chance of making these particles, but if they are six times as common as ordinary matter in outer space then it ought to be possible to detect them in the wild, as it were. That is what Boulby is trying to do. Unfortunately, they are hard to detect.

The Zeplin detectors are filled with liquid xenon. The hope is that occasional dark-matter particles called neutralinos will run into the nuclei of the xenon atoms, releasing detectable amounts of energy as they do so. Drift-II is more ambitious. If it works, it will be able to track such a recoiling nucleus through a device filled with gas. It will therefore be possible to work out which direction the neutralino that caused it to recoil came from and thus engage in a form of dark-matter astronomy.

And if Boulby does come up trumps, then it will be a delightful victory for cheap and cheerful science over the billion-dollar variety. ■

2009 IN BRIEF
The **total solar eclipse** in July will last for six minutes and 39 seconds, and will be the longest this century.

Geoffrey Carr: science and technology editor, *The Economist*

A fin-tuned design

Jan Piotrowski

The propeller will soon be replaced with something decidedly fishy

A new kind of aquatic beast will start making waves in 2009. Spawned by a team of researchers from Boston's Franklin W. Olin College of Engineering and Boston Engineering, GhostSwimmer is the latest in biomimetics, which involves looking to nature for clues in solving technical conundrums. A so-called autonomous underwater vehicle, it swims by wagging a tail fin like its biological brother, the tuna, and may be able to cover three times the distance of propeller-driven devices running on the same battery. Though designed with oceanographic research in mind, the United States Navy, which helped fund the endeavour, is eyeing the possibility of deploying it on reconnaissance missions, and eventually using the technology to construct a new generation of fuel-efficient submarines.

A predecessor of GhostSwimmer was born in 1993 at the Massachusetts Institute of Technology. RoboTuna, affectionately known as Charlie, took its first dip in 1995. The idea was to create a machine that would mimic how big members of the family *Scombridae* (which includes the genus *Thunnus*) rip through the water. The genus comprises a vast range of similarly shaped fish which vary in length from the 1.5-metre albacore to the bluefin, which can measure more than three metres. This dimensional diversity was one reason for choosing tuna from an array of marine fauna, for it suggests that the basic tuna-esque shape must possess some desirable hydrodynamic properties. These are evident in the fish's speed (up to 70kph) and extreme swimming efficiency, evolution having honed its body to reduce drag and thus conserve strength during transoceanic migrations. Also, tuna's physical attributes are readily replicable by engineers. As Charlie's creators put it, they were after "a fast submarine-shaped fish with a relatively rigid torso that swims with fairly small body and tail motions".

The first generation of robotic tuna had to be tethered to a heap of electronics the size of a fridge. But GhostSwimmer, set to make a splash in early 2009, is controlled by "flexstack", a pocket-sized computer made by Boston Engineering. However, the major improvement will be replacing the cumbersome motor-powered tangle of pulleys and cables previously used to move the tail fin with something more elegant. One option is to use sequentially triggered vertebrae made of electroactive polymers, whose shape is modified by applying a voltage.

All this makes the robotic tuna's new incarnation ever more reminiscent of the real thing. A few more years and sushi chefs may need to watch out. ■

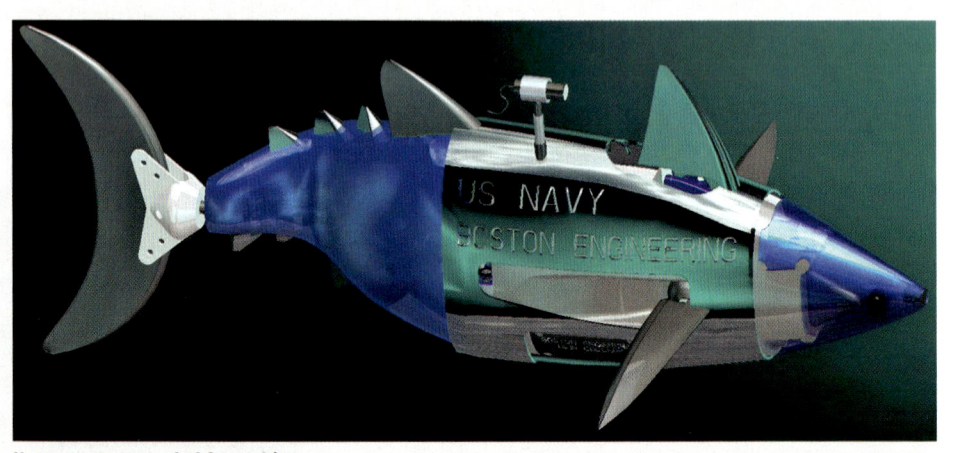

Not yet recommended for sushi

Piece of mind

Paul Allen, co-founder of the Allen Institute for Brain Science (and of Microsoft), believes a tipping-point is near in brain research

A new generation of implantable pacemakers for the brain will be widely used to treat everything from depression to addiction and Parkinson's disease

The mystery of how the brain works is the most compelling question in science. We can discover new planets around distant stars and find water on Mars, but over 95% of the workings of the brain remain unexplored and unexplained.

So six years ago I brought together a group of leading neuroscientists to find the basis for an approach that could advance the entire field of brain research. It was clear there needed to be a comprehensive database of information on where genes are turned on (or expressed) in the mouse brain—a map, or atlas, of the brain's frontiers that would provide more encyclopedic information than any individual lab could afford to generate.

It seemed achievable. With the help of several noted researchers, I founded the Allen Institute for Brain Science in 2003 to undertake this project. Three years later, the institute had completed an atlas of gene expression in the mouse brain.

The scientists used state-of-the-art technology to dissect a mouse brain, photographed it sliver section by section, then reassembled it in a computer database that would allow easy access. But it was the speed at which the project was accomplished and what they did with it afterwards that changed the game.

They released it to the public. Over the internet. Free.

When we first put the mouse-brain atlas online free, it was met by the research world with suspicion. People wondered what the catch was. Scientific research has long been a solitary endeavour—one researcher, one microscope. Findings are protected so that discovery credit can be clearly defined and awarded. This is a successful model and will continue to be.

However, the Human Genome Project demonstrated a different path: multiple teams working collaboratively towards a common goal. I believe a real acceleration in progress and innovation comes from the open sharing of ideas and collaboration. We wanted the mouse atlas to be free and available for all to use as the basis for foundational research and discovery.

If we thought it would be a hit right out of the gate, we were slightly wrong. It took a while for people to trust that it really was free to use. No one believed in a free lunch.

Now, things have changed. Today we have many scientists using the atlas for their research into Alzheimer's, bipolar disorders, Down's syndrome, Parkinson's, fragile x mental retardation and epilepsy. The atlas is also giving scientists insight into alcoholism, obesity, sleep, hearing and memory.

The greatest testament to what we did was that researchers of spinal-cord diseases, trauma and disorders approached the institute and asked us to create a spinal-cord atlas, which is now close to completion. We will launch the first phase of a human-brain atlas, a four-year project, in 2010.

Like the Human Genome Project, the Allen Brain Atlases and Spinal-Cord Atlas have helped democratise the scientific landscape. When you can log on to a map of gene expression from anywhere in the world, more people can enter the scientific conversation. The result is a massive saving in time, since without the atlas each researcher could spend a lifetime trying to gather complete gene-expression data for his or her work.

Brainstorming

Clearly the model of providing a freely accessible database is a successful one. In a sense, we have challenged other researchers to offer greater access to their findings. Will they take the challenge? My bet is that over the next 18 months we are going to see more open access and more collaboration.

In the next decade we will make great strides in uncovering the complex network of gene interactions that govern every major brain disease and will create effective therapies through traditional drug discovery or new methods for modifying gene activity. Just as the use of cardiac pacemakers or artificial knees is common today, a new generation of implantable pacemakers for the brain will be widely used to treat everything from depression to addiction and Parkinson's disease.

Our increasing knowledge will shed light on how information is processed and stored in the human brain at a molecular level. Even now, scientists are already mimicking the brain's information-processing capabilities to create a new generation of computer processes. We are going to get far better at this as our understanding of the brain improves.

Private philanthropy will continue to grow and help to accelerate scientific discovery. I believe we are nearing a tipping-point in brain research where the discoveries, treatments and cures will come more quickly than the questions. Private dollars, combined with broader adoption of open collaboration and data-sharing models, will help push us over the top. Success will follow. ■

Obituary

End of an aura

Ann Wroe

The Bush administration will come to an end on January 21st

With Jimmy Carter it was the teeth, big, straight and white as a set of country palings. With Richard Nixon it was the eyebrows, surely brooding on Hell. Abe Lincoln had the ears (and the beard, and the stove-pipe hat); Bill Clinton had a nose that glowed red, almost to luminousness, as his allergies assailed him. But George Bush's most extraordinary feature was his nostrils, and they will be missed.

It is not just that they were large, and lent his face a certain simian charm. They were also uncontrollable. When the rest of the presidential body was encased in a sober suit, and the rest of the presidential face had assumed an expression appropriate to taking the oath of office, or rescuing banks, or declaring to terrorists that they could run but they couldn't hide, the nostrils would suddenly flare and smirk, as if Mr Bush was about to burst out with something outrageous or obscene, or flash a high-five, or hail his deputy chief of staff as "Turd blossom".

Occasionally, a real gaffe was about to emerge. Watched closely, the nostrils no doubt gave advance warning of the moment when, addressing the Pentagon's top brass, Mr Bush said: "Our enemies...never stop thinking about new ways to harm our country and our people, and neither do we." More often, nothing exceptional was on the way to being said. But the nostrils ran ahead, twitching like a bull in a rodeo or a frisking wild horse, hinting at danger to come.

When he was debating with Al Gore in 2000, Mr Bush's language was polite and the policy statements well coined, but the nostrils declared they couldn't take the whole thing seriously. With hindsight, when the 2000 election became the closest ever, the Florida shenanigans seemed prefigured in that sniggering expression, which less became the 43rd president than Alfred E. Neumann of *Mad* magazine.

Being bigger and better than most people's, the presidential nostrils were also more acute. They could sniff out WMD in Iraq as snappily as hot dogs at a football game, though it took the UN many years to come up with nothing. Yellow-cake uranium could be nosed as far as Niger, and Saddam Hussein's connections to al-Qaeda were as odorous as a Texas feedlot. The nostrils could smell victory, too, especially on that morning in May 2003 when, standing on an aircraft-carrier with "Mission Accomplished" fluttering on a banner behind him, Mr Bush breathed in the tang of the ocean and of power.

Much else alerted those nostrils when others were indifferent. Oil, for example, even when buried under hundreds of feet of environmentally protected Arctic

> The nostrils ran ahead, twitching like a bull in a rodeo or a frisking wild horse, hinting at danger to come

tundra. Cheese, as eaten by the feckless French and other effete gastronomes of old Europe. Red meat, when demanded by the right-wing base which so often found this president disappointing, in the form of tax cuts and suspended regulations. And danger, as personified by suspicious individuals from faraway countries, whose proper place was to be in orange pyjamas at Guantánamo Bay, well out of reach of a lawyer.

An aroma of pork

Disloyalty, or the whiff of it, set off a particular quivering. When Paul O'Neill, Mr Bush's ex-treasury secretary, revealed that Saddam had been targeted from day one of Mr Bush's first term, and when Scott McClellan, his former press secretary, wrote that the Bush White House lacked both candour and competence, the nostrils assumed an air of outraged innocence: the same look, in fact, they had assumed on the worst day of Mr Bush's presidency, when an aide leaned down to tell him of the attack on the twin towers and the president, busy reading "The Pet Goat" to a class of Florida children, could not for a moment engage either his brain or his mouth to take the news.

All the stranger, therefore, that the noble orifices had their shortcomings. They could not smell the putrid mud that covered the ninth ward of New Orleans after Hurricane Katrina passed, or the stink of subprime mortgages leaching their poison into the financial system. They found nothing especially noisesome about the presence of Dick Cheney and his oilman cronies in charge of the national energy task-force. Sensitive as they were, they were unimpressed by levels of arsenic in drinking water or particulates in the air. And though Mr Bush had sold himself as a lean-spending, small-government man, they could not resist the aroma of a trillion-dollar budget stuffed with choicest pork.

Most curiously, they failed to detect the poisonous atmosphere that swirled around him abroad. Granted, the most revolting protesters were kept away. But even so the nostrils, proudly set even when the eyes blinked and the mouth pursed and wavered, maintained an extraordinary belief in the wisdom of the president and the rightness of his cause. One day the rest of the world would wake up and be grateful. One day the Bush administration would come up smelling like a rose. ∎

Ann Wroe: obituaries and briefings editor, *The Economist*